The Rational Restoration:

Reframes in the pursuit of clarity, charity, and understanding

LDS Nonfiction by Jonathan Neville

The Lost City of Zarahemla (2d Edition)
Moroni's America
Brought to Light
Letter VII: Joseph Smith and Oliver Cowdery Explain the Hill Cumorah
The Editors: Joseph, Don Carlos and William Smith
Whatever Happened to the Golden Plates?
Because of this Theory
Mesomania
Moroni's America (pocket edition)
The 2020 "seeing clearly" trilogy
- *A Man that Can Translate: Joseph Smith and the Nephite Interpreters*
- *Infinite Goodness: Joseph Smith, Jonathan Edwards, and the Book of Mormon*
- *Between these Hills: A Case for the New York Cumorah*
Lemurs, Chameleons and Golden Plates: An African Perspective on the Restoration (with William Rasoanivo)
By Means of the Urim and Thummim: Restoring Translation to the Restoration (with James Lucas)

LDS fiction by Jonathan Neville

Before the World Finds Out
The Joy Helpers
Moroni's Keys
Among All Nations
In Earthly Things

Blogs
http://www.lettervii.com/
www.mobom.org
www.nomorecontention.com

The Rational Restoration:

Reframes in the pursuit of clarity, charity, and understanding

Jonathan Neville, MS, JD

DIGITAL LEGEND
Toll Free: 1-877-222-1960

The Rational Restoration: Reframes in the pursuit of clarity, charity and understanding
Copyright © 2023 by Jonathan Neville
All rights reserved.
First Edition
11-8-23
This is a work of nonfiction. The author has made every effort to be accurate and complete and welcomes comments, suggestions, and corrections, which can be emailed to **lostzarahemla@gmail.com**.

All opinions expressed in this work are the responsibility of the author alone.

ISBN: 978-1-937735-67-8

Front cover: Conceptual depiction of light in the forest

www.digitalegend.com

To open-minded people everywhere.

———

This book is dedicated to the Joseph Smith Papers and everyone who has created, discovered, preserved, organized and presented historical records.

———

18 Come now, and let us reason together, saith the LORD: (Isaiah 1:18)

10 And now come, saith the Lord, by the Spirit, unto the elders of his church, and let us reason together, that ye may understand;
11 Let us reason even as a man reasoneth one with another face to face.
12 Now, when a man reasoneth he is understood of man, because he reasoneth as a man; even so will I, the Lord, reason with you that you may understand. (Doctrine and Covenants 50:10–12)

And now, how much more cursed is he that knoweth the will of God and doeth it not, than he that only believeth, or only **hath cause to believe**, and falleth into transgression? (Alma 32:19)

———

"… it acts directly on their emotions, below the logical level. You can sway a thousand men by appealing to their prejudices quicker than you can convince one man by logic. It doesn't have to be a prejudice about an important matter, either."
Robert A. Heinlein, *Revolt in 2100*, p. 90.

———

"Humans are never so irrational as when protecting their pet ideas."
Steven Pinker, *Rationality*

"The crucial difference in the church today is not between so-called believers and nonbelievers, but between the dwellers and seekers."[1]

Reasoning will never make a Man correct an ill Opinion, which by Reasoning he never acquired.[2]

THE Principles on which Christian Churches are built, are so plain, so natural and easy, and so much the same with those which give Rise to all the well-formed Societies in the World that one would think there should not be such Matter of Debate and Controversy among Christians, upon these Subjects, as we have unhappily found.[3]

Sometimes we fall into a trap of dealing with false dichotomies. For instance, we might believe that observation or reason are the only valid ways to learn truth, or we might believe that observation and reason undermine Faith to such an extent that they should have no role in religious life.

This is a false dichotomy because **observation and reason work synergistically with faith.** Faith without works will not amplify itself. Faith will only grow by observation and reasoning coupled with other spiritual work.[4]

---

[1] Father Tomas Halik, New York Times, in The New Copernicans.
[2] Jonathan Swift, "A Letter to a Young Gentleman," (January 9, 1720), London. (Google Books) [link](#)
[3] Isaac Watts, Preface, The Rational Foundation of a Christian Church, 1747. https://archive.org/details/rationalfoundati00watt/page/n5/mode/2up
[4] Dale G. Renlund, "Observation, Reason, Faith, and Revelation," BYU Education Week, August 2023, https://speeches.byu.edu/talks/dale-g-renlund/observation-reason-faith-and-revelation/

Table of Contents

Contents

The Rational Restoration: i
    Reframes in the pursuit of clarity, charity, and understanding i
Table of Contents iii
Table of Figures vi
Why *this* Book vii
Section I – Rationality 1
1. Something for everyone. 3
2. The Nature of the Restoration 9
3. Rational Explanations 11
    The Age of Reason 15
    Observation, Reason, Faith, and Revelation 18
    Cause to believe 20
    Pursuit of an ideal society 21
    Rationality in Religion 23
    Pascal's Wager 26
    The Nature of Religious Belief 28
    Truth Claims 29
4. Clarity, charity and understanding 31
5. The FAITH model 35
    Facts 38
    Assumptions 39
    Inferences 40
    Theories 40
    Hypotheses 40
6. All, Some, None 41
    Application – Lucy Mack Smith 44
    Narrative Poison 47
Section II – Reframes 49
7. Rational Living 51
    Reframing thinking patterns 52
    Reframing life challenges 55

  Gospel scholarship.. 57
8. Reframing Church..61
  Reframing the Restoration as fulfillment................................ 61
  Reframing Zion 64
  Reframing Church wealth 67
  Reframing Church structure 69
  Reframing Church interaction with members........................ 71
  Reframing Church leadership.. 72
9. Reframing Church History...73
  How Do We Know the Past?... 73
  Reframing the beginning of the Restoration........................... 77
  Reframing Joseph's preparation as a prophet........................ 79
  Reframing the plates 82
  Reframing the translation.. 89
  Reframing the witnesses.. 96
  Reframing changes in the D&C... 98
  Reframing the origins of the Urim and Thummim................ 103
  Reframing the term "Urim and Thummim"........................... 105
10: Reframing Scripture... 107
  Reframing Moroni 10 107
  Reframing relevance of geography 110
  Reframing Cumorah-Identification 115
  Reframing Cumorah-requirements.. 116
  Reframing Cumorah-Repository.. 117
  Reframing Cumorah and M2C... 123
  Reframing Crossing to America.. 124
  Reframing the setting... 126
  Reframing physical evidence 129
  Reframing volcanoes 130
  Reframing Nephite civilization 130
  Reframing the Moundbuilder myth....................................... 131
  Reframing Zelph 132
  Reframing Zarahemla: D&C 125:3.. 134
  Reframing Zarahemla: Iowa 135
  Reframing the term Jaredites 135
  Reframing Jaredite civilizations... 137
  Reframing Asian DNA... 144
  Reframing "the Americas"... 149
  Reframing Book of Mormon Language................................. 149

Reframing the purpose of the Book of Mormon 150
  Reframing Joseph's knowledge 151
  Reframing Cumorah teachings 151
  Reframing the hemispheric model 152
  Reframing the Times and Seasons 153
  Reframing Joseph as Editor 155
  Reframing Joseph as author in the Times and Seasons 156
  Reframing Joseph as author generally 158
  Reframing William Smith 159
11: Reframing Mortality 161
  A Window into Eternity 161
  For Thy Good 165
  Reframing how God operates 166
  Reframing sin 168
  Reframing the creation 169
12: Critics and Apologists 171
  Reframing The Faith Crisis Study 174
  The Grievance grifters 178
  Reframing Mormon Stories 180
  Reframing the CES Letter 181
  Reframing apologists 182
  Reframing the Interpreter 183
  Reframing Book of Mormon Central 184
13: Reframing the Gospel Topics Essays 187
  Gospel Topics entry on Book of Mormon Geography 189
  Gospel Topics Essay on Book of Mormon Translation 201
14: Reframing *Saints*, volume 1 233
15: Reframing *Rough Stone Rolling* 249
16: All/Some/None—Book of Mormon geography 253
17: All/Some/None—Book of Mormon translation 260
Appendix 1: Recommended Reading 263
Appendix 2: The Restoration according to Joseph Smith and Oliver
   Cowdery 265
Appendix 3: Restoration Timeline Summary 267
Appendix 4: The *New* New Mormon History 270

Table of Figures

Figure 1 - The FAITH model 36
Figure 2 - Church Structure 69
Figure 3 - Church Structure metaphor 70
Figure 4 - Two Sets of Plates 88
Figure 5 - Church History issues at MOBOM 101
Figure 6 - M2C map by L. E. Hills 111
Figure 7 - Overview of Nephite lands 127
Figure 8 - Two Final Battles - BYU Studies 140
Figure 9 - Historical Record on Mary Whitmer 243

Why *this* Book

We all want to make the world a better place. This book is my small contribution to that cause. It's not easy to write a book—lots of "fun" activities compete and life is short—so we need a good reason to write and read books. Here's mine:

> The reframes in this book will enhance understanding and goodwill among everyone interested in the Restoration—believers, critics, and curious bystanders alike—by shifting consciousness toward unity.

By "Restoration" I refer to the specific Restoration movement started by Joseph Smith and Oliver Cowdery, based on their truth claims about divine intervention leading to the formation of a church in 1830.[5]

Like you, I've read, watched, and listened to lots of content about the Restoration from many perspectives. Most of it, whether faithful or critical, aims for a particular audience who agrees with them.

Such content reinforces the barriers between people. Confirmation bias serves a useful purpose for group cohesion. But times are changing. People like you and me prefer to make our own informed decisions instead of simply choosing a team and sticking with it no matter what.

That's not to say I'm not on a team, because I am. We all are, one way or another. But my teammates disagree among themselves, and people on other teams also have good ideas and objectives. I figure, why not learn from everyone?

This book originated as a series of reframes derived from my previous books that describe a rational approach to the Restoration. To me, the Restoration is the fulfillment of centuries of Christian hopes and faith. It offers what most people around the world seek: **peace, prosperity, and purpose**.

But the message is often obscured by ancillary distractions. And certainly, critics view the Restoration much less positively. Having been

---

[5] This is distinct from other Christian Restoration movements that preceded and followed what they started, but it includes all the groups who accept what they started.

raised in a "mixed-faith" family, including a stepbrother who was so "anti-Mormon" that he addressed letters to me on my mission as "Younger Neville," I'm fully conversant with both the critics and the apologists.

The reframes in my books offer a way to "think different," to quote the old Apple slogan. I wrote the books partly to respond to modern narratives developed by faithful Latter-day Saint scholars—apologists—that have made the Restoration less rational, and therefore less credible.

Reframes are prompted by conversations, contemplations, and even contentions.

Contention—strong disagreement over beliefs, ideas, and values—is driven by the human compulsion to prevail by converting, persuading, or compelling others to change *their* minds because, after all, we are "right." But, as Joseph Smith observed, "all their good feelings one for another, if they ever had any, were entirely lost in a strife of words and a contest about opinions."

We all want less of that in the world.

In this book, we'll discuss practical ways to "reframe" contention to mitigate and avoid that problem. Instead of papering over differences, we want to solve for clarity, charity and understanding.

Naturally, we'll each have our own opinions about what makes the world a better place and whether this book contributes to that effort.

Which is exactly how it should be. Let's see if we can enhance good feelings—be "of one heart and one mind" —*because* of our differences.

That's not as paradoxical as it might seem at first.

———

Throughout this book I embrace this aphorism, and I invite you to do likewise.

> "I will ask no man to believe as I do".
>
> Joseph Smith[6]

---

[6] https://www.josephsmithpapers.org/paper-summary/discourse-9-july-1843-as-reported-by-willard-richards/3

Section I – Rationality

The following excerpt from a letter written by Matthew L. Davis to Mary Greene Davis describes a discourse Matthew listened to, delivered by Joseph Smith in Washington, D.C., on 5 February 1840. Emphasis added.

He [Joseph Smith] commenced, by saying, that he knew the prejudices which were abroad in the world against him; but requested us to pay to no respect to the rumors which were in circulation respecting him and his doctrines…

I believe, said he, that there is a God, possessing all the attributes ascribed to him by Christians of all denominations. That he reigns over all things in Heaven and on Earth; and that all are subject to his power. He then spoke, **rationally**, of the attributes of Divinity, such as foreknowledge; mercy, &c &c

He then took up the Bible. I believe, said he, in this sacred volume— In it the Mormon faith is to be found. We teach nothing but what the Bible teaches. We believe nothing but what is to be found in this Book…

There was much in his precepts, if they were followed, that would soften the asperities of man towards man, and that **would tend to make him a more rational being than he is generally found to be.**

There was no violence; no fury; no denunciation. His religion appears to be the religion of meekness; lowliness, and mild persuasion.

https://www.josephsmithpapers.org/paper-summary/discourse-5-february-1840/1

1. Something for everyone.

A few months ago, my wife and I sat down for breakfast at our hotel in Fiji. Two college-age women shared our table. Australians. Except one was born in Russia and the other in South Africa. They had immigrated with their families when they were young.

As it was a spectacular morning, I commented on how everything is awesome: the ocean, the sunrise, the food on the plates before us.

They seemed surprised. They listed a string of worries ranging from catastrophic climate change to the economy, war, inequality, etc.

I responded by pointing out that air and water are cleaner than they have been in decades, despite the increase in human population and wealth; forests are expanding; we have abundant nutritious food and relatively clean energy (that is becoming cleaner all the time); and that health, environment and poverty statistics are improving everywhere in the world.

They seemingly had never heard such optimism, having been fed a steady stream of negativity by the media and their college professors. They thanked us for the new perspective—the reframe.

Media narrative	Reframe
Conditions in the world are terrible and are getting worse.	Conditions in the world are not ideal but are improving and are better than ever before in history.

I had a similar after-dinner conversation with a couple of Latter-day Saint (LDS) missionaries. We talked about how we're living in the Golden Age: high-tech, education, and communication have combined to produce unprecedented global prosperity and opportunity. In many ways, we live at the height of human civilization.

And yet, we recognized that anxiety and depression seem pervasive. People are dissatisfied, looking for something they can't find. They're not even sure what, exactly, they seek, but they sense something is missing.

And they don't know where to find it.

One of the Elders (both 19 years old) said, "You've lived a long life. What has kept you faithful in the Church for so many years?"

I mentally sorted through a variety of scenarios:

- A 19-year-old LDS missionary who constantly encounters questions about faith from active LDS, nominal LDS, former LDS, and never LDS, any of whom could be curious, antagonistic, or apathetic.
- A non-LDS Christian who accepts the Bible but rejects the Book of Mormon.
- A non-Christian who knows nothing about the Bible and has a different (or no) religious tradition.
- A life-long faithful LDS who faces a difficult health, financial, or faith crisis.
- A former LDS who can't understand why anyone stays in the Church, given all the "problems with Church history" or other issues.
- An LDS teenager who wonders whether to go on a mission or even whether to continue attending church.
- A new or prospective convert who is confused by conflicting narratives or paradoxes.
- A faithful LDS who enjoys sharing accounts of conversion, testimony, life experiences, and insights.

I'm empathetic with these circumstances and recognize they would each elicit a different discussion. Sometimes it seems that people are so different—so fundamentally different—that it is impossible for them to even communicate, let alone find common ground on anything.

Despite our many individual differences, one thing you and I have in common with people everywhere is the capacity to reason. In this time of contention and distrust, rationality leads to understanding one another. Understanding, and *not* conformity or agreement, is the common ground that we all seek. Or *should* seek, if we are rational.

In this book I propose that rationality is a tool God uses as well.

You may identify with one or more of these scenarios or another of the myriad we could think of. Regardless of where you're coming from, I

The Rational Restoration

wrote this book to offer perspectives that may be new to you—but not to persuade you of anything.

We humans resist persuasion anyway. We want to think for ourselves. As we should.

To paraphrase Newton's third law of motion, "For every argument there is an equal and opposite, or contrary, argument." To explore new ideas, we'll discuss them as "reframes" or different ways of understanding and interpreting facts and hypotheses.

Whether by nature or nurture (or both), I'm usually skeptical. I follow the adage of "trust, but verify."

I hope this book helps you think about how *you* think about these issues. I'm just explaining how I see things and I invite you to do the same. Make notes in the book. Post thoughts on social media. Email me or another friend to explore alternatives. Let's promote rational understanding of one another.

You are already familiar with reframes. You've had many in your life already. Every time you learned something in school and thought "I didn't know that," you saw the world a little differently.

Reframes can be incremental or abrupt and life changing. Think of the first time you fell in love. Your world changed.

Reframes occur at individual, family, group, and social levels. Succeeding generations may share a language but not a worldview. Contemporary generations may share a worldview but not a language.

When the ordinary clash of worldviews between generations reaches a breaking point, reframes can help restore mutual understanding. In our day, younger generations today have been shaped by

> exposure to cultural, racial, religious, and sexual diversity (which promotes a nonjudgmental approach to how others live their lives)... [they] don't view life in traditional binaries of sacred versus secular, biblical versus nonbiblical, left versus right, and so on. They are comfortable with both/and. They are the champions of non-dualistic unitive thinking.[7]

---

[7] The New Copernicans, page x.

Unitive thinking embraces reframes aiming at clarity, charity and understanding.

Rationality. I assume you already know what "rationality" means. And yet, even experts disagree about whether people are mostly rational or mostly irrational.

In this book, we discuss rationality as the common bond of humanity, despite our frequent confusion, emotions, and erratic behavior. Rationality underlies language, culture, and social structure. We interact with the physical world, itself a rational, rules-based system. Matter and energy obey laws of physics. Imagine the chaos if they didn't!

We all think we are rational, more or less, but we wonder about everyone else who acts or thinks differently. Human actions that appear irrational from one perspective might be rational from another perspective. We choose among rational alternatives, with our choices being driven by the narratives through which we understand the world.

But we also acknowledge that we often rationalize decisions *after* we make them based on irrational factors. We constantly confirm and reaffirm our biases. Distinguishing between *rational* decisions and *rationalized* decisions can be difficult and unnerving.

That's why reframes are handy.

Another key point: rationality is not synonymous with materialism. Rational outcomes flow from logically following facts, assumptions, inferences, etc. Multiple working hypotheses can all be rational.

Restoration. The "Restoration" in the title refers to the events described by Oliver Cowdery and Joseph Smith, Jr., involving what they called "a marvelous work and a wonder."[8] If you're not familiar with Oliver and Joseph, you should read Appendix 2 for background.

Basically, they made truth claims regarding angelic ministrations related to the origin and setting of the Book of Mormon, the Restoration of the Priesthood and the Restoration of specific keys for the gathering of Israel, temple sealings, etc. They founded a church, now known as the

---

[8] https://www.josephsmithpapers.org/paper-summary/history-1834-1836/68

The Rational Restoration

Church of Jesus Christ of Latter-day Saints.⁹ I'm a member, partly because, in my view, the Restoration is rational. (See Chapter 3).

Obviously, other people do not think the Restoration is rational. Critics arose simultaneously with the Restoration, accusing Joseph Smith of lying about his experiences and labeling the movement a fraud and an imposition. They proposed alternative naturalistic theories for the origin of the Book of Mormon.

Christian ministers claimed the Restoration was blasphemous and contrary to the Bible. "Mormons" were not Christian because they did not accept the Nicaean creed and taught a "different Jesus."

The same dichotomy of opinion persists today, albeit with more nuances. To clarify and simplify the various positions, I summarize these in the "all, some, none" model of analysis discussed in chapter 6. This model categorizes beliefs based on how the proponent approaches the truth claims made by Joseph and Oliver.

The current iteration of the Church's website reframes past narratives by emphasizing three main benefits the Church offers.¹⁰

1. Learn about Jesus Christ: get to know and follow Him.
2. Find meaning in your life: seek God's perspective.
3. Navigate life's challenges: discover strength, direction, and peace.

What We Believe   Learn about The Church of Jesus Christ of Latter-day Saints

Learn About Jesus Christ
Get to know and follow Him

Find Meaning in Your Life
Seek God's perspective

Navigate Life's Challenges
Discover strength, direction, and peace

---

⁹ There are numerous other denominations in the Restoration. For a list, see https://en.m.wikipedia.org/wiki/List_of_denominations_in_the_Latter_Day_Saint_movement

¹⁰ https://new.churchofjesuschrist.org/?lang=eng (accessed August 2023).

Some might complain that this reframe glosses over the historical record, but I consider it a more accurate explanation of the Restoration—an explanation that is consistent with what the Restoration was supposed to accomplish all along.

You will notice this book is not one long narrative. I started with a discussion of rationality so that you and I are on the same page, not only literally but conceptually. I do this in the pursuit of clarity, charity, and understanding.

Clarity. One cause of contention and confusion is word thinking. If we have different definitions of terms and concepts, we'll never communicate effectively, so I'll define terms as we go.

Charity. I assume you are reading and engaging in good faith, and I hope you see that I'm doing the same.

Understanding. Finally, I seek understanding, not persuasion. I'm fine with you believing whatever you want. I challenge everything I read and hear. Whenever my wife points out that I'm oppositional, I immediately respond "No I'm not." (Running joke.) But seriously, I expect you to disagree with me about lots of things, and that's fine.

If you spot errors in the book, please contact me and let me know. I'm continually revising my books in response to reader feedback and new information. That said, please don't rehash old arguments. We don't want to emulate Tolstoy's Anatole. "Anatole, with the partiality dull-witted people have for any conclusion they have reached by their own reasoning, repeated the argument he had already put to Dolokhow a hundred times." Leo Tolstoy, *War and Peace*

One last point. The table of contents directs you to specific reframes that might interest you more than others. For example, you can jump to reframes about LDS Church history or rational living or critics and apologists. Don't think you need to read from beginning to end.

2. The Nature of the Restoration

This year marks the 200th anniversary of Moroni's visit to Joseph Smith in 1823. In the ensuing years, the Restoration has generated narratives ranging from vociferous opposition to sublime embraces. It has changed the lives of millions of people.

Joseph said Moroni told him that "my name should be had for good and evil among all nations, kindreds, and tongues, or that it should be both good and evil spoken of among all people." (JS-H 1:33)

It was an audacious claim in 1823. Even when it was first published in 1842 (having been written by scribes in 1838), Joseph's name was only somewhat known in a few parts of the United States, Canada, and England, where most people were Christians. Today, Joseph's name trends on Twitter and other social media, and is "both good and evil spoken of among all people" around the world.

Before delving into specific topics and reframes, let's discuss the nature of the Restoration.

Many people think of the Restoration as a threat or enemy to their existing beliefs, customs, traditions, and worldviews. Others see it as an escape from their existing beliefs, customs, traditions, and worldviews.

Before framing it as a threat to, or an escape from, our comfortable traditions, we can look at what Joseph Smith said in the last year of his life as he looked back on all that had happened.

In July 1843, less than a year before his death, Joseph Smith gave a sermon that exemplifies the spirit of the Restoration. One of his scribes took the notes below. I've bolded significant passages.

I think most people would feel affinity with what Joseph expressed. See what you think.

―――

Joseph remarked that **all was well between him and the heavens, that he had no enmity against anyone**. And as the prayer of Jesus, or his pattern, so prayed Joseph. Father forgive me my trespasses as I forgive those who trespass against me. For I freely forgive all men.

If we would secure & cultivate the love of others we must love others. Even our enemies— as well as friends.

People ask, "why is it this babler gains so many followers & retains them"?

Because **I possess the principle of love.** All I can offer the world is a good heart & a good hand. Mormons can testify whether I am willing to lay down my life for a Mormon.

If it has been demonstrated that I have been willing to die for a Mormon I am bold to declare before heaven that I am just as ready to die for a Presbyterian, a Baptist or any other denomination.

It is a love of liberty which inspires my soul. Civil and religious liberty were diffused into my soul by my grandfathers while they dandled me on their knees.

And shall I want friends? no!

"Wherein do you differ from others in your religious views?"

In reality and essence we do not differ so far in our religious views but that we could all drink into one principle of love.

One of the grand fundamental principles of Mormonism is to receive truth let it come from where it may.

...

If I esteem mankind to be in error shall I bear them down? no!

I will lift them up, and in his own way, if I cannot persuade him my way is better.

And I will ask no man to believe as I do.[11]

Later that month, Joseph added, "**Friendship is one of the grand fundamental principles of Mormonism** to revolutionize and civilize the world, and cause wars and contentions to cease, and men to become friends and brothers."[12]

---

[11] https://www.josephsmithpapers.org/paper-summary/discourse-9-july-1843-as-reported-by-willard-richards/1

[12] https://www.josephsmithpapers.org/paper-summary/history-1838-1856-volume-e-1-1-july-1843-30-april-1844/50

3. Rational Explanations

One influence on my thinking about rationality is Matt Ridley's book, *The Rational Optimist: How Prosperity Evolves*. As a natural optimist and a trained economist,[13] I found Ridley's book insightful. In the opening pages, he includes this diagram.

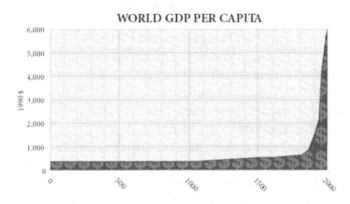

Other studies show similar results, with a tremendous burst of knowledge and prosperity beginning in the early 1800s.

Ridley's view of the world—his operating framework—attributes this progress to social evolution.

After observing that human society did not materially change until, "at some point, human intelligence became collective and cumulative in a way that happened to no other animal," Ridley asserts that

> Humanity is experiencing an extraordinary burst of evolutionary change, driven by good old-fashioned Darwinian natural selection. But it is selection among ideas, not among genes. The habitat in which these ideas reside consists of human brains.

---

[13] I have a degree in Agricultural Economics and a Master's in Agribusiness and I worked professionally in the field.

Ridley further developed his framing in the book *The Evolution of Everything: How Ideas Emerge*, which argues that evolution, not design, shapes culture, technology and society.

Ridley is a careful and persuasive proponent of his worldview, but when I looked at exactly the same data he did, I reached a much different conclusion or hypothesis. That and other similar examples led me to explore how rational people, looking at identical facts, can reach such different outcomes.

Eventually, I developed an approach that looks at the Facts, Assumptions, Inferences, and Theories that lead to a rational worldview or Hypothesis. Hence the FAITH model that we'll discuss in Chapter 5.

In this case, when I look at Ridley's graph of world GDP per capita, I see something different than he does. A reframe that makes sense to me but that apparently didn't occur to Ridley.

You can probably already guess what it is.

Go ahead and fill in the blank: _____.

But before we find out if you guessed correctly, let me explain an experience I had in India.

I was in India on business. At the time, I was co-owner of a computer animation business. We did projects around the world, including in India.

My customers were gracious. They hosted a luncheon for me and introduced me as "a Mormon, and Mormons are just like Hindus." They were referring to their experiences attending business meetings and conferences in California. They were uncomfortable; they cooked their own food in their hotel room to avoid contamination. Later, they told me I was the only American they had met who didn't drink, smoke, and/or carouse. When they visited me in Salt Lake City, they were impressed to discover lots more Americans who were focused on family.

Obviously, their impressions of America were tainted by California business conferences and Hollywood portrayals. Millions of non-LDS Americans also focus on families and avoid the "vices" my hosts deplored.

But nevertheless, they had known nothing about Mormons previously and they felt an immediate affinity. I soon discovered why.

During this visit to India, my hosts took me to visit Swaminarayan Akshardham (Gandhinagar), a large complex that includes a Hindu temple and an extensive visitor center. I walked down a hallway, turned the corner, and confronted a display of God, floating in the air in human form, appearing to Swaminarayan, who was kneeling on the ground looking up. Apart from the Hindu apparel and design, the display would have fit in Temple Square in Salt Lake City.

It turned out that Swaminarayan (1781-1830) was a contemporary of Joseph Smith, Jr. He introduced religious reforms and produced a scriptural text in 1826 containing dietary instructions and prohibition of alcohol or drugs that remains the basis for a Hindu sect that continues today. He taught that God has a physical form; hence the diorama.

I don't relate this to suggest that Swaminarayan and Joseph Smith taught the same things, but only to point out that God inspires people throughout the world. As the Book of Mormon says, "I bring forth my word unto the children of men, yea, even upon all the nations of the earth." (2 Nephi 29:7)

Let's return to Ridley's diagram.

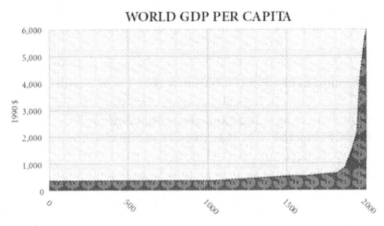

What Ridley sees as "an extraordinary burst of evolutionary change" looks to me like an abrupt enhancement of human intelligence of the sort that had long been anticipated by Christians (see Chapter 8).

I understood Ridley's argument, but I reframed the evidence as the fulfillment of Biblical prophecy. As soon as I did, all of the facts Ridley cited to support his hypothesis also fit my own. We looked at the same facts, applied our respective assumptions, interpretations, and theories, and developed a hypothesis as our filter to understand the world.

Burst of human prosperity in early 1800s	
Ridley narrative	My reframe
The rapid rise of human prosperity in the early 1800s is an extraordinary burst of evolutionary change	The rapid rise of human prosperity in the early 1800s reflects the Restoration of divine inspiration in the fulfillment of prophecy

Yes, if you wrote Restoration in the blank above, you were correct.

Obviously, people can choose between these or other worldviews to explain the data. To be rational, the conclusion or hypothesis should logically flow from the facts, assumptions, inferences and theories one applies.

This is where critics may complain that it is not "rational" to assume or infer divine (supernatural) factors. But that's not really an argument based on rationality. It's an argument based on strict materialism.

A key component of my reframe is that I agree with Ridley in the sense that these technological changes are the natural outcome of enhanced human communication and cooperation. They are probably not *all* divinely directed. But that doesn't mean *none* are inspired. Those who have experienced unexpected insights of the sort that leads to new discoveries may relate to this explanation from Joseph Smith:

> A person may profit by noticing the first intimation of the Spirit of Revelation for instance when you feel pure Intelligence flowing unto you it may give you sudden strokes of ideas that by noticing it you may find it fulfilled the same day or soon.[14]

Here's a related reframe that fits the observable data:

---

[14] https://www.josephsmithpapers.org/paper-summary/discourse-between-circa-26-june-and-circa-2-july-1839-as-reported-by-willard-richards/1

Industrial Revolution	
Naturalistic narratives	Reframe
The industrial revolution arose from the introduction of tea and coffee to the English business community, replacing the alcoholic beverages people consumed to kill off water-borne diseases.	God can work better with a clear mind than with an inebriated one.

As you can tell already, there are innumerable reframes that we can use to understand how and why people think differently. You've probably already thought of a few just by considering this example.

The Age of Reason

Ridley's chart corresponds with another development in western society called the Age of Reason after the book of that name.

Thomas Paine first published *The Age of Reason* in 1794. The book, which questioned the legitimacy of the Bible and Christianity generally, sold thousands of copies in the United States. Paine, who was not atheist, advocated that reason should replace revelation and that God does not suspend natural laws to perform miracles. He also opposed organized Christianity, arguing it had become corrupted by priests who insisted on rituals and doctrines such as original sin that made people dependent on the priests.

> The evidence I have produced, and shall still produce in the course of this work, to prove that the Bible is without authority, will, whilst it wounds the stubbornness of a priest, relieve and tranquillize the minds of millions: it will free them from all those hard thoughts of the Almighty which priestcraft and the Bible had infused into their minds, and which stood in

everlasting opposition to all their ideas of his moral justice and benevolence.[15]

The book provoked a backlash, contributing to the Second Great Awakening. Paine was denounced by ministers and the media; Harvard students received a copy of a book rebutting *The Age of Reason*.

An intimate example of the conflict was related by Lucy Mack Smith, who reported that her father-in-law used *The Age of Reason* as a cudgel to keep her husband away from church.

> I endeavored to persuade my husband to attend the Methodist meeting with me he went a few times to grat[ify] me for he had so little faith in the doctrines taught by them that my feelings were the only inducement for him to go— But as soon as his Father and brother Jesse [Smith] heard that we were attending methodist meeting they were much displeased and his father came to the door one day and **threw Tom Pain's age of reason into the house** and angrily bade him read that until he believed it they also told him that he ought not to let his wife go to the meetings and it would be far better for him to stop going accordingly my husband requested me not to go[16]

Some authors have proposed that the Restoration arose from Joseph Smith's understandable desire to defend the legitimacy of the Bible. This view sees the Book of Mormon as partly a response to *The Age of Reason*, such as in the way it affirms the validity of Matthew 27:51-53.[17]

I see it differently. The age of rationality was a necessary precursor for the restoration of the gospel because to fulfill its purpose, the Restoration needs to overcome centuries of irrationality, tribalism, etc.

---

[15] Thomas Paine, *The Age of Reason*, p. 88, https://klymkowskylab.colorado.edu/Readings/Thomas%20Paine%20-%20The%20Age%20of%20Reason.pdf

[16] https://www.josephsmithpapers.org/paper-summary/lucy-mack-smith-history-1844-1845/250

[17] Grant Adamson, "Joseph Smith, Thomas Paine, and Matthew 27:51b–53," *Dialogue*, Volume 54, No. 4 (2021), online at https://www.dialoguejournal.com/articles/joseph-smith-thomas-paine-and-matthew-2751b-53/

The Rational Restoration

Paine made some legitimate objections to what Christianity had become. His worldview—his framing—was an understandable reaction to the abuses and even irrationality of what was being taught.

In that sense, he helped open the door to the Restoration.[18]

The Age of Reason	
Naturalistic narratives	Reframe
The Age of Reason affirmed a rational framework that rejected doctrinal and supernatural elements of Christianity. The Restoration was partly Joseph Smith's response to *The Age of Reason* as he sought to reaffirm the truthfulness of the Bible, not God's miraculous intervention with human affairs.	*The Age of Reason* affirmed a rational framework that was necessary to overcome centuries of tradition and oppression. The Restoration relies on and incorporates rational thinking together with God's miraculous intervention with human affairs.

An 1831 revelation, now D&C 45, summarized the Restoration and explained how reasoning would help people understand the Restoration.

> 9 And even so I have sent mine everlasting covenant into the world, to be a light to the world, and to be a standard for my people, and for the Gentiles to seek to it, and to be a messenger before my face to prepare the way before me.
> 10 Wherefore, come ye unto it, and with him that cometh I will **reason** as with men in days of old, and I will show unto you my strong **reasoning**.
> 11 Wherefore, hearken ye together and let me show unto you even my wisdom—the wisdom of him whom ye say is the God of Enoch, and his brethren,
> 12 Who were separated from the earth, and were received unto myself—a city reserved until a day of righteousness shall come—a day which was

---

[18] Critics might say that Paine's criticisms apply to the Restoration as well. Such obvious and predictable NPC (non-player character) arguments are the type of ping-pong debates that go nowhere so I don't take the time to address them here.

sought for by all holy men, and they found it not because of wickedness and abominations;
13 And confessed they were strangers and pilgrims on the earth;
14 But obtained a promise that they should find it and see it in their flesh.
15 Wherefore, hearken and I will **reason** with you, and I will speak unto you and prophesy, as unto men in days of old.
(Doctrine and Covenants 45:9–15)

In what ways has the Lord reasoned with us?

Eight months later, on November 3, 1831 at Hiram, Ohio, the Lord expanded his explanation.

57 And for this cause, that men might be made partakers of the glories which were to be revealed, the Lord sent forth the fulness of his gospel, his everlasting covenant, **reasoning in plainness and simplicity**—
58 To prepare the weak for those things which are coming on the earth,
(Doctrine and Covenants 133:57–58)

Now we can ask, how does the Lord reason "in plainness and simplicity?"

That's what the rest of this book is about.

Observation, Reason, Faith, and Revelation

At BYU Education Week in August 2023, Elder Dale G. Renlund delivered an address titled "Observation, Reason, Faith and Revelation." It's an exceptional description of the interplay of these sources of knowledge. Everyone should watch or read it. Key excerpts:

Sometimes we fall into a trap of dealing with false dichotomies. For instance, we might believe that observation or Reason are the only valid ways to learn truth, or we might believe that observation and reason undermine Faith to such an extent that they should have no role in religious life. This is a false dichotomy because observation and reason work synergistically with faith. Faith without works will not amplify itself. Faith will only grow by observation and reasoning coupled with other spiritual work.

The Rational Restoration

When we start with an inclination to believe, observation leads to Faith. As Faith grows, reason facilitates the transformation of faith into revelatory knowledge. And revelatory knowledge produces added faith. (D&C 8).

Studying it out in one's mind—coupling faith and observation with reason—was necessary for spiritual impressions to come. We focus on a problem, study it out and think about it. We formulate various solutions. It seems that only then can personal revelation reliably come.

The Holy Ghost communicates in different ways to different people at different times. Observing how he speaks to us is critical to receiving further revelation.[19]
...

Personal revelation is facilitated by understanding and formulating questions from multiple angles. Formulating and reframing questions requires observation, reason and faith. At one time or another many of us have asked ourselves, "How do I know whether the thought I have is my own or if it's from the Holy Ghost?" This is a reasonable question.

Perhaps a better question and certainly more actionable is this: "Should I act on this particular thought?"

President Dallin H. Oaks taught we should study things out in our minds using our reasoning Powers the creator has placed within us then we should pray for guidance and act upon it if we receive it. If we don't receive guidance we should act upon our best judgment.
...

President Dallin H. Oaks cautioned persons who persist in seeking revelatory guidance on subjects on which the Lord has not chosen to direct us may concoct an answer out of their own fantasy or bias or they may even receive an answer through the medium of false revelation. The Prophet Joseph Smith warned "nothing is a greater injury to the children of men than to be under the influence of a false Spirit when they think they have the spirit of God." We shouldn't try to force spiritual things.

---

[19] Elder Dale G. Renlund, "Observation, Reason, Faith, and Revelation," BYU Education Week, August 2023. https://www.youtube.com/watch?v=NTOIx-_4QSg

Cause to believe

Many people say they cannot believe in God or religion without tangible evidence. They don't believe that faith is a legitimate basis for knowledge. That's a rational approach, if you assume that the only reality is what we can perceive with our physical senses. This is strict materialism. It seems axiomatic, really; when we *know* something, we no longer have to *believe*.

Others see the lack of tangible evidence as actual evidence of God. Instead of tangible evidence, God gives us "cause to believe." Then we can choose whether or not to believe. The rationale is that a loving God knows it would be worse to know the will of God and reject it than to only believe and reject it.

Alma explained it this way.

> 17 Yea, there are many who do say: If thou wilt show unto us a sign from heaven, then we shall know of a surety; then we shall believe.
> 18 Now I ask, is this faith? Behold, I say unto you, Nay; for if a man knoweth a thing he hath no cause to believe, for he knoweth it.
> 19 And now, how much more cursed is he that knoweth the will of God and doeth it not, than he that only believeth, or only hath cause to believe, and falleth into transgression?
> 20 Now of this thing ye must judge. Behold, I say unto you, that it is on the one hand even as it is on the other; and it shall be unto every man according to his work. (Alma 32:17–20)

John Lennox, a professor of Mathematics at Oxford University, observes that

> either human intelligence ultimately owes its origin to mindless matter; or there is a Creator. It is strange that some people claim that it is their intelligence that leads them to prefer the first to the second.[20]

---

[20] https://www.johnlennox.org/

Pursuit of an ideal society

For four years I taught Chinese students at a Chinese university, first in person, then online. My students were as idealistic as students in any other country.

One of my Chinese university students wrote:

> Human nature is not easy to change. But I really want humanity to be better, so that the world will be a better, friendly, happy place. We have experienced so much human ugliness, so we yearn for a better world.

This universal human desire for an ideal society is one of the purposes for the Restoration. Through the Restoration, we not only learn principles of living that change human thinking and behavior to bring about an ideal society, but we see the development of a worldwide church capable of organizing people effectively and rationally to make such a society possible.

Human societies today are more prosperous than ever before in human history, yet people are dissatisfied, unhappy, angry. They sense something is missing, but they don't know what it is. They have aspirations and ideals but don't know how to achieve them.

As we saw at the outset, many of "the rising generation, and all the pure in heart... are only kept from the truth because they know not where to find it."

In a materialistic world, *The Rational Restoration* includes a response to revisionist history, cynical skepticism and magical thinking, but it is more than that. It offers a rational, evidence-based explanation for the ongoing Restoration, making the Restoration understandable and attractive.

The concept of Zion, rightly understood, fulfills the universal desire for a just, harmonious society that facilitates the pursuit of happiness for all people.

The Lord explained, "it is my purpose to provide for my saints, for all things are mine. But it must needs be done in mine own way."

In his book *Of One Heart*, Neal A. Maxwell used a fictional exchange of letters to describe aspects of a Zion society that are part of the Restoration.

There appear to be no new or complex doctrines that would account for the unique outcome in the city of Enoch. One will look in vain in the scriptures for a single spectacular teaching that accounts for this singular and spectacular event. Clearly, what made these people unique was their serious and steady application of the simple teachings of Jesus Christ. p. vi

"You know from our sharings in the past that while I have not been religious, I am not one of those who believe that life is explainable without acknowledging the existence of a God, though I have resisted the efforts of factions to capture God as if he were their own private trophy. Enoch does not give me that tribal feeling. Men seem to me to belong to such factions solely to increase the strength of their own voices, to give them the courage they otherwise lack, or to get gain by multiplying their power. p. 5.

Enoch's followers are not long-faced and sad; they are a happy and smiling people who pay much heed to the needs of each other. Their striking individuality seems to be heightened, not lessened, by their faith in Jesus Christ, who, they say, is the ultimate Redeemer to come. Their unity is not the conformity that you and I have seen imposed by the sword; it rests upon mutual esteem and mutual desires. p. 8.

You write that your countrymen are not steady and consistent. The adversary need not be consistent, Omner. Indeed, evil is not only erotic, it is erratic, since it must entice so many in such a multitude of ways. Thus, persuade a man possessed of one truth that he has all truth. Convince another that there is no truth whatsoever. Let another believe that all truths are of equal importance to man. Notice, Omner, that the result is the same in all cases: the searching for truth stops. Allow one person to think that no matter what he does, it is not wrong. Tell another that he has done wrong, but it is not serious. Persuade another that he has erred so gravely that there is no hope for him. Again, the result is the same: the sinning continues. p. 25.

The principles of a Zion society are rational. They respond to human psychology, physiology, and spirituality. The pursuit of an ideal society can be simplified into a simple phrase:
Live rationally with God.

Rationality in Religion

Philosophers have extensively debated the problem of evil. A common explanation by Hume, derived from the ancient Greek named Epicurus, goes like this:

Is God willing to prevent evil, but not able? Then he is not omnipotent.
Is he able, but not willing? Then he is malevolent.
Is he both able and willing? Then from whence comes evil?
Is he neither able nor willing? Then why call him God?[21]

Debates swirl around the definitions of terms (what is evil?), God's unwillingness to override free will (agency), comparisons of lesser vs. greater evil, and so forth. These debates are never resolved because they rely on subjective criteria, including assumptions, inferences, and theories.

It may be useful to consider this reframe.

Atheist narrative	Reframe
There is great evil in the world, which proves that either God does not exist or God is powerless or malevolent.	There is great evil in the world, but imagine how much worse it would be without God's influence to offset it.

If you're coming from the atheist framework, the reframe might be impossible to consider. But you don't have to agree with it or adopt it. Just use the reframe to understand how other people see the world.

If you're a believer but you think God does not do enough to prevent evil, maybe the reframe will enable you to appreciate that God does a lot more to mitigate and prevent evil than we realize.

This reversal reframing appears in the scriptures, when Alma and Korihor cited the same facts but reached opposite conclusions. In both

---

[21] A useful overview is here: https://en.wikipedia.org/wiki/Problem_of_evil.

cases, they relied on the facts of what is visible, but they applied different assumptions and inferences from those facts.

Atheist narrative	Reframe
[Priests threaten believers] that they should, if they did not do according to their words, offend some unknown being, who they say is God—a being who never has been seen or known, who never was nor ever will be. (Alma 30:28)	all things denote there is a God; yea, even the earth, and all things that are upon the face of it, yea, and its motion, yea, and also all the planets which move in their regular form do witness that there is a Supreme Creator. (Alma 30:44)

Harvard cognitive scientist Steven Pinker opened his book *Rationality* with the declaration that "Rationality ought to be the lodestar for everything we think and do."[22]

Would you agree or disagree?

His deliberately provocative sentence works, ironically, because we humans are not completely rational—and we shouldn't be.

Later in his book Pinker admits that rationality is only one element of human thought and behavior—one tool among many to enable us to find fulfillment in our individual and social lives. I suspect he knows a more accurate—a more *rational*—sentence would have been this:

"Rationality ought to be *a* lodestar for *many* things we think and do."

How much of a lodestar, and for what things we think and do, is an open question.

―――

I assume that you, like me, are fascinated by the variety of beliefs people have. I've conversed with innumerable Catholics and atheists in France, Coptic Christians in Cairo, a Druze scholar in Lebanon, Hindus in India and Africa, Buddhists in Asia, Orthodox and atheists in Russia, as well as Jews, Muslims, Evangelicals, Jehovah's Witnesses, and more.

―――

[22] Steven Pinker, Rationality: What it Is, Why it Seems Scarce, Why it Matters, (Viking: New York, NY) 2021, Preface.

The Rational Restoration

Whether by disposition or training and experience (having been a lawyer for decades), I not only enjoy but I seek out multiple working hypotheses, pursuant to the FAITH model we'll discuss in this book.

But there is a threshold question for every person on earth—Christian and otherwise: did Jesus Christ really rise from the dead?

If so, or if not, what does that mean for me?

Questions about moral and political values, history, doctrine, interpersonal relationships... all these and more pale in comparison.

Question 20th. What are the fundamental principles of your religion?

Answer. The fundamental principles of our religion is the testimony of the apostles and prophets concerning Jesus Christ, "that he died, was buried, and rose again the third day, and ascended up into heaven;" and all other things are only appendages to these, which pertain to our religion.[23]

If Jesus did rise from the dead, we naturally ask if others have also risen from the dead. And if they did, can we? And if so, how?

Despite perennial (and new) problems in the world, we live in a Golden Age of knowledge and opportunity. Yet like other Latter-day Saints, I'm aware of challenges and obstacles we face with the ongoing Restoration.

I wrote this book to offer some new perspectives on the origins and destiny of the Restoration. Based on evidence—anecdotal and statistical—new perspectives may be useful.

As Charles Dickens observed in *A Tale of Two Cities*, every age presents contrasts. "It was the best of times, it was the worst of times..."

Best of times	Worst of times
Age of wisdom	Age of foolishness
Epoch of belief	Epoch of incredulity
Season of light	Season of darkness
Spring of hope	Winter of despair

---

[23] Joseph Smith, Questions and Answers, May 8, 1838, in *Elders' Journal*, July 1838. https://www.josephsmithpapers.org/paper-summary/questions-and-answers-8-may-1838/3

Latter-day Saints relate.

We live in a day when hundreds of temples make sacred ordinances readily accessible, the Pathway program is expanding to give quality university education to everyone on the planet, and missionaries use social media to reach the ends of the earth.

Tens of thousands of missionaries are serving, yet the growth of the Church has stalled (23 of 50 states in the USA lost membership between 2019 and 2021),[24] and social media videos by critics and former members attract millions of views.

For some people, religion is primarily, if not purely, a matter of faith. And that's great.

For others (including me), religion implicates reason and rationality. One Church leader explained it this way:

> "Each of us must accommodate the mixture of reason and revelation in our lives. The gospel not only permits but requires it. An individual who concentrates on either side solely and alone will lose both balance and perspective."[25]

Pascal's Wager

When he died in 1662, the French mathematician Blaise Pascal left notes that were published posthumously in a book titled *Pensées* (Thoughts). The book included a philosophical argument that has come to be known as Pascal's Wager.

According to the wager, a rational person would live as though God exists because of the infinite gain of heaven that ensues, versus the finite (temporary) losses of wealth, pleasure, etc. if God does not exist.

---

[24] See https://ldschurchgrowth.blogspot.com/2022/04/membership-by-us-state-in-2021-percent.html

[25] Boyd K. Packer, "I Say unto You, Be One," *BYU Speeches*, February 12, 1991 https://speeches.byu.edu/talks/boyd-k-packer/say-unto-one/

Those who wager against God's existence risk infinite loss (hell) versus only finite gains of wealth, pleasure, etc.

Pascal's wager looks like this:

Live according to:	God Exists	God does not Exist
Belief in God	Infinite gain	Finite loss
Disbelief in God	Infinite loss	Finite gain

Pascal's Wager does not prove the existence of God, but it's a logical framework for approaching the question. People still weigh gains and losses differently. For some people, living as though God exists is both logical and appealing regardless of what they actually believe; e.g., the Ten Commandments are common sense, rational rules for living. For others, adhering to religious teachings feels confining and not worth an infinite gain they don't believe in.

At any rate, Pascal's famous argument frames religion in a logical, rational context.

Critics have raised objections to Pascal's Wager, such as the myriad religions that each claim to represent God.[26] Pascal, a Catholic, suggested that people should study diligently to make informed decisions about what to believe about God and what to do about it.

One critic observed, "perhaps this god is not satisfied with the mere belief that there is a god, but adopts the principle... where the church within which alone salvation is to be found is not necessarily the Church of Rome, but perhaps that of the Anabaptists or the Mormons or the Muslim Sunnis or the worshipers of Kali or of Odin."[27]

The Rational Restoration teaches that God speaks to people everywhere in the context of their respective societies and individual background, psychology, etc.

---

[26] For more analysis, see https://plato.stanford.edu/entries/pascal-wager/ or https://en.wikipedia.org/wiki/Pascal%27s_wager

[27] Mackie, J. L., *The Miracle of Theism* (Oxford 1982), pg. 203, https://archive.org/details/TheMiracleOfTheismArgumentsForAndAgainstTheExistenceOfGodJLMackie/page/n207/mode/2up.

10 Wherefore, because that ye have a Bible ye need not suppose that it contains all my words; neither need ye suppose that I have not caused more to be written.

11 For I command all men, both in the east and in the west, and in the north, and in the south, and in the islands of the sea, that they shall write the words which I speak unto them; for out of the books which shall be written I will judge the world, every man according to their works, according to that which is written. (2 Nephi 29:10–11)

The Nature of Religious Belief

Around the world, people readily embrace new technology (electronics, medicine, agriculture, machinery, etc.), regardless of nationality, language, politics, or religion. People quickly see the advantages of better products, systems, and techniques. They respond to evidence. Once people see what a cell phone can do, they don't need to be persuaded to acquire one.

But religious preference, like language, remains largely regional. In the western world, Latin America and much of Europe is predominantly Catholic. The United States, Scandinavia, Australia/New Zealand, and southern Africa are mostly Protestant. Eastern Europe and Russia are Orthodox. Northern Africa, the Middle East, and Indonesia are mainly Muslim. India is mainly Hindu. Asian countries are largely Buddhist.

Why?

Religious preference, like language, is typically cultural, social and familial. Children acquire a worldview based on the religious traditions they inherit. They filter everything they learn through that worldview, effectively confirming their beliefs. When religious people experience joy, good fortune, etc., they attribute the experience to their respective concepts of the divine.

Just as people can communicate with a variety of languages, they can make sense of the world and find purpose through their respective religions. Religions endure when they improve, or at least maintain, society. They bless the lives of believers in many ways, so people retain their beliefs.

The Rational Restoration

Because the foundations of most religions are obscured by the fog of history, faith is a matter of subjective belief and trust in tradition. Faith is not a result of assessing evidence. People don't automatically embrace a different religion the way they would embrace new technology.

And yet, people do change their religious beliefs when they find compelling reasons to do so.

To achieve its full potential, the Restoration must persuade—the Book of Mormon uses the term *convince*—people that Jesus is the Christ and that the way to happiness and fulfillment is through Him. But so long as the Restoration is obscured by overgrown hedges, few will see the Restoration for what it is.

The term *convince* is rooted in Latin words meaning "conquer with" and was coined in English to mean "overcome, defeat in argument." No one is converted by being defeated in argument. Defeat raises too many psychological objections.

But people do enjoy learning for themselves. They happily embrace new ideas when they understand the benefits. Once the Restoration become clear, they readily and eagerly join in.

Truth Claims

The Restoration is, or should be, different because of truth claims.

Religious belief is complex, but the Restoration is unique because it began with physical evidence of God's reality and intervention in human affairs. The Restoration is not just another philosophy or interpretation. It's not merely a suggestion.

Sacred books such as the Bible and Koran have murky origins. Believers accept them not because they have personally observed Moses or Mohammed receiving revelations and writing them down, but because people they trust have told them these books originated with prophets.

In the early days of the Restoration, things were different.

Joseph Smith, led by an angel, found an ancient record. He translated it into English and had it published. Unlike other religions, the Restoration was supported by objective evidence. Only God could have revealed the existence of such an ancient record.

Moroni explained the hill where the plates was found was the Cumorah mentioned in the record, tying the events in the book to the real world in which Joseph lived. Joseph and his successors reiterated this critical fact for over 150 years.

Joseph also explained that he translated the characters on the plates. Witnesses saw the plates Joseph translated. As directed by Moroni, Joseph translated "by means of the Urim and Thummim" and the text he dictated was "after the manner of [his] language." Joseph explained that the mounds in Ohio, Indiana and Illinois were evidence of the divine authenticity of the Book of Mormon.

That the book fulfilled the hopes and expectations of Christians was all the more impressive. A fulfillment of prophecy.

In recent years, however, LDS scholars have put forth an alternative narrative. Abandoning (de-correlating) these truth claims waters down the Restoration so it becomes like other religions, with a murky origin that depends primarily on faith in traditions.

Changing the narrative so that Joseph didn't really translate the plates but instead read words off a stone (or words he saw in vision) transforms the Book of Mormon into a mystical text, akin to the Koran. With no disrespect to that holy book, turning the Book of Mormon into a mystical text opens the door to claims of pious fraud, composition, and other alternatives to an actual translation of an ancient record.

De-correlating the New York Cumorah detaches the narrative from the real world. It causes confusion and leads to such speculative "internal" maps as those used currently by BYU and CES to teach the Book of Mormon. Faced with this fantasy setting, students (and converts) naturally find it difficult to believe the book is an actual history.

Evidence of the Restoration abounds in the progress of the Church. Faithful communities are found throughout the world and members are prospering through self-reliance and their faith in Christ. But this progress is stunted by the de-correlation of foundational truth claims which undermines belief.

The reframes in this book offer rational narratives based on the historical and other extrinsic evidence that corroborates the traditional truth claims.

4. Clarity, charity and understanding

"There is a beauty and clarity that comes from simplicity that we sometimes do not appreciate in our thirst for intricate solutions."
Dieter F. Uchtdorf

At the beginning of this book I set out my objective:

The reframes in this book will enhance understanding and goodwill among everyone interested in the Restoration—believers, critics, and curious bystanders alike—by shifting consciousness toward unity.

By "unity" I don't mean conformity or agreement. Instead, I mean a higher level of consciousness that doesn't merely acknowledge or tolerate diversity but *enjoys* it. We are sincerely interested in how others view the world, how their reality functions for them, and whether they have insights we can incorporate. We are confident with our own worldview and therefore don't seek reassurance by needing others to agree with us, yet we continually seek "truth let it come from where it may."

Now let's see how this works in the real world. How does any group of people achieve harmony and unity in diversity?

With the tremendous variation of backgrounds, education, culture, and worldviews among people generally, and Latter-day Saints specifically, what does it mean to have harmony and unity instead of disputations and contention?

It's easy to say everyone should agree to get along, but what does that mean? No two people agree perfectly on everything. People don't even agree with themselves; we all change our minds, our preferences, our priorities, etc. Our very brains are diverse.

Temporally, my right brain existed solely for the present moment, with no past regrets, present fears, or future expectations… My left hemisphere, on the other hand, had functioned like a bridge across time: it was responsible for linking this present moment to the past moment and then to the next moment....

By having both of these hemispheres working together inside of one head, we experience a natural duality. As a result, it is normal for us to endure an ongoing internal conflict, based completely on the two uniquely autonomous perspectives of our left and right brains. For example, my left brain might want to jump on that homework immediately and get it done, while my right brain would rather go out and play, leaving the work for the last minute.[28]

We don't resolve the "ongoing internal conflict" in our own brain through lobotomy—removing one or the other side of our brain. Instead, we harmonize that internal conflict through choice and action.

That models the way we can harmonize our relationships with others by implementing clarity, charity, and understanding.

Clarity. Whenever there is a disagreement, the first objective must be clarity. Often disagreements arise from misunderstanding, and clarity can resolve misunderstandings, suspicions, and confusion. "Oh, you meant that? Then we agree after all!"

Clarity reveals whether there really is a disagreement, and whether it is material. If so, clarity lets everyone see if the disagreement is about objectives, values, and ideals, or if it is about the means to achieve a common objective. Many political and business disputes revolve around different means to an end that all parties agree upon.

In cases where contention is entertainment of the sort that produces dopamine (a verbal/intellectual "sporting" contest typical of social media and much of the media), clarity ensures that all parties recognize the "contest" for what it is so they don't take it seriously.

When a disagreement involves the underlying facts, assumptions, inferences, and theories, clarity narrows the issues to specific points that can be addressed and understood in a spirit of charity.

---

[28] Jill Bolte Taylor, Whole Brain Living: the Anatomy of Choice and the Four Characters that Drive our Life (Hay House, New York: 2021).

Charity. After clarifying the issue(s), those involved with the disagreement can invoke harmony by giving one another the benefit of the doubt, including the mutual assumption that everyone is acting in good faith.

This means implementing the six principles President Nelson offered in a Facebook post while observing that "Charity is the antidote to contention." He explained,

> Differences of opinion are part of life. I work daily with people who sometimes see an issue differently. My two noble counselors, Dallin H. Oaks and Henry B. Eyring, have taught me how to disagree in a Christlike way. Over the last five years of working together, we haven't always agreed. Still, they know I want to hear their honest feelings about everything we discuss—especially sensitive issues.
> From their examples, I have learned six ways to disagree:
>
> - Express feelings with love.
> - Don't think you know best.
> - Don't compete.
> - Don't rigorously defend your position.
> - Let the Spirit guide your conversations.
> - Be filled with charity, the pure love of Christ.

People who don't share the value of charity are engaged in a sporting contest for dopamine rather than a pursuit of truth or common ideals.

Understanding (reframing contention). The fundamental reason for contention is the impulse to seek conformity to one's own position, beliefs, priorities, etc. People contend because they want someone else to change, without realizing (or accepting the possibility) that maybe they are the ones who should change.

Usually, the pursuit of conformity includes an element of insecurity; the person seeks reassurance by having someone else agree. Mature confidence prefers clear, charitable understanding over conformity.

When parties to a disagreement seek to "understand" instead of to "convince," they eliminate the utility of contention. They may come to a meeting of the minds and replace disagreement with agreement. Or they might not.

And it doesn't matter.

People who fully understand one another can live in harmony and unity despite their differences. Liberated from the compulsion to "win," they are free to exchange the best ideas and attributes from their respective worldviews.

One of the classic "7 Habits" is "Seek first to understand, then to be understood."[29]

This habit involves listening effectively. But to completely eliminate contention, understanding is not enough. We must be comfortable with different ideas—multiple working hypotheses.

Multiple working hypotheses. Even after people achieve clarity, charity, and understanding, they may realize they still disagree for any number of reasons. Often the differences involve gaps in knowledge. While we await more information, we fill in the gaps according to our own assumptions, inferences, and theories.

In this situation, people can accept the concept of "multiple working hypotheses," whereby different people are all at peace knowing that other people see things differently. This involves a paradoxical combination of confidence and humility; confidence in one's own views together with a humble recognition that someone else might be correct.

The concept of multiple working hypotheses does not deny the existence of truth. "truth is knowledge of things as they are, and as they were, and as they are to come." (Doctrine and Covenants 93:24)

In the absence of complete and universal knowledge, we work with the limited knowledge we do have, much like the proverbial story of the blind men describing an elephant by touch. By sharing our experiences, ideas, beliefs, and hopes, always seeking clarity, charity and understanding, the multiple working hypotheses gradually coalesce as we come closer and closer to the whole truth.

---

[29] https://www.franklincovey.com/the-7-habits/habit-5/

5. The FAITH model

Most of us are generally satisfied with our worldview. Otherwise, we'd change it. That's why many of us are perplexed that other people who seem rational and reasonable have different opinions than we do.

Because we all live on the same planet, share the same basic genetics, and interact with the same laws of physics, we wonder, "How can you think *that?*"

We have no problem with personal preferences: apples over oranges, mathematics over poetry, cutting hair for a living over cutting logs. Diversity of talents and interests makes human society functional, interesting, and meaningful.

Worldviews are more fundamental to our reality than are mere preferences. Different views on politics, religion, science and moral values seem threatening. They generate contention, even war.

People inherit worldviews along with the language they acquire to express themselves. Religion, like language, remains largely regional around the world. We can all see that people with entirely different worldviews live productive, happy lives. We can think of disparate worldviews as multiple working hypotheses.

But we can't help wondering, what if another worldview is better or correct? Does that mean I'm wrong? In what ways? Would I have the courage and humility to change to a "truer" worldview?

And, for purposes of this book, how can we compare one view of the Restoration with other views?

I propose the FAITH model to achieve clarity, charity and understanding.

F – Facts (demonstrable, objective facts everyone can agree upon)
A – Assumptions (what we assume about those facts, given our worldview, often treated as facts)
I – Inferences, interpretations (how we fill gaps and place the facts into a comfortable context)
T – Theory (overall explanation of the facts)
H – Hypothesis (a narrative basis for further investigation)

The optimum outcome of the FAITH analysis is a set of multiple working hypotheses, all based on the same facts, that people can assess for themselves by tracing back upriver from the hypotheses to the facts through the network of inferences and assumptions. While enabling us to make informed decisions, the analysis also hopes to help us understand how and why others reach different conclusions.

Figure 1 - The FAITH model

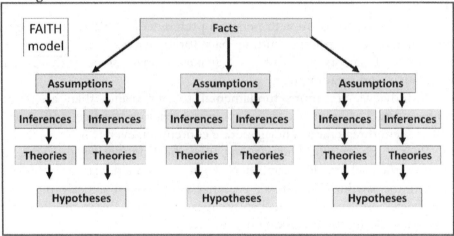

We usually see that the end result—the hypothesis—correlates to the initial assumptions. The hypothesis is driven not by facts, but by assumptions, inferences, and theories.

This surprises many people because we all like to think our opinions are based on facts.

But once we use the FAITH model to separate actual facts from the other elements of our thought process, we can all see that what we may think is *obvious* is merely *confirmation bias*.

Confirmation bias. Steven Pinker defines "confirmation bias" as "the bad habit of seeking evidence that ratifies a belief and being incurious about evidence that might falsify it."[30]

---

[30] *Rationality*, Kindle at 339.

The Rational Restoration

Because the FAITH model lays all the facts out for everyone to see and address, it solves the evidence problem of bias confirmation. Now everyone can see all the facts.

Because the FAITH model requires proponents to articulate their assumptions, inferences and theories, everyone can accurately compare and contrast multiple working hypotheses. Everyone can make informed decisions that comport with their own priorities, values, desires, and experiences of life.

As Christ said, "Ye shall know the truth, and the truth shall make you free." (John 8:22)

Cognitive dissonance. The clarity achieved through the FAITH model presents a risk of cognitive dissonance, which is the mental discomfort we feel when we have two conflicting beliefs or perceive contradictory information. Among Latter-day Saints and their critics, this is sometimes referred to as putting something "on the shelf."

One way to diminish cognitive dissonance is through apathy or indifference.

I have a friend who is normally competitive, but when he sees he's going to lose a game, he often says, "Well, it's only a game, it doesn't really matter." Reminding himself of that (out loud, no less!) may be a healthy antidote to tense competition, but indifference rings hollow when applied to weighty matters.

Certainly, there are times when we legitimately decide something doesn't matter—we have higher priorities elsewhere—so we don't spend time or effort on it. And we don't want to let others set our priorities. As the saying goes, "The business model of the media is to make every problem your problem."

But there are few things more important than finding meaning, purpose, and happiness in life. By reading and sharing this book, you show you care enough about worldviews—frames—to consider these topics seriously.

Regarding the Restoration, whether we are believers or critics there are inevitably some questions we cannot answer. But we want to make informed decisions for ourselves, and we want to understand how and why others see things differently.

Let's turn to the elements of the FAITH model.

Facts

If we seek a rational approach to life and we engage with other people, even if we seek mainly to understand them, we need to be clear about what we believe and why.

And a lot of that has to do with what we think are facts.

Lawyers spend a lot of time sifting evidence to filter "facts" from the "quasi-facts" of assumptions, inferences, and theories. (Here, the term "quasi-fact" refers to types of evidence that people may deem facts even though they are subjective.)

A classic "fact" is the *existence* of a document, which is not the same as the *contents* of a document, which may or may not be factual.

A classic "quasi-fact" is a witness statement in the absence of cross-examination. The statement itself is a fact. That leads us to think the contents, too, are facts. And they may appear factual. But the contents may consist of hearsay, assumptions, inferences, speculation, etc.

Typically, any advocate for a point of view combines facts and quasi-facts. Given the constraints of time and effort, we take intellectual shortcuts to confirm our biases. And that's all normal. Quasi-facts are part of the grease that lets the gears of civilization turn smoothly.

But when we engage in persuasion mode—when we think we need to convince others of something—the quasi-fact shortcut doesn't work. It's counterproductive because it *generates* instead of *resolves* differences. That's the contention we all want to minimize or eliminate.

The perplexity and complexity of religious belief suggests that evidence, by itself, is not persuasive. What one person finds convincing leaves the next person unmoved. Even people who read, study, and pray about the Bible or the Book of Mormon receive varying responses.

The complex psychological, physical, and emotional factors at play cannot be easily summarized or applied. The scientific method does not work because religious beliefs are not subject to objectivity, repeatability, or even testing.

Nevertheless, this FAITH model offers insights into how people actually engage with evidence. In most cases, their assumptions guide their analysis so that the facts confirm their biases (their beliefs).

In the context of historical analysis, the scientific method is a little more useful because science can help authenticate historical evidence. But the utility and meaning of that evidence veers into subjectivity. We can say that a historical fact (such as a document) is *evidence* of a historical reality, and everyone can agree that the document exists, but they can (and usually do) disagree about its relevance and significance.

Notice also that the model uses the term "fact" in the sense of *evidence* of an actual event or occurrence, pursuant to meaning #2 in the Merriam-Webster Dictionary:[31]

> 1a: something that has actual existence: e.g., space exploration is now a *fact*
> 1b: an actual occurrence: e.g., prove the *fact* of damage
> 2: a piece of information presented as having objective reality: e.g., These are the hard *facts* of the case.
> 3: the quality of being actual: ACTUALITY: e.g., a question of *fact* hinges on evidence
> 4: a thing done, such as a crime: e.g., accessory after the *fact*

The alternative definitions of the term "fact" enable controversy about what is and what isn't a fact, so they are not useful for this model.

Assumptions

With our backpack full of facts, we next choose which path through the forest to pursue. We choose from the array of assumptions before us and embark on our journey.

Metaphors aside, assumptions range from obvious to entirely subjective. We assume the laws of physics are consistent through recorded history. Everyone agrees with that assumption. But whether we assume a historical figure is credible or not depends on subjective factors. In the FAITH model we explain our reasoning, but others are free to disagree—so long as they also explain their reasoning. Ideally, our

---

[31] "fact," https://www.merriam-webster.com/dictionary/fact

reasoning incorporates facts, but the subjective nature of assumptions leaves open a range of rational possibilities.

Inferences

We've traveled down the path of our assumptions. We sit by a stream and open our backpack. As we remove the facts, we discover lots of gaps. There are pieces missing. Some don't join together.

To assemble the puzzle, we pick up a tree branch and carve our own pieces, as needed to make everything fit.

These gap-fillers are the inferences we draw from the available evidence, consistent with our assumptions. We use them to construct our narrative. If we're not careful, we conflate them with the facts. But by isolating them through the FAITH model, we allow everyone (including ourselves) to discern facts from imagination, however plausible and reasonable our imagination may be.

Theories

In science, a theory is formed to explain the things already shown in data. Using facts, assumptions and inferences as our components, we now assemble our theories, or narratives, to explain them. Ideally, everything seems clear to us, and we've made it possible for anyone else to trace our steps back to the facts everyone agrees upon.

Hypotheses

A scientific hypothesis is an assumption to be tested by research. Here, I use the term for the final step in the process of merging our fact-originated theories into an overall hypothesis that has predictive utility and a broader scope. It's our overall worldview. Our hypotheses are tested by comparison with other working hypotheses, further research, and exploration.

Next, we'll discuss a framework for categorizing different approaches to the Restoration.

6. All, Some, None

This chapter applies the FAITH model by presenting a simplified method of analysis to clarify different beliefs.

Two basic narratives have arisen about the truth claims made by Joseph Smith and Oliver Cowdery regarding the foundational events of the Restoration. These truth claims offer a binary choice.

> (i) The truth claims demonstrated divine intervention,
> OR
> (ii) The truth claims were not divine because they were
> (a) unproven and delusional or deceitful claims that have naturalistic explanations or
> (b) the product of sinister supernatural influences.

Within category (i), believers accept all or some of what Joseph and Oliver taught, leaving them free to entertain a range of narratives depending on how closely they adhere to what Joseph and Oliver taught.

Within category (ii), nonbelievers accept none of the truth claims made by Joseph and Oliver, but they may object on either naturalistic or supernatural grounds.

Relative belief in what Joseph and Oliver claimed		
All	Some	None
Believe all of what Joseph and Oliver claimed.	Believe some, but not all, of what Joseph and Oliver claimed.	Believe none of what Joseph and Oliver claimed.

Advocates of each narrative can find historical evidence to support their respective interpretations. Everyone is looking at the same facts, but then people diverge based on assumptions, inferences and theories.

For example, consider this tweet from well-known critic:

> The leaders of the Mormon church continue to blame the youth leaving on them having 'anti-Christ' teachings when in reality it's because the youth are

not as afraid of looking at information about the LDS church as older generations are... and they're finding out it's not true.

When we run this through the FAITH model, we can quickly isolate facts from assumptions, inferences, and theories. There are no clear facts stated—even though the tweet claims it is giving us facts. When it says "in reality," that's a rhetorical opinion, not a fact.

Is it a fact that youth "are not as afraid" as older generations? Aside from the overgeneralization, the substance of the claim is dubious. To the youth, everything is new under the sun. They're naturally curious and uninformed. Many in the older generation have seen and heard the critical narratives so many times that they don't feel a need to rehash them yet again. They may be "weary" rather than "afraid." Labeling them as "afraid" is pejorative and argumentative, not factual.

Besides, today every generation has equal access to the Internet and thus the same information.

When the tweet says the youth are "looking at information about the LDS church," information can be supportive or critical. Presumably people are looking at both categories. And if so, which category are they "finding out" is "not true" here?

The author, as a critic, presumably wants readers to infer that young people are "looking at" critical information and "finding out" the church's truth claims are "not true." That would be his framing.

But what he actually wrote supports the opposite conclusion; i.e., that the youth are looking at the information the author promotes and are finding out that his critical information is not true. That would be my framing.

We start with the identical facts, but after applying our assumptions, inferences, etc., we reach completely opposite conclusions or hypotheses.

With that clarity, charity, and understanding, there is no incentive to contend about our differences.

―――――

Because we start with a focus on issues involving the Restoration, particularly those related to the keystone of our religion (the origin and setting of the Book of Mormon), we've identified three broad categories of people who have engaged with these issues.

The Rational Restoration

In doing so, we recognize everyone is different. These categories serve as analytical tools only. Any individual may find affinity with any group on a given specific topic.

The objective is to seek greater understanding by enabling side-by-side comparison. It produces greater clarity and charity.

Important: the tool does not impose a value judgment on which approach is better or worse, but it assists others who assess a particular issue to make their own informed decisions.

> Under the right circumstances—the alternatives are available for comparison side by side, and the wording of the alternatives leaves nothing to the imagination—people can think their way out of the fallacy.
>
> Steven Pinker[32]

Clarity requires isolation of facts, assumptions, inferences, theories, and hypotheses (the FAITH model). The understanding process is nonjudgmental. If anyone brings errors to our attention, they will be promptly noted and appropriate corrections made.

These are the three broad categories, using terminology familiar to those involved with these discussions. The groups are organized as a continuum, but there is no implied preference for "All" just because A is the first letter in the alphabet.

The order could be reversed just as easily.

Believe what Joseph and Oliver claimed		
All	Some	None
Believe **all** of what Joseph and Oliver claimed about the origin and setting of the Book of Mormon	Believe **some**, but not all, of what Joseph and Oliver claimed about the origin and setting of the Book of Mormon	Believe **none** of what Joseph and Oliver claimed about the origin and setting of the Book of Mormon

---

[32] *Rationality* at 584

Each of these groups is overbroad. People who generally identify themselves within the description in one box may have a variety of views about how to interpret the teachings of Joseph and Oliver that puts them in one or two of the other boxes on some issues. But the classifications are useful for analytical and clarity purposes.

Application – Lucy Mack Smith

The all/some/none model can be applied to any historical evidence. In the following example, everyone agrees on the facts, but they divide into three categories because of their assumptions, inferences, and theories, which lead them to reach entirely different hypotheses (multiple working hypotheses). To repeat, obviously the all/some/none classification is a generalized summary. Any individual may have a different set of assumptions, inferences, etc.

Fact (an objective fact everyone agrees upon): Because we can all see the original document in the Joseph Smith Papers, everyone agrees that the document exists. We can all see that the handwriting is by Martha Jane Knowlton Coray and Howard Coray, who later reported they acted as scribes for Lucy's dictation. Lucy Mack Smith wrote a letter to her son William, explaining that

> People are often enquiring of me the particulars of Joseph's getting the plates seeing the angels at first and many other thing which Joseph never wrote or published I have told over many things pertaining to these matters to different persons to gratify their curiosity indeed have almost destroyed my lungs giving these recitals to those who felt anxious to hear them I have now concluded to write down every particular as far as possible and if those who wish to read them will help me a little they can have it all in one piece to read at their leasure—[33]

With this historical background, presumably we can all agree that Lucy dictated her history in 1844. That's the easy part.

---

[33] https://www.josephsmithpapers.org/paper-summary/lucy-mack-smith-history-1844-1845/41#historical-intro

The Rational Restoration

We can also agree to the fact that she reported that the first night he appeared to Joseph Smith, the divine messenger told Joseph that

> the record is on a side hill on the Hill of Cumorah 3 miles from this place remove the Grass and moss and you will find a large flat stone."34

Where people diverge is how to handle what Lucy reported. Next, we look at the typical assumptions, inferences, theories and hypotheses employed by three different categories of people, grouped according to their pre-existing beliefs about Cumorah.

Relative acceptance of what Lucy Mack Smith said		
Assumption		
All	Some	None
Lucy was correct because Cumorah is in New York.	Lucy was mistaken because Cumorah is not in New York.	Lucy was mistaken because Cumorah is imaginary.
Inferences and interpretations		
All	Some	None
We infer that Lucy heard this directly from Joseph Smith, that Joseph heard it correctly in the first place, and that Lucy accurately reported what Joseph told her. The words speak for themselves; i.e., Moroni identified the hill where the plates were deposited as *Cumorah*.	This is not a direct quotation so we infer Lucy paraphrased what she heard or added anachronistic details years after the fact. She said "hill *of* Cumorah" which is not the same as the Hill Cumorah, so we interpret it to mean a hill "like" Cumorah, reminiscent of Cumorah, etc.	We infer that Lucy probably wanted to believe it, and wanted others to believe it, because she naturally trusted her own son. But there's nothing believable about this account because resurrected beings don't come to earth to convey messages.

---

34 https://www.josephsmithpapers.org/paper-summary/lucy-mack-smith-history-1844-1845/41

Theory/explanation		
All	Some	None
Because Lucy was generally a reliable witness, there is no reason to doubt her claim in this case. Even though Lucy related this 20 years after the fact, she had a good memory and she repeated the account many times during the lifetime of Joseph Smith and he never corrected or contradicted her. Lucy related a similar account about Cumorah that took place about 3 years later.	Although Lucy was generally a reliable witness, she was not in all cases. Lucy related this 20 years after the fact so she must have heard the Cumorah theory from someone other than Joseph Smith, but even if she heard it from Joseph, Joseph was speculating along with Oliver Cowdery.	Lucy was generally a reliable witness, but at best, Lucy is relating hearsay (what Joseph told her), so it's not even admissible in court. Her belief in resurrected beings doesn't make her belief a reality. Besides, even scholars who believe the Book of Mormon is "true" don't accept what Lucy said here.
Hypothesis		
All	Some	None
The actual Hill Cumorah is in western New York.	The actual Hill Cumorah is in southern Mexico or somewhere else.	Any hill Cumorah is fictional, whether it's in New York or anywhere else.

Predictably, the concluding hypothesis confirms the beginning assumption held by each of the three groups. As we discussed previously, this is called "confirmation bias," defined as a cognitive bias "that results from the tendency to process and analyze information in such a way that it supports one's preexisting ideas and convictions."[35]

---

[35] https://www.dictionary.com/browse/confirmation-bias

But that doesn't matter because the FAITH model is not designed to produce convergence of ideas. It solves for clarity, charity and understanding. To review:

Clarity. The FAITH model enables everyone to see exactly what are the assumptions, inferences and theories which lead to the hypothesis or conclusion. Often, it clarifies these elements for the proponent of a particular hypothesis as well.

With the "ancestry" of each hypothesis clearly spelled out, everyone can understand alternative working hypotheses. People can make informed choices without the confusion that typically results from argument and contention.

Charity. The FAITH model also promotes charity. Instead of speculating about possible ulterior motives, everyone can see exactly how others reached their conclusions.

Understanding. The FAITH model brings people together based on mutual understanding and respect without requiring agreement, adherence, or conformity to one particular outcome.

This approach is far beyond merely agreeing to disagree. Once people understand one another with clarity and charity, we can all work together without underlying suspicions, distrust, or animosity; i.e., we can have "no more contention."

Chapters 16 and 17 apply the All/Some/None approach to the origin and setting of the Book of Mormon.

―――――

Narrative Poison

Without clarity, charity and understanding, people sharing one belief often consider the assumptions and inferences of other groups to be "wrong" or "bad" in some way. Rather than taking a sincere interest and seeking to glean insights and understanding, people look to attack, judge, and condemn. The resulting narratives poison the analysis and lead to confusion, anger, mistrust, etc.

We see this in politics and science as well as religion.

Confusion is actually a business model. Try to compare cell phone plans. The companies use different terminology, time frames, incentives, and other tactics to make comparisons nearly impossible. Medical bills, insurance plans, building contractors and many more use complexity and confusion to frustrate consumers into simple acceptance.

Narratives can be poisonous in another sense. A particular narrative can taint our perception of reality, our interpretation of facts, and our interaction with other people and ideas.

When we consider the purpose of life, the nature of reality, and the pursuit of happiness, we want to eliminate narrative poisons.

The famous physicist Richard Feynman set out five signs of intelligence that can help us avoid narrative poison.

1. You're not afraid or ashamed to find errors in your understanding of things.
2. You take mistakes as lessons.
3. You don't get offended with accepting the facts.
4. You are highly adaptable and very curious.
5. You know what you don't know.

My publisher, Boyd Tuttle, once articulated it this way:

"A key mark of intelligence is the capacity to alter one's worldview when presented with superior information."

Section II – Reframes

For me and many others, Gospel living is simply the most rational way of life. As Nephi wrote, "we lived after the manner of happiness." (2 Nephi 5:27)[36] On a daily basis, we observe the sad, preventable consequences of people making choices to live contrary to Gospel principles.

One impediment to Gospel living is the perception that the truth claims of the Restoration are false or that belief in God is irrational.

The reframes we discuss below offer alternatives to what seem (to me) to be irrational (or less rational) propositions advanced by critics and some apologists.

To be sure, rationality depends on the worldview we start with. As we can see through the FAITH model, everyone starts with the same facts. Based on facts, we can all make rational—and different—assumptions, draw inferences, and apply theories consistent with our worldview.

This process leads to greater clarity, charity, and understanding.

Speaking of critics and apologists (see Chapter 12), Austin Farrer wrote a memorable passage on the utility of rational argument in the face of criticism, including complaints that Christianity disrupts society.

---

[36] Jonathan Edwards offered an eternal perspective on happiness. "we consider the degree and manner in which [God] aimed at the creature's excellency and happiness in his creating the world; viz. the degree and manner of the creature's glory and happiness during the whole of the designed eternal duration of the world he was about to create: which is in greater and greater nearness and strictness of union with himself, and greater and greater communion and participation with him in his own glory and happiness, in constant progression, throughout all eternity."

You cannot well oppose the accusation of social disruptiveness without making a case for the cohesive tendencies of the gospel; you cannot clear the charge of silliness without establishing a claim to rationality.

...

It is commonly said that if rational argument is so seldom the cause of conviction, philosophical apologists must largely be wasting their shot. The premise is true, but the conclusion does not follow. For though argument does not create conviction, the lack of it destroys belief. What seems to be proved may not be embraced; but what no one shows the ability to defend is quickly abandoned. Rational argument does not create belief, but it maintains a climate in which belief may flourish. So the apologist who does nothing but defend may play a useful, though preparatory, part...

[C.S.] Lewis did better. He provided a positive exhibition of the force of Christian ideas, morally, imaginatively, and rationally. The strength of his appeal (we have said) lies in the many-sidedness of his work. Christian theism, to those who believe it, commends itself as fact, not theory, by the sheer multiplicity of its bearings.[37]

The reframes in this book are intended to provide a "positive exhibition" of the Restoration in all its facets. Although we can touch only on a few topics here, readers can think of additional reframes to better explain how and why the Restoration offers everyone a life "after the manner of happiness."

Perhaps in a future volume we will look at reframes for many more aspects of the Restoration.

---

[37] Austin Farrer, "The Christian Apologist," in *Light on C.S. Lewis*, edited by Jocelyn Gibb (New York: Harcourt Brace Jovanovich, 1965), 23, 26.

7. Rational Living

How is the abundant life to be obtained? The abundant life involves an endless search for knowledge, light, and truth. President Hugh B. Brown said: "God desires that we learn and continue to learn, but this involves some unlearning."
James E. Faust, 'The Abundant Life,' *Ensign*, November 1985

Learning to think rationally can improve the quality of life for people everywhere. It makes people more productive while also enhancing their enjoyment of life.

To fulfill its purpose, the Restoration provides a framework for rational living, which includes reframes to help us transition from the "natural man" to the more refined, intentional, and capable people we want to become.

People commonly "know" they should develop positive habits and goals. Get an education. Exercise and eat healthy food. Interact positively with other people. Pursue interests and develop a variety of talents and abilities.

Yet it's also common for people to think and act contrary to all of these ideals. Progressing often means "unlearning" what we take for granted. It can mean replacing counterproductive habits with productive ones. We can develop talents and systems that lead where we want to go.

This is a complex topic, but the Restoration shows us that knowing what to do is not always sufficient. Every individual is different, but a common factor in living an abundant life is social interaction and a belief system that nudges us in the direction we want to go.

Neuroplasticity. A fundamental principle of Christianity is that people can change. The Greek noun *metanoia*, translated as repentance, literally means "a change of mind." The verb form, *metanoéō*, literally means "to think differently after."

The ability to "think different" or "reframe" our understanding of the world is explained by the scientific term neuroplasticity.

> Neuroplasticity is the brain's capacity to continue growing and evolving in response to life experiences. Plasticity is the capacity to be shaped, molded, or altered; neuroplasticity, then, is the ability for the brain to adapt or change over time, by creating new neurons and building new networks.
>
> Historically, scientists believed that the brain stopped growing after childhood. But current research shows that the brain is able to continue growing and changing throughout the lifespan, refining its architecture or shifting functions to different regions of the brain.
>
> The importance of neuroplasticity can't be overstated: It means that it is possible to change dysfunctional patterns of thinking and behaving and to develop new mindsets, new memories, new skills, and new abilities.[38]

Optimism about neuroplasticity is tempered by everyday reality in our own lives and the lives of those around us. Those of us who embrace and enjoy the Restoration adopt a reframe such as this.

Old narratives	Reframe
Church imposes rules that inhibit my freedom and individuality. OR Society should not tell anyone how to live.	The Restoration teaches basic principles and habits that lead to mental, spiritual and physical health and prosperity.

Reframing thinking patterns

> "They found that people's reasoning skills did indeed predict their life outcomes: the fewer fallacies in reasoning, the fewer debacles in life."
>
> Steven Pinker, *Rationality*

---

[38] https://www.psychologytoday.com/us/basics/neuroplasticity

The Rational Restoration

One of the impediments to a happy, healthy life is counterproductive thinking patterns.

The Restoration offers a solution.

The Church's program for Emotional Resilience alone could revolutionize the daily lives of Latter-day Saints, and, eventually, the entire world. It is available everywhere and should be high on the list of priorities for everyone.

Each week, participants study and discuss these topics:

1. Exercise Faith in Jesus Christ
2. Healthy Thinking Patterns
3. Our Bodies and Emotions
4. Managing Stress and Anxiety
5. Understanding Sadness and Depression
6. Overcoming Anger
7. Managing Addictive Behaviors
8. Building Healthy Relationships
9. Providing Strength to Others.
10. Moving Forward with Faith

Let's look at 2. Healthy Thinking Patterns.

Emotional Values and Skills
1. Our Thoughts Influence Our Emotions
2. Recognizing Inaccurate Thinking Patterns
3. Responding to Triggers
4. Creating More Accurate Thinking Patterns
5. Changing Our Thinking Takes Practice

Number 2, Recognizing Inaccurate Thinking Patterns, includes this insight:

> We might frequently find ourselves focusing our thoughts on what is wrong or negative. Inaccurate thinking patterns may lead us to see the worst possible outcomes to a situation. These distorted thoughts cause us to feel bad about ourselves and others. We all experience negative thoughts, but

sometimes we get stuck in them and don't see the inaccurate thinking pattern and how it is hurting our emotional health.[39]

The manual identifies common inaccurate thinking patterns that plague individuals and societies everywhere in the world. Among these are mislabeling, jumping to conclusions, overgeneralizations, and "should" statements.

Examples of reframes:

Old narrative	Reframe
Believe the thinking error	Create more accurate thoughts
All or nothing: Seeing something or someone as all good or all bad. Look for phrases with words like *always* and *never*.	Recognize that people (including ourselves) are complex and changeable with both good and bad qualities.
Jumping to conclusions: Interpreting others' thoughts or assuming the worst possible outcome.	Mindreading takes place in our own heads. In reality, we don't know what others are thinking. Assume a positive situation.

The Church encourages all 30,000 units around the world to participate in these programs. Participants don't have to be members of the Church, either.

In this way, the Restoration is raising people to a higher level of consciousness. It is fulfilling the aspiration found in D&C 121:33

> How long can rolling waters remain impure? What power shall stay the heavens? As well might man stretch forth his puny arm to stop the Missouri river in its decreed course, or to turn it up stream, as to hinder the Almighty from pouring down knowledge from heaven upon the heads of the Latter-day Saints.

---

[39] https://www.churchofjesuschrist.org/study/manual/emotional-resilience-for-self-reliance/2-healthy-thinking-patterns/2-learn?lang=eng

Reframing life challenges

"Self-image is the prison. Other people are the guards."
Naval Ravikant @naval

The Church's website explains the way the Restoration reframes life experiences from barriers and impediments to opportunities to learn and serve.

Life Help
Everyone needs help sometimes. Life is like that. In fact, God planned it to be that way. Mortality presents each of us with a wide variety of experiences, and some are easier to manage than others. No matter the experience, there is always help. That's part of God's plan too. [40]

One Area in the Church conducted a survey of leaders about what needs their members had. They surveyed Stake Presidents, Stake Relief Society Presidents, High Councilors, Bishops, Ward Relief Society Presidents, and Elders Quorum Presidents.

These were the top ten needs with the number of votes for each.

Anxiety or Depression	388
Financial Hardship	226
Pornography	208
Marital Difficulties	203
Chronic Illness (Physical)	193
Housing and Utilities	192
Inadequate Income	183
Gender Identity	182
Disabilities (Physical or Mental)	156
Clinical Mental Illness	155

How does the Church help with these needs?

---

[40] https://www.churchofjesuschrist.org/topics/families-and-individuals/lifes-challenges/hope-and-help?lang=eng

Church participation offers the social interaction and support people need to handle life's challenges. Beyond that, the Church provides specific guidelines and programs for all of the following topics and more.

Abuse
Addiction
Adoption
Death, Grieving, and Loss
Disabilities
Divorce
Education
Employment
Family and Relationships
Finances
Media Safety
Mental and Emotional Health
Parenting
Physical Health
Pornography
Preparedness
Pregnant and Single
Same-Sex Attraction
Self-Reliance Services
Single-Parent Families
Suicide

The Self-Reliance programs: Personal Finances, Education for Better Work, Starting and Growing a business, and Finding a Better Job.[41]

The Word of Wisdom—abstaining from alcohol, tobacco, and addictive drinks and drugs, along with good nutrition and regular exercise—is a key element of rational living that avoids innumerable personal and social problems. Monthly fasting for 24 hours and giving offerings turns our hearts and means toward others, an ideal for the entire world.

---

[41] https://www.churchofjesuschrist.org/study/manual/emotional-resilience-for-self-reliance/2-healthy-thinking-patterns?lang=eng

Gospel scholarship

President Gordon B. Hinckley reminded us, "As a Church, we encourage gospel scholarship and the search to understand all truth. Fundamental to our theology is belief in individual freedom of inquiry, thought, and expression. Constructive discussion is a privilege of every Latter-day Saint." (*Ensign,* Sept. 1985, p. 5.)

Old narratives	Reframe
Faithful. Gospel scholarship requires years of preparation and credentials to access and understand the original sources and then write and present conclusions consistent with high standards of academia. OR Critical. Gospel scholarship is inherently an exercise in bias confirmation, with peer review that consists mainly of peer approval.	Gospel scholarship remains useful but the credentialed class no longer deserves deference because everyone can readily access the original sources. Bias confirmation is a risk in every field that can be overcome with clarity, charity, and understanding.

People frequently tell me that such-and-such must be true because so-and-so, a professional and faithful scholar, said so.

Deference to the credentialed class is understandable. None of us has the time to become experts in multiple fields. We go to a doctor instead of medical school. We buy food at a market instead of operating a farm. We buy a ticket on an airline instead of attending flight school.

Gospel scholarship is somewhat different.

We can all study the scriptures; in fact, that's an individual responsibility. No Church leader has urged us to study the works of the scholars; instead, we study the scriptures and the teachings of the prophets.

For Church history, we can all access the original documents without the traditional filters.

Plus, we've seen that some scholars, both faithful and critical, have abused their trust by manipulating sources, withholding sources, engaging in sophistry and obfuscation, and other tactics designed to promote their personal agendas. In our day, most people prefer to make informed decisions by evaluating multiple working hypotheses in side-by-side comparisons as much as possible.

Besides, living the gospel is far more meaningful than studying the gospel. Study is useful primarily to encourage people to live better lives.

But we can all benefit from the work of gospel scholars, provided we retain our agency and keep their work in perspective.

Professional historians. No qualifications are necessary to research history (or any other topic). Professional historians are great at finding, collecting, preserving, organizing, and presenting historical documents, but their training doesn't seem to give them any special talent or skills for *interpreting* historical information.

Some are better than others at explaining context, such as what people generally thought during a particular time, how people lived, what current events were, etc. Context is often overlooked when people focus on a particular quotation. But in reality, very few historical events are fully documented.

Think of how little of your own life is documented, even with the ever-present smart phones that can record every moment you want to remember. We have tiny snippets of evidence from the historical record that leave an enormous gap that we fill with assumptions and inferences, leading to a wide range of possible conclusions.

Professional linguists. Experts in other language, particularly biblical languages, have a lot to offer in terms of understanding the original texts of the Bible and related materials. They both concur and disagree about a particular translation or meaning of biblical terms.

Lawyers. By training, I'm a lawyer and agricultural economist. In a sense, lawyers are historians because we spend a lot of time researching facts and constructing narratives, but we also spend a lot of time assessing the credibility of witnesses, which seems to be a different approach than professional historians take. Economists focus on comparing things. These are useful skills for assessing evidence, but lawyers also tend to "make a case" for whatever position they are advocating, a tendency to be wary of unless they explain their bias clearly.

Consequently, I ignore "qualifications" when I assess someone's opinions. It doesn't matter to me whether they are part of the credentialed class or not. All I care about is whether authors deal with all the relevant evidence and explain their assumptions, inferences, and theories, or if they (i) ignore evidence that contradicts their theories, (ii) present their theories as facts, and (iii) fail to clearly explain their assumptions, inferences, theories, etc.

One of the most prominent lawyer/scholars in the Church today is John W. (Jack) Welch. As the founder of FARMS and Book of Mormon Central, editor of *BYU Studies*, and a long-time law professor at BYU Law School, Brother Welch has published voluminous scholarly materials.

In 2010 he published a thoughtful piece titled "Toward Becoming a Gospel Scholar."[42] I highly recommend it. Here are some useful excerpts:

> To a gospel scholar, truth is like any other tool: it can either be used to build up or to tear down. Thus, truth alone is not the objective of a gospel scholar, because knowledge and truth -- until put to some purposeful use -- remain morally inert. At the same time, a gospel scholar knows that, no matter how well intended or motivated, building on a sandy foundation will ultimately lead to collapse.
>
> Do a little bit every day.
> Have a pen and piece of paper with you everywhere you go.
> Have a good place to study.
> Begin with prayer.
> Read, read, and read.
> Slow down, read slowly, and read it again.
> Always leave the scriptures open.
> Create and keep files.

---

[42] John W. Welch, "Toward Becoming a Gospel Scholar," Patheos.com, https://www.patheos.com/resources/additional-resources/2010/09/toward-becoming-a-gospel-scholar

Jonathan Neville

While it is always important for gospel readers to contemplate and ponder the scriptures for pure enjoyment and general inspiration, gospel scholars read and study with specific points in mind.

Scholarship exists to answer questions, or at least to attempt to find answers. To become a gospel scholar, you must adopt a purpose for your pursuits. There must be a point to your endeavors.

Good scholars ask themselves, "Why do I accept certain ideas and reject others?" Good scholars also articulate those reasons openly and honestly to themselves and to their audiences....

Good questions help people to see insights that they had not seen before. They offer explanations. They help people unpack the complexity of textual material. They make obscure materials clear....

Gospel scholars also have enough perspective and have read widely enough to recognize faddish, passing, and momentary influences in our thinking....

Nothing is more important in becoming a gospel scholar than reading the scriptures. Gospel scholarship is thoroughly grounded in the four standard works....

When reading articles and books written by Jewish, Catholic, Protestant, or secular scholars, a Latter-day Saint gospel scholar needs, of course, to be highly sensitive to some of their assumptions, purposes, methodologies, skepticism, criteria, and biases, for most Mormons probably would not join in all of their thinking. Their problems are not necessarily your problems. Their purposes are not likely the same as your purposes....

8. Reframing Church

Reframing the Restoration as fulfillment

Since New Testament times, Christians have looked forward to the victory promised in the Book of Revelation and other biblical passages.

Old narrative	Reframe
The Restoration came out of nowhere to thwart traditional Christianity. OR The Restoration is a product of Joseph Smith's imagination and/or Satanic influence.	The Restoration fulfills the long-held aspirations of Christians and is well within the Christian tradition.

Writing in 1742, Jonathan Edwards articulated the great Christian hope—and anticipated that the "work will begin in America."

> It is not unlikely that this work of God's Spirit, that is so extraordinary and wonderful, is the dawning, or at least, a prelude of **that glorious work of God**, so often foretold in scripture, which in the progress and issue of it shall renew the world of mankind… we cannot reasonably think otherwise, than that **the beginning of this great work of God must be near**. And there are many things that make it probable that **this work will begin in America**…It is exceeding manifest that this chapter [Isa. 60] is a prophecy of the **prosperity of the church, in its most glorious state on earth in the latter days**; and I can't think that anything else can be here intended but America by **"the isles that are far off"**… This prophecy therefore seems plainly to **point out America**, as the first fruits of that glorious day.[43]

---

[43] Jonathan Edwards, *The Works of President Edwards*, Vol. III (1808) p. 153. The 8-volume set was on sale at TC Strong, Bookseller and Printer, in Palmyra in 1818-23.

"Prosperity of the church" is a non-biblical Book of Mormon phrase (Mosiah 27:9, Helaman 3:25) that Edwards used to describe the latter-day state of the Christian church in the world. The work would "renew the world of mankind."

But modern Christians wouldn't recognize it when it happened.

Jewish readers of the Old Testament prophets long anticipated the coming of the Messiah, but when Jesus Christ was born as a baby in Bethlehem, he did not fulfill their expectations. Nor did Christ deliver the Jews from bondage as they expected. Instead, he suffered an ignominious death at the hands of the Roman oppressors, thereby deflating the hopes of the Jews for deliverance—at least, the type of deliverance they sought.

Following the death of Christ, believers looked forward to the "restitution of all things" (Acts 3:21) without specifying, exactly, how, where or when that would take place.

In the ensuing centuries, Christian authors proposed a variety of interpretations of Acts 3:21. Like the Jews who interpreted the Old Testament, however, these Christians had to be content to await the fulfillment of prophecy, whether events agreed with their own ideas or not.

Naturally, Christians sought a fulfillment in line with their own situations. As we saw in the opening quotation, the prominent Christian theologian and minister Jonathan Edwards (1703-1758) discussed the connection between the New World (America) and the glorious future of God's church. Edwards was born a hundred years before Joseph Smith. Obviously, he did not have Joseph Smith or the Book of Mormon in mind when he wrote about this topic.

The biblical authors Edwards quoted did not have America in mind when they wrote, either. Yet Edwards applied the ancient texts to his current situation, seeing in his times the fulfillment, or at least movement *toward* the fulfillment, of the prophecies of the restoration.

The excerpt above is from Edwards' famous "Revival of Religion in Newengland [sic]," which appears in Vol. 3 of the 1808 edition, on sale in the T.C. Strong bookshop Joseph frequented. These extracts start on p. 153.

The Rational Restoration

The passage begins with Edwards setting the stage for the dawning of that glorious work of God. At least one edition of Edwards' works (but not the 1808) captions this section as "The Millennium Probably To Dawn in America," an apt interpretation.

Edwards' readers, if they had eyes to see, would have expected a "restoration" to begin in America. The Restoration Joseph Smith described was a complete fulfillment of Edwards' anticipatory thinking

If the beginning was "near" for Edwards, writing around 1742, then it would be that much nearer for Joseph in 1818. Edwards identifies America as the site for the commencement of the great work.

In the excerpt above, Edwards cites Isaiah 60:9 to explain that the work "shall begin in some very remote part of the world, that the rest of the world have no communication with but by navigation."

Edwards presents Isaiah as describing America. He paraphrases Isaiah by writing "the isles that are far off" and explains his reasoning that Isaiah points to America.

Edwards' focus on "the isles" surfaces in the Book of Mormon, which uses that term eight times in Nephi's commentary. Nephi identified his people as "those who should inhabit the isles of the sea" (1 Nephi 19:10). Jacob declares, "we are upon an isle of the sea" (2 Nephi 10:20), directly affirming Edwards' interpretation of Isaiah.

Next Edwards compares the old and the new worlds, asserting that the new world

> has been till of late wholly the possession of Satan, **the church of God having never been in it**, as it has been in the other continent, from the beginning of the world.

This point deserves a brief discussion. European settlers explained the Indians through their biblical worldview, assuming they were among the lost ten tribes. For context, Edwards was sandwiched between the 1650 book *Jews in America* and James Adair's 1775 *History of the American Indians*, both of which taught the theory that the Indians were Hebrews. This was not unknown to Edwards; his son, Jonathan Jr., proposed a Hebraic origin of the Indian languages he learned.

Any Hebrew connection, however, would not constitute the establishment of the Christian church among them.

Thus, when Moroni visited Joseph the first time and "gave a history of the aborigenes [sic] of this country,"[44] it would be no surprise to Joseph when Moroni "**said** they were literal descendants of Abraham." But then Moroni "**represented** them as once being an enlightened and intelligent people, possessing a correct knowledge of the gospel, and the plan of restoration and redemption." It's an interesting choice of words because "represent" connotes more nuance than just stating a fact; it means to "describe," "portray" or "depict." It suggests Joseph's surprise, and possibly skepticism, that the Indians once had "a correct knowledge of the gospel." Indians as part of the Ten Tribes was a common theme, but Indians as ancient Christians was unheard of.

Edwards proceeds to suggest that the new world would see a "new and most glorious state of God's church."

> This new world is probably now discovered, that **the new and most glorious state of God's church on earth might commence there**; that God might in it **begin a new world in a spiritual respect**, when he creates the new heavens and new earth....

"Commence" is a non-biblical word that Joseph used in the Book of Mormon 17 times and three times in the D&C. We have "the work of the Father shall commence," "my work shall commence," "the Lord God shall commence his work," and so on.[45]

Reframing Zion

The Tenth Article of Faith, which Joseph Smith wrote and published in Nauvoo, Illinois, in March 1842, originally held that "Zion will be built upon this continent." Joseph also taught that "We ought to have the building up of Zion as our greatest object."

---

[44] https://www.josephsmithpapers.org/paper-summary/history-1834-1836/68.
[45] For more on the connections between Jonathan Edwards and Joseph Smith, Jr., see https://www.mobom.org/jonathan-edwards.

The Rational Restoration

Old narratives	Reframe
Zion as a perfect society is an impractical idea that won't be established until Christ returns OR Zion is a mythical fiction that can't exist in the real world	The establishment of Zion is currently underway, both within and outside the Church, as people of good will seek to make the world a better place. https://howtozion.blogspot.com/

Zion societies have been described in latter-day scripture. "And the Lord called his people Zion, because they were of one heart and one mind, and dwelt in righteousness; and there was no poor among them." (Moses 7:18)

A similar society existed among the Nephites.

> the people were all converted unto the Lord, upon all the face of the land, both Nephites and Lamanites, and there were no contentions and disputations among them, and every man did deal justly one with another.
> And they had all things common among them; therefore there were not rich and poor, bond and free, but they were all made free, and partakers of the heavenly gift. (4 Nephi 1:2–3)

In our day, several passages explain the Zion ideal, such as this:

> 19 For, behold, the beasts of the field and the fowls of the air, and that which cometh of the earth, is ordained for the use of man for food and for raiment, and that he might have in abundance.
> 20 But it is not given that one man should possess that which is above another, wherefore the world lieth in sin. (Doctrine and Covenants 49:19–20)

Latter-day Saints around the world are actively working toward the establishment of Zion—even if many of them do not realize it. Modern Church leaders discuss it frequently, as in these examples.

> As the long-prophesied latter-day gathering of the Lord's covenant people gains momentum, the Church will truly be composed of members from every nation, kindred, tongue, and people. This is not a calculated or forced

diversity but a naturally occurring phenomenon that we would expect, recognizing that the gospel net gathers from every nation and every people.

How blessed we are to see the day that Zion is being established simultaneously on every continent and in our own neighborhoods. As the Prophet Joseph Smith said, the people of God in every age have looked forward with joyful anticipation to this day, and "we are the favored people that God has made choice of to bring about the Latter-day glory."[46]

In this dispensation, although we live in a special time, the world has not been blessed with the righteousness and unity described in 4 Nephi. Indeed, we live in a moment of particularly strong divisions.

However, the millions who have accepted the gospel of Jesus Christ have committed themselves to achieving both righteousness and unity. We are all aware that we can do better, and that is our challenge in this day. We can be a force to lift and bless society as a whole. At this 200-year hinge point in our Church history, let us commit ourselves as members of the Lord's Church to live righteously and be united as never before.

President Russell M. Nelson has asked us "to demonstrate greater civility, racial and ethnic harmony and mutual respect." This means loving each other and God and accepting everyone as brothers and sisters and truly being a Zion people.

With our all-inclusive doctrine, we can be an oasis of unity and celebrate diversity. Unity and diversity are not opposites. We can achieve greater unity as we foster an atmosphere of inclusion and respect for diversity.[47]

---

[46] D. Todd Christofferson, 'The Doctrine of Belonging,' General Conference, October 2022.

[47] Quentin L. Cook, 'Hearts Knit in Righteousness and Unity,' General Conference, November 2020.

Reframing Church wealth

Old narratives	Reframe
The Church has accumulated substantial wealth for a rainy-day fund. OR The Church has improperly accumulated substantial wealth that it hoards instead of helping the poor.	The Church has accumulated substantial wealth to use for the establishment of Zion, and the wealth is being put to productive uses.

Popular media has published several articles about the accumulated wealth of the Church. An article in the *Wall St. Journal* reported that:

> A whistleblower revealed a few years ago that the Church of Jesus Christ of Latter-day Saints had an estimated $100 billion investment portfolio, and at the time, church officials called the holdings a rainy-day account.
>
> They now say the money also has provided a financial foundation that gives the Mormon Church confidence to construct more than 100 temples, from Cape Verde to Guam, a series of stone-clad monuments exhibiting the church's vast and expanding wealth.[48]

Critics frame this wealth as a sort of hoarding that deprives the poor of the assistance the Church could provide. The article gives some examples of Church assistance, such as the millions of dollars donated to charities and the Church allowing use of chapels for hospital beds during the Covid-19 pandemic. But it also points out that some members share the concerns of the critics.

---

[48] Jonathan Weil, "Inside the Mormon Church's Globe-Spanning Real-Estate Empire: From Guam to Cape Verde, the Church of Jesus Christ of Latter-day Saints is using the financial cushion of its $100 billion investment portfolio to go on a temple-building spree," *Wall St. Journal,* June 29, 2023.

Jana Riess, a 53-year-old church member and columnist for Religion News Service, said she stopped tithing to the church and instead donates the money to charities that feed hungry children. "Our church is supposed to be following Jesus, and there is no example of Jesus hoarding wealth while children are starving in the world," she said.

While people can argue the Church should give more of its wealth directly to the poor, claiming the Church is hoarding wealth reflects ignorance of basic economics. Money invested in productive real estate and the stock market directly creates wealth that in turn feeds far more families than direct payments would. Such investment improves material wellbeing for everyone, as we saw in the Matt Ridley graph.

Christ gave a parable in the New Testament that explains this basic concept of economics. It starts this way:

14 For the kingdom of heaven is as a man travelling into a far country, who called his own servants, and delivered unto them his goods.

15 And unto one he gave five talents, to another two, and to another one; to every man according to his several ability; and straightway took his journey.

16 Then he that had received the five talents went and traded with the same, and made them other five talents. 17 And likewise he that had received two, he also gained other two. 18 But he that had received one went and digged in the earth, and hid his lord's money.

19 After a long time the lord of those servants cometh, and reckoneth with them. 20 And so he that had received five talents came and brought other five talents, saying, Lord, thou deliveredst unto me five talents: behold, I have gained beside them five talents more.

21 His lord said unto him, Well done, thou good and faithful servant: thou hast been faithful over a few things, I will make thee ruler over many things: enter thou into the joy of thy lord. (Matthew 25:14–21)

Church wealth is a complex topic. At the macro level, investment portfolios might seem complex and excessive, but the recent disclosures assure us that this wealth is neither hoarded nor used to enrich anyone. At the micro level, each of the 30,000 units in the Church has resources to help members in need. Local leaders balance the competing interests in providing assistance and encouraging self-reliance.

And, of course, nothing prevents anyone from directly giving to the poor or any other causes they support.

Reframing Church structure

Old narratives	Reframe
The Church is the gateway to God.	The Church is part of a triangle of a two-way streets between Christ and people.

On April 26, 1838, Joseph Smith received a revelation that held a key for testing religious experience and organizations everywhere.

4 For thus shall my church be called in the last days, even The Church of Jesus Christ of Latter-day Saints. (Doctrine and Covenants 115:4)

The name establishes an ideal system for God's relationship with mortals. The system works through a structure of checks and balances.

Figure 2 - Church Structure

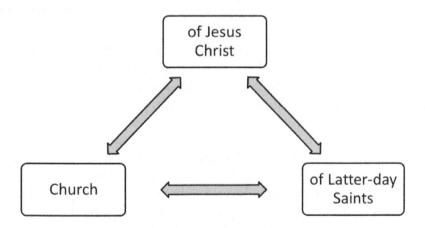

Each Latter-day Saint is entitled and encouraged to access Christ directly. We seek and obtain personal revelation this way. We obtain spiritual energy, comfort and strength. But human weaknesses and the ebb and flow of spirituality leave us susceptible to vagaries. "We see through a glass darkly" as Paul put it.

I like to compare this direct access to God with energy from a solar panel. We each have an individual solar panel that works great when the sun is shining on a clear day. But we receive intermittent spiritual guidance on cloudy days and at night.

Figure 3 - Church Structure metaphor

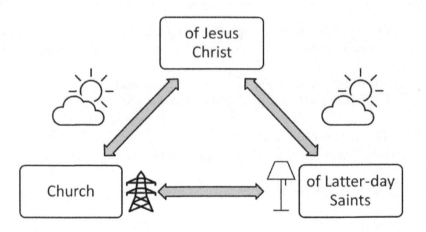

As wonderful as it is when the sun is shining, we all recognize the inconsistency and unreliability of direct access. So does God.

For that reason, we need a steady power source to supplement the direct sunlight. The Church and the scriptures are the power source in this metaphor. The scriptures are the record of previous revelations—bright, sunny days of revelation—that we can rely upon when our solar panels are obscured. Church leaders seek and obtain revelation for the organizational and management issues they confront.

Accessing the divine through organizations is important "backup" but it can leave people susceptible to abuse, misdirection, complacency, confusion, etc. This is why the arrows point both ways between Church and members. Church leaders at all levels seek feedback just as members seek guidance.

All mortals are imperfect. Just as the New Testament documents difficulties in Church leadership, difficulties arise today. The pursuit of clarity, charity and understanding resolves difficulties and unites the Latter-day Saints in the common cause of Zion.

Reframing Church interaction with members

Old narratives	Reframe
Critical. The Church uses psychologically abusive tactics to control its members	The Church teaches members to be self-reliant physically, financially, intellectually, emotionally, and spiritually

Critics who don't understand why people embrace and participate in the Restoration attribute their faithfulness to victimhood, citing examples of psychologically abusive tactics to control members.

Elements of coercion are inherent in family, community and group setting, as parents, societies, and organizations set parameters for behavior and criteria for membership. The scriptures (e.g., D&C 121:37) warn members of the risk of abusive tactics so they can be identified and addressed. The Church seeks to empower individuals by teaching self-reliance and agency.

> He has also given you a church that strengthens families for mortality and binds them together for eternity. It provides more than 31,000 wards and branches where people gather and sing and fast and pray for each other and give of their means to the poor. This is where every person is named, accounted for, and ministered to and where lay friends and neighbors voluntarily serve each other in callings that range from clerical work to custodial duty.
>
> Young adults—and senior couples as well—serve missions by the thousands at their own expense with no say whatsoever as to where they will labor, and members young and old trundle off to temples to perform sacred ordinances necessary to bind the human family together—a bold activity in such a divided world but one which declares that such divisiveness is only temporary. These are a few of the reasons we give for "the hope that is in [us]."[49]

---

[49] Jeffrey R. Holland, 'Fear Not: Believe Only!,' General Conference, April 2022

Reframing Church leadership

Old narratives	Reframe
The Church claims its leaders have all the answers and must be strictly obeyed	Church leaders focus on basic principles and administration, trusting members to obtain and pursue revelation for their own lives

Church leaders serve several functions: pastoral, ecclesiastical, doctrinal, and managerial. They teach members self-reliance in both spiritual and temporal affairs.

Neil L. Andersen explained the calling from the perspective of an Apostle.

> Some view the First Presidency and the Quorum of the Twelve as having worldly motives, like political, business, and cultural leaders.
>
> However, we come very differently to our responsibilities. We are not elected or selected from applications. Without any specific professional preparation, we are called and ordained to bear testimony of the name of Jesus Christ throughout the world until our final breath. We endeavor to bless the sick, the lonely, the downhearted, and the poor and to strengthen the kingdom of God. We seek to know the Lord's will and to proclaim it, especially to those who seek eternal life.
>
> Although our humble desire is for the Savior's teachings to be honored by all, the words of the Lord through His prophets are often contrary to the thinking and trends of the world. It has always been so.[50]

---

[50] Neil L. Andersen, 'Following Jesus: Being a Peacemaker,' General Conference, April 2022.

9. Reframing Church History

How Do We Know the Past?

Old Soviet dissident saying: the future is known, it's the past that is always changing.

Unknown origin, but frequently cited

Who controls the past controls the future: who controls the present controls the past.

George Orwell, 1984

Often I see people on social media, including podcasts and YouTube videos, describe their interpretation of historical events as facts. Even leading professional historians do this.[51] While the practice does make a narrative easier to read, it can be misleading when it is not clear that the material is a mixture of opinion and fact.

We distinguished between facts and assumptions/inferences in chapter 5, the FAITH model. They are quite different, but they are also easily mingled because we all want to fill in the gaps in our knowledge.

To appreciate how many gaps there are, ask yourself: How many of your activities in the last week have been documented? 10, 50, 100 years from now, will people with full access to your documentation be able to recreate your week's worth of activities?

How about yesterday's activities?

What about your activities exactly ten years ago?

Now, ask yourself: if your life in this age of ubiquitous cameras, electronic calendars, and communications cannot track everything you say, hear, and do, how much of a person's life circa 1820s can we expect to learn about by examining the sketchy historical record?

---

[51] See chapter 15 for an example.

The sum total of all the contemporaneous accounts of Joseph's life from his birth through September 1827 when he got the plates is... Zero.[52]

Because I am not a professional historian, I need to explain my approach to studying history.

Historical events are set in stone—we can't change the past. But our *understanding* of those events is fluid. To see why, let's consider this question:

How do we know the history of the Church?

In a brilliant essay that everyone should read, LDS historian Richard Bushman explained the challenge of interpreting historical events.

> it is disconcerting to observe the oscillations in historical fashion and to recognize how one's own times affect the view of the past. Anyone unfamiliar with the writing of history may wonder why historians are such vacillating creatures. Are not the facts the facts and is not the historian's task no more than to lay them out in clear order? Why the continual variations in opinion? It seems reasonable that, once told, the story need only be amended as new facts come to light.
>
> **The reason for the variations is that history is made by historians.** The facts are not fixed in predetermined form merely awaiting discovery and description. They do not force themselves on the historian; he selects and molds them. Indeed he cannot avoid sculpturing the past simply because the records contain so very many facts, all heaped together without recognizable shape. The historian must select certain ones and form them into a convincing story. Inevitably scholars come up with differing accounts of the same event.[53]

---

[52] Documents relating to his school attendance, his family's property and finances, birth records, etc., do not describe Joseph's daily activities.

[53] Richard L. Bushman, "Faithful History," in *Dialogue*, https://www.dialoguejournal.com/wp-content/uploads/sbi/articles/Dialogue_V04N04_13.pdf

The Rational Restoration

We are fortunate to have lots of records, including journals, documents, correspondence, newspaper reports, and official histories. But none of these tells a complete story unless put in context, which introduces subjectivity.

In a sense, trial lawyers are historians. They seek to understand past events and make them understandable to a fact-finding authority (judge or jury) in a manner favorable to their clients. Litigation is usually a debate about history.

When I practiced law, I had stints as both a criminal prosecutor and a criminal defense lawyer. My opponents and I would examine every known bit of evidence to assemble a coherent and consistent account of what happened in the past. Often, the facts were so indisputable that a guilty verdict was a foregone conclusion, and a guilty plea resulted. But other times, extensive research leads the two sides to completely different versions of history, and the only way to resolve the dispute is at trial.

That's what I see happening with some details in Church history. The facts are subject to contradictory assumptions and inferences, and we end up with multiple theories about what happened and why.

My work in Church history has focused on specific details that didn't fit traditional narratives. When I investigated the authorship of the anonymous articles in the *Times and Seasons*, the detail was a list of books donated to the Nauvoo Library in 1844 (see *The Lost City of Zarahemla*). When I investigated Book of Mormon passages about geography, the detail was a reference to "west sea south" (Alma 53:8) (see *Moroni's America*).

The detail that didn't fit in the plates narrative was an unusual comment by David Whitmer about encountering an old man bearing a knapsack. In June 1829, David was driving his wagon from Harmony to Fayette with Joseph and Oliver as passengers. He stopped to give the man a ride, but the man declined, explaining he was going to Cumorah.

That comment nagged at me. The few historians who even mentioned the event dismissed it as a product of David's faulty memory, probably conflated with a false tradition about Cumorah.

But that didn't make sense to me. I pulled on the thread, and the result was the book *Whatever Happened to the Golden Plates*, from which the next paragraphs are taken.

Jonathan Neville

History begins every second; you can't go back in time even to the moment you read the previous sentence. The persistence of memory makes life seem fluid, similar to the way persistence of vision makes a movie seem continuous. Movies consist of a series of still images displayed at the rate of 24 frames per second. We don't perceive each discreet image separately because our mind interpolates between each image. We make a connection. We smooth it out.

Likewise, we process events as discreet moments. We usually don't notice the details of an event unless we relate it or write it down—or unless we're asked about it. Then we draw on our memories to see what our brains may have recorded about the event.

Defects in perception and recall make even eyewitness testimony problematic. On a daily basis, courts around the world confront discrepancies between the testimony of multiple people whose eyes may have witnessed the same event, but whose brains recorded it differently. *Much* differently in many cases.

Often a particular historical narrative takes on the qualities of "truth" because it is widely accepted, but all understanding of history is inherently subjective. We have no photographs from the 1830s. No video or audio recordings. All we have are personal accounts, historical documents, and limited physical evidence.

Records kept by eyewitness accounts are usually the only sources for historical information, but no two people can observe the same event in identical ways. Each person has a unique perceptual filter, based on past experience, expectations, and priorities. Memories are imperfect and fade over time. Relatively few people keep journals, and even the most meticulous and detailed journals are inherently incomplete.

We examine historical records in the totality of the circumstances, considering not only the words on a page but the personalities and motivations of the authors and the circumstances in which they lived. Sometimes a new historical document surfaces that completely changes our understanding of past events. Other times a fresh look brings an entirely new interpretation of existing documents.

The Rational Restoration

Church historians and private collectors have done a remarkable job acquiring, assembling, and organizing most of the sources I use in this book. Many are relatively obscure and unknown to most readers, but whether or not you have read them before doesn't matter. We're going to take that fresh look.

I think of historical references as keys on a piano. Each key strikes the same wire no matter who presses it, but together they can be played in unlimited variations. Like piano keys, the words in historical sources are fixed. But as we interpret them through our own filters of unique experiences, priorities, interests, and insights into human nature, we can derive multiple interpretations.

Ideally, the more perspectives we consider, the closer we'll come to the truth. But whether we actually reach the truth is for the factfinder—you, in this case—to decide.

Reframing the beginning of the Restoration

Old narratives	Reframe
Faithful: The Restoration began with Joseph Smith's First Vision when he saw God the Father and Jesus Christ in the Sacred Grove near Palmyra, New York. Critical: Joseph Smith never told anyone about this First Vision. It wasn't until he claimed an angel visited him in 1823 that he started his Restoration movement.	The Restoration began when Joseph Smith became a religious seeker as a result of his life-threatening leg surgery. The First Vision was a step forward in the Restoration but was rarely discussed during Joseph's lifetime because lots of people claimed to see God.

Joseph's journal relates an event from November 14, 1835, that includes an interesting detail about his young life.

> A Gentleman called this after noon by the name of Erastus Holmes of Newbury Clemon [Clermont] Co. Ohio, he called to make enquiry about the establishment of

77

the Church of the latter-day Saints and to be instructed more perfectly in our doctrine &c I commenced and gave him a brief relation of my experience while in my juvenile years, say from 6, years old up to the time I received the first visitation of Angels which was when I was about 14, years old and also the the [sic] visitations that I received afterward, concerning the book of Mormon, and a short account of the rise and progress of the church, up to this, date.[54]

Holmes inquired about the "establishment of the Church," so it is curious that Joseph began with his juvenile years, "say from 6." That time frame corresponds with his leg surgery, but what did that surgery have to do with the establishment of the Church?

There is circumstantial evidence that Joseph read Christian materials while staying in Salem. Samuel Deane delivered a series of four sermons for young men that were collected and published as a booklet in Salem, Massachusetts, in 1774.[55] Joseph's uncle Jesse was known for his strong religious beliefs,[56] suggesting that he would give such reading material to his recuperating nephew. The Deane booklet contains non-biblical language that appears in the Book of Mormon, including *design, anxious, tendency, rising generation, opposite, in other words, on the other hand, garb, regulation, faculties, lay before, state of probation, everlasting damnation, soften, reluctance, look forward, ignominious, thoughtless*, and more. As suggested by this terminology, the sermons focus on Book of Mormon themes.

Joseph's convalescence didn't conclude in Massachusetts. He wrote that after the doctors removed "a large portion of the bone from my left leg… fourteen additional pieces of bone afterwards worked out before my leg healed, during which time I was reduced so very low that my mother could carry me with ease. & after I began to get about I went on crutches till I started for the State of New York."[57]

---

[54] Joseph Smith, Journal, 1835-1836, p. 36-7. Online at https://www.josephsmithpapers.org/paper-summary/journal-1835-1836/37

[55] *Four Sermons to Young Men, from Titus II.6.* preached at Falmouth, by Samuel Deane. Salem (Samuel and Ebenezer Hall) 1774.

[56] John W. Welch, "Jesse Smith's 1814 Protest," *BYU Studies* Vol. 33, 1 (1993): 131, https://scholarsarchive.byu.edu/cgi/viewcontent.cgi?article=2892&context=byusq

[57] Joseph Smith, *History, 1838-1856*, volume A-1, Addenda, Note A (handwriting of Willard Richards) https://www.josephsmithpapers.org/paper-summary/history-1838-1856-volume-a-1-23-december-1805-30-august-1834/137

These years of disability compromised Joseph's usefulness for farm work, leaving him more time to read Christian materials and engage in what his mother Lucy Mack Smith later called "meditation and deep study."

In this way, Joseph's life-threatening leg surgery prompted him to become a religious seeker.

Reframing Joseph's preparation as a prophet

Old narratives	Reframe
Faithful: Joseph Smith was an unlearned farm boy with a "blank slate" mind upon which God could write.	Joseph Smith was prepared by God from a young age to translate an ancient document and articulate modern revelation.
Faithful: The Book of Mormon is a miracle because Joseph was so ignorant, he couldn't even write a coherent letter.	Although "unlearned" in the sense of little formal education, Joseph had "an intimate acquaintance" with Christian writings that enabled him to translate the plates "after the manner of his language."
Critical: Joseph Smith was a clever scoundrel who lied about spiritual experiences.	
Critical: Joseph Smith was tutored for years by Hyrum, who attended Dartmouth, and was well-versed in the Bible.	

Two basic hypotheses (narratives) have arisen about the early events of the Restoration.

1. Faithful: Joseph Smith as ignorant farm boy who couldn't even write a letter, chosen by God because of a sincere prayer and his future potential.

2. Critical: Joseph Smith as clever treasure-digger trying to make money, and well-versed enough in Christian thinking to compose and dictate a religious text.

There are numerous variations of these two narratives. Advocates of each can cite historical facts that, when filtered through their assumptions, inferences and theories, support their respective interpretations.

To itemize all the facts would take an entire book or two, but we can separate a few facts that everyone can agree upon and see how assumptions, inferences and theories lead to the respective hypotheses.

Any list of accepted historical facts would include these.

1. Joseph's leg surgery and recuperation, and his reference to that event when explaining the Restoration.

2. Joseph's proximity to Dartmouth during his recuperation and his brother Hyrum's attendance there. (Assumptions and inferences about the extent of Hyrum's education vary.)

3. Joseph's early years in Palmyra, his exposure to ministers from different denominations, and the ready availability of Christian writings, including the works of Jonathan Edwards and James Hervey.

4. Joseph's aversion to writing, as well as his abilities to exhort, preach, and narrate stories.

5. The intensity of Joseph's religious seeking, reflected in his 1832 history and his mother's history.

Some commonly cited facts are debatable. For example, many people cite Emma Smith's "Last Testimony" as relating facts, such as Joseph Smith's inability to write a letter. Again, we know the document exists, but whether it relates facts is a separate question.

The "Last Testimony" is in Joseph Smith III's handwriting. Emma died shortly after the interview and never publicly acknowledged it. The testimony was published six months after her death. The parts of the interview regarding plural marriage were directly contradicted by others who were present at the events. When Joseph Smith III later discussed the translation, he didn't even cite the "Last Testimony."

Emma's claim about Joseph's ability to write a letter contradicts two known letters Joseph did write: one to his uncle before beginning the translation, and one to Oliver Cowdery shortly afterward.[58] These and other aspects of the "Last Testimony" undermine the credibility of the document's truth claims, suggesting it was more of an apologetic statement and leaving its interpretation as a matter of assumption, inference, etc.

Reframe. The reframe incorporates all the historical facts and sees Joseph Smith as a religious seeker from a young age. This is a pragmatic approach, based on historical evidence but also common human experience.

This is a relatively naturalistic approach, but it supports and does not contradict Joseph's claim that he translated an ancient record.

At the same time, the reframe makes Joseph Smith more relatable to the rest of us. It shows that his earnest efforts to study and learn prepared him to become the instrument in the hands of God that he eventually became.

When asked about the Restoration, Joseph said it began when he was around six years old. Presumably he referred to his leg surgery, which left him disabled for nearly three years. Even when the family moved to Cumorah, Joseph was still using crutches. A disabled boy would naturally occupy his time by reading.

The move to Palmyra exposed Joseph to a variety of books on sale in the T.C. Strong bookstore that Joseph visited weekly to get the newspaper for his father. A coworker there later described Joseph as an "inquisitive lounger."

Among the books on sale at the bookstore was an 8-volume set of the works of Jonathan Edwards, the most prominent American theologian in the 1700s. Edwards was highly influential on other Christian authors and ministers, particularly in New England and New York. His work was republished in pamphlets, newspapers, magazines, and books.

---

[58] https://www.josephsmithpapers.org/paper-summary/letter-to-oliver-cowdery-22-october-1829/1

The 8-volume set was published in 1808. Most of the non-biblical language (words and phrases) in the Book of Mormon, Doctrine and Covenants, and Joseph's personal writings can be found in the works of Jonathan Edwards.[59]

In his 1832 history, Joseph wrote that his "goodly Parents... spared no pains to instructing me in the Christian religion."[60] He also explained that he had "an intimate acquaintance with those of different denominations." While some have interpreted that to refer to various ministers or members of various churches, Joseph later explained he did not care much for church meetings.

For a detailed discussion of this point and all the relevant sources, including alternative interpretations, see my book *A Man that Can Translate: Joseph Smith and the Nephite Interpreters* and the book I wrote with James Lucas titled *By Means of the Urim and Thummim: Restoring Translation to the Restoration*.

Reframing the plates

As I mentioned a few pages ago, I was re-reading historical accounts about the plates when I was struck by the account by David Whitmer that I'd known about for decades.

Before describing David's account, it's important to review the order in which Joseph translated the plates.

Our current Book of Mormon follows a chronological narrative, beginning with Lehi's family leaving Jerusalem and ending at Cumorah, but it is not organized according to the order in which Joseph translated it.[61]

---

[59] See my book *Infinite Goodness* and the database here: https://www.mobom.org/nonbiblical-intertextuality-database

[60] Joseph Smith, History, circa Summer 1832, https://www.josephsmithpapers.org/paper-summary/history-circa-summer-1832/1

[61] We know Joseph translated the plates of Nephi in Fayette because the Original Manuscript for 1 Nephi features the handwriting of John and Christian Whitmer, who never visited Harmony. See https://www.mobom.org/translation-chronology.

Table 1 - When and where translated

Source		Harmony, Pennsylvania	Fayette, New York
Abridged plates	Book of Lehi (lost 116 pages)	Spring 1828	
Abridged plates	Mosiah – Moroni and Title Page	Nov 1829-May 1829	
Original plates	1 Nephi – Words of Mormon		June 1829

Note that Joseph translated the abridged plates in Harmony and the original plates of Nephi in Fayette. David's narrative of the trip to Fayette helps us understand why.

David Whitmer explained that, as requested by Joseph and Oliver, he went to Harmony to pick them up and bring them to his father's home in Fayette, New York. On the journey from Harmony toward Fayette, they met a man along the road. David offered him a ride, but the man declined, saying "No, I am going to Cumorah." David reported that "This name was something new to me, I did not know what Cumorah meant." Of course, he wouldn't have known about Cumorah because he hadn't read the manuscript that Joseph had just dictated to Oliver, which contained what is now Mormon chapters 6 and 8.

David also said the man "had on his back a sort of knapsack with something in, shaped like a book. It was the messenger who had the plates, who had taken them from Joseph just prior to our starting from Harmony." He asked Joseph about the man and Joseph "said their visitor was one of the three Nephites to whom the Savior gave the promise of life on earth until He should come in power."

Years ago, most Latter-day Saints knew about this encounter because it was included in Seminary and Institute manuals.

However, younger and newer Latter-day Saints don't know about this event. The book *Saints*, Volume 1, Chapter 7, mentions the trip to Fayette but omits David's account, as does the book *Opening the Heavens*, which purports to include all known accounts about the translation.

In Chapter 14 we'll discuss why this account has been omitted, but here we'll focus on how this seemingly insignificant event has led to a reframing of the saga of the plates that resolves longstanding confusion and uncertainty.

Table 2 - Reframing the Plates

Old narratives	Reframe
Faithful: There was only one set of ancient golden plates and Joseph got them from Moroni's stone box. OR Critical: There were never any authentic ancient plates because witnesses gave inconsistent descriptions.	There were two sets of plates: the abridged plates in Moroni's stone box that Joseph translated in Harmony, PA, and the original plates of Nephi from the repository in the Hill Cumorah that Joseph translated in Fayette, NY

The saga of the golden plates generated considerable discussion even before Joseph obtained them in 1827. It's easy to see why critics disbelieve there were any ancient plates. Not only are the plates unavailable for examination, but witnesses gave inconsistent descriptions. Joseph said "a portion" of the plates were sealed (and Moroni warned him not to touch the sealed things Ether 5:1). Yet none of the eight witnesses who claimed they handled the plates reported any sealed portion. Some witnesses said the plates weighed 60 pounds, but Joseph's father reported that he weighed them at 30 pounds.

The Title Page itself claims the set of plates included two abridgments (Nephite and Jaredite), plus Moroni's sealing, but never mentions any original plates. Plus, Joseph translated the Title Page, which he said was the "last leaf" of the plates, before he translated the plates of Nephi, leaving everyone guessing where, exactly, those original plates might have been in the stack of abridged plates.

Thanks to David Whitmer's account of the messenger, we can reframe the saga of the plates to reconcile the inconsistencies and corroborate the accounts of the witnesses.

The reframing goes like this.

The Rational Restoration

1. Moroni took his father's abridged plates and added content (the last 2 chapters in Mormon, all of Ether, including the sealed portion, and all of Moroni). Then he summarized the contents on the Title Page, which was the last leaf of the collection. He deposited the plates in the stone box he constructed on the Hill Cumorah in New York.

2. Moroni appeared to Joseph Smith in 1823 and explained that "a history of the aborigines of this country… was written and deposited not far from"[62] Joseph's home. He said, "the record is on a side hill on the Hill of Cumorah 3 miles from this place remove the Grass and moss and you will find a large flat stone pry that up and you will find the record under it laying on 4 pillars of cement."[63] Joseph obtained these abridged plates, together with the Urim and Thummim (interpreters), brought them home, and then took them to Harmony, Pennsylvania.

3. In Harmony, Joseph copied and translated the characters (JS-H 1:62). He then began translating the plates by means of the Urim and Thummim. In the Preface he wrote for the 1830 edition, Joseph explained that "I would inform you that I translated, by the gift and power of God, and caused to be written, one hundred and sixteen pages, the which I took from the Book of Lehi, which was an account abridged from the plates of Lehi, by the hand of Mormon."[64]

4. Martin Harris took the 116 pages back to Palmyra but lost them in the summer of 1828. Joseph forfeited the plates and the Urim and Thummim.

5. In the fall of 1828, Moroni returned the plates and the Urim and Thummim to Joseph Smith. He resumed translating the abridged plates

---

[62] https://www.josephsmithpapers.org/paper-summary/history-1834-1836/69
[63] https://www.josephsmithpapers.org/paper-summary/lucy-mack-smith-history-1844-1845/41
[64] Facsimiles of the 1830 edition are online here: https://bookofmormon.online/fax/1830 and here: https://www.josephsmithpapers.org/paper-summary/preface-to-book-of-mormon-circa-august-1829/1

with Emma as a scribe. In April 1829, Oliver Cowdery arrived in Harmony and began working as a scribe.

6. Oliver desired to translate. The Lord authorized it, but Oliver was unable to translate. The Lord explained that

> I would that ye should continue [as scribe] until you have finished this record [i.e., the abridged plates], which I have entrusted unto him [Joseph]. And then, behold, **other records have I**, that I will give unto you power that you may assist to translate. (D&C 9:1–2)

Question: What were the "other records" referred to here? They were records that the Lord had but Joseph did not.

7. In May, Joseph and Oliver translated to the end of the abridged plates. They contemplated going back to the beginning to retranslate the Book of Lehi.

8. The Lord instructed them not to do that. Instead,

> you shall **translate the engravings which are on the plates of Nephi**, down even till you come to the reign of king Benjamin, or until you come to that which you have translated, which you have retained; And behold, you shall publish it as the record of Nephi." (D&C 10:41–42)

9. D&C 10 tells us three things regarding the plates:

a. The plates of Nephi were the "other records" mentioned in D&C 9:2 and were original plates, not abridged plates.
b. Joseph was translating "the engravings on the plates" and therefore needed the actual plates to translate.
c. Joseph and Oliver **did not have the plates of Nephi in Harmony**. D&C 9:2 explained that the Lord had them.

On the Title Page, Moroni described only abridged plates, plus his own words (he sealed them). Moroni did not list the original plates of Nephi on the Title Page because he did not put the plates of Nephi in the stone box.

10. Question: Where were the plates of Nephi?

Answer: They were in the repository of Nephite records back in the Hill Cumorah near Palmyra.

Oliver described his visit to the repository to Brigham Young, who related it in a conference in Utah shortly before he died. Orson Pratt explained that there were two separate departments in the Hill Cumorah: one was Moroni's stone box and the other was the repository of all the original Nephite records (Mormon 6:6).[65]

11. Question: How and where did Joseph get the plates of Nephi?

Answer. From a divine messenger Joseph described as one of the Nephites, who took the abridged plates to the repository in Cumorah and there picked up the plates of Nephi to take to Fayette.

Sequence of events:

a. Lucy Mack Smith reported[66] that one morning in Harmony, as Joseph applied the Urim and Thummim to his eyes to look on the plates, he was commanded instead to write a letter to David Whitmer (whom he had not met) and ask David to take Joseph and Oliver to Fayette until the translation was complete. Joseph was also instructed to give the abridged plates to "an angel."

b. Joseph gave the abridged plates to the messenger before leaving Harmony. (JS-H 1:60)

c. David Whitmer arrived in Harmony and picked up Joseph and Oliver. On their journey back to Fayette, they encountered the messenger who had the plates. The messenger declined David's offer of a ride, explaining that he was going to Cumorah.

Key point: Why would the messenger go to Cumorah with the abridged plates before going to Fayette? Because he had to get the plates of Nephi for Joseph to translate as instructed in D&C 10.

d. David, Joseph and Oliver continued their journey to Fayette. Soon after their arrival, the messenger met Joseph and gave him the plates to translate. Because Joseph translated the plates of Nephi in Fayette, we infer that the messenger picked up the plates of Nephi from the

---

[65] References available here: https://www.mobom.org/church-history-issues

[66] https://www.mobom.org/resources-fayette-trip

repository in Cumorah. The messenger also showed these plates to David's mother, Mary. She said he introduced himself as "Brother Nephi."[67]

This scenario explains how Joseph obtained the plates of Nephi and why the messenger took the abridged plates to Cumorah.

The figure below explains the composition of today's Book of Mormon.

Figure 4 - Two Sets of Plates

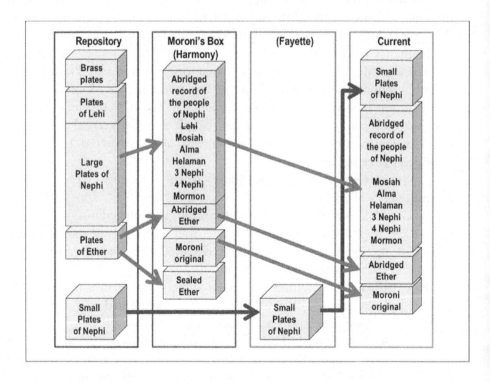

---

[67] The *Saints* book claims it was Moroni who showed the plates to Mary Whitmer. For a discussion of that point, see chapter 14, "Reframing *Saints*."

Reframing the translation

You might wonder, why reframe the translation of the Book of Mormon? Everyone knows Joseph Smith dictated the text of the Book of Mormon. People either believe that it was divinely inspired or they don't. If they do believe it, what difference does it make *how* he did it?

Many faithful Latter-day Saints say they have a spiritual witness of the truthfulness of the Book of Mormon, and they don't care how Joseph produced it. That's a rational position for those who believe a spiritual witness suffices.

For many other faithful Latter-day Saints, as well as for non-Latter-day Saints, the credibility of the restoration narrative is directly affected by the credibility of the origins of the Book of Mormon. They, too, recognize the importance of spiritual manifestations, but they also recognize that people of all faiths—and no faith—also receive spiritual manifestations that confirm their beliefs. For them, the Restoration is distinctive because in addition to the spiritual confirmation, there is extrinsic evidence to corroborate their faith.

Among that evidence is Joseph's own explanation of the Book of Mormon.

Joseph said he was asked almost on a daily basis how he obtained the Book of Mormon. He answered in the *Elders' Journal*.

> How, and where did you obtain the book of Mormon?
> Moroni, the person who deposited the plates, from whence the book of Mormon was translated, in a hill in Manchester, Ontario County, New York, being dead; and raised again therefrom, appeared unto me, and told me where they were, and gave me directions how to obtain them. I obtained them, and the Urim and Thummim with them, by the means of which, I translated the plates; and thus came the Book of Mormon. (*Elders' Journal*, July 1838)[68]

---

[68] https://www.josephsmithpapers.org/paper-summary/elders-journal-july-1838/10

Some people accept Joseph's statement. Others, both believers and critics, reject or modify his statement.

Even if your mind is already made up in either direction, you should be able to articulate alternative narratives.

Old narratives	Reframe
Faithful. To produce the Book of Mormon, Joseph Smith read words that appeared on the stone in the hat (SITH). He did not use the plates or the Urim and Thummim that came with the plates._____OR_____**Critical**. To produce the Book of Mormon, Joseph Smith used an occult device to deceive people or to turn people away from biblical Christianity._____OR_____**Critical**. To produce the Book of Mormon, Joseph read from an existing manuscript (such as the Spalding story) as he dictated from behind a screen, curtain, or veil._____OR_____**Critical**. To produce the Book of Mormon, Joseph performed a narrative he had developed over many years, using mnemonic cues.	Joseph Smith studied the characters on the plates by copying them and translating them by means of the Nephite interpreters that came with the plates (the Urim and Thummim), which God had prepared for that specific purpose.With that knowledge, and with the "gift and power of God," Joseph translated the engravings on the plates.Reports that Joseph used the stone in the hat (SITH) were based on demonstrations he conducted to satisfy the curiosity of his supporters, but Joseph did not use SITH to produce the Book of Mormon.SITH became an apologetic argument to contradict the Spalding theory.

By applying the FAITH model, we can separate facts from assumptions, inferences, and theories. There is a finite (although extensive) set of facts to consider, including a range of witness

The Rational Restoration

statements, the existing Original Manuscript, and other circumstantial evidence. There are numerous compilations of the available facts.[69]

Translation is an inherently mental process. Even when we observe someone who is ostensibly translating, we can't read that person's mind to determine distinguish between translating, composing, reciting from memory, etc.

If we have the source material, we can compare it with the translated material and conclude that it was, in fact, translated. Obviously, in the case of the Book of Mormon, we don't have the source material.

To know what mental process produced the text, we have (i) the statements from Joseph Smith, who claimed he translated the text, and (ii) extrinsic evidence such as possible source material, statements from observers and others, and the text itself.

Because Joseph (and Oliver) consistently explained that Joseph translated the plates, and their explanation is the most parsimonious explanation for the text, contrary extrinsic evidence demonstrates either that (i) Joseph and Oliver were deceptive, or (ii) the extrinsic evidence is misunderstood, fabricated, or otherwise unreliable.

Believers and critics alike have a range of theories about what Joseph meant when he said he translated the plates and what he actually did to produce the Book of Mormon. Everyone cites historical evidence for their widely divergent views. Different outcomes result from different weighing of the evidence, so (as usual) one's conclusions depend on what one wants to believe. The FAITH model clarifies the assumptions and inferences that lead to the conclusions.

In recent years, critics and many believers alike have converged on an explanation for the translation that I refer to as the "stone-in-the-hat" narrative (SITH).

Although it is based on historical accounts, SITH does not reconcile the historical evidence. It directly contradicts the traditional faithful narrative that prevailed for over 180 years, based on Joseph's claim that

---

[69] See, e.g., *Opening the Heavens* and *the Joseph Smith Papers*, but always check references and distinguish between facts and editorial commentary.

he actually translated ancient plates. Likewise, the traditional explanation does not reconcile the seemingly conflicting evidence from witnesses.

Because I was dissatisfied with SITH and the other faithful and critical theories, I delved into the historical evidence for myself.

The questions I asked were, (i) is there a way to reconcile what seems to be contradictory historical evidence and (ii) what is the most rational explanation?

My research led to me writing a book on the translation in which I compiled and addressed all the known historical references, and then proposed a reframing that (at least for me) answers the questions I posed.[70] The reframing is an example of "neo-traditional" thinking; i.e., the reframe re-establishes a traditional narrative by offering a new approach to old evidence. Then, with my co-author James Lucas, we developed the reframe further and proposed a reframing of the translation process itself that offers a rational explanation of how that worked.[71]

We can't summarize these entire books here, but to simplify the discussion, the question boils down to whether or not Joseph translated ancient plates. If he did not, then it doesn't matter much which alternative theory you choose to accept because all the alternatives mean he misled everyone about the origin of the Book of Mormon. Indeed, even some faithful LDS scholars now think that Joseph and Oliver *did* mislead everyone because, according to some accounts, Joseph used only SITH to produce the text we have today, even if he used the Urim and Thummim to produce the lost 116 pages.[72]

In this section, we'll briefly assess the historical record and then we'll turn to the witnesses.

The Preface in the 1830 edition is the earliest known public statement Joseph made about the translation.[73]

---

[70] See *A Man that Can Translate*.

[71] See *By Means of the Urim and Thummim: Restoring Translation to the Restoration*.

[72] See my paper here: https://www.academia.edu/67756647/Agenda_driven_editorial_content_in_the_Joseph_Smith_Papers

[73] Prior revelations (D&C 2-19) were not published until 1833.

The Rational Restoration

To the Reader—
As **many false reports have been circulated** respecting the following work, and also many unlawful measures taken by evil designing persons to destroy me, and also the work, I would inform you that **I translated**, by the gift and power of God, and caused to be written, one hundred and sixteen pages, **the which I took from the Book of Lehi**, which was an account abridged from the plates of Lehi, by the hand of Mormon... **thou shalt translate from the plates of Nephi**, until ye come to that **which ye have translated**, which ye have retained...

What were those "false reports" that were circulating even before the Book of Mormon was published in April 1830?

Although Joseph didn't itemize the false reports, his emphatic declaration that he *translated* 116 pages, which he *took* from the Book of Lehi, is as plain as words can be. Or, in other words, Joseph translated a specific ancient record.

From his statement we rationally infer that the "false reports" included claims that Joseph *did not* translate ancient records.

Sure enough, "false reports" were newspaper reprints of an article first published in Palmyra by Jonathan Hadley in August 1829. Based on interviews with Martin Harris and/or other "proselytes," the article claimed that "by placing the spectacles in a hat, and looking into it, Smith interprets the characters into the English language."[74]

These newspaper articles could not have been based on anyone's personal observation because Joseph had been commanded not to show the "spectacles" (a descriptive term he sometimes used for the Nephite interpreters known as the Urim and Thummim) to anyone until after the translation was finished.[75] Furthermore, neither Martin Harris nor anyone

---

[74] The article and its implications are available here: http://www.ldshistoricalnarratives.com/2023/08/the-jonathan-hadley-account-and-sith.html

[75] 42 Again, he told me, that when I got those plates of which he had spoken—for the time that they should be obtained was not yet fulfilled—I should not show them to any person; neither the breastplate with the Urim and Thummim; only to those to whom I should be commanded to show them; if I did I should be destroyed.
(Joseph Smith—History 1:42)

else claimed to have seen the Urim and Thummim during the translation process (except Oliver Cowdery, who attempted to translate).

Hadley was highly antagonistic toward the "whole Mormon gang." While it's impossible to know for sure, Hadley may have conflated reports that Joseph found "spectacles" with reports that he used the stone-in-the-hat technique for finding lost treasure. Regardless of the origin of Hadley's article, Joseph's efforts to refute such "false reports" in 1830 did not succeed because variations of the "stone-in-the-hat" narrative (SITH) persisted to the present day.[76]

An anti-Mormon book published in 1834 titled *Mormonism Unvailed* described SITH this way:

> The translation finally commenced. They were found to contain a language not now known upon the earth, which they termed "reformed Egyptian characters." The plates, therefore, which had been so much talked of, were found to be of no manner of use. After all, the Lord showed and communicated to him [Joseph] every word and letter of the Book. **Instead of looking at the characters inscribed upon the plates, the prophet was obliged to resort to the old "peep stone," which he formerly used in money-digging.** This he placed in a hat, or box, into which he also thrust his face. Through the stone he could then discover a single word at a time, which he repeated aloud to his amanuensis, who committed it to paper, when another word would immediately appear, and thus the performance continued to the end of the book.[77]

Continuing on the same page 18, *Mormonism Unvailed* provided readers a second, alternative description of the way Joseph produced the Book of Mormon, again emphasizing that Joseph did not refer to the plates.

> Another account they give of the transaction, is, that it was performed with the big spectacles before mentioned, and which were in fact, the identical

---

[76] For an analysis, see http://www.ldshistoricalnarratives.com/2023/08/the-jonathan-hadley-account-and-sith.html

[77] See https://archive.org/details/mormonismunvaile00howe/page/18

Urim and Thumim [sic] mentioned in Exodus 28 — 30, and were brought away from Jerusalem by the heroes of the book, handed down from one generation to another, and finally buried up in Ontario county, some fifteen centuries since, to enable Smith to translate the plates without looking at them![78]

In response to the publicity given to SITH by *Mormonism Unvailed*, Oliver Cowdery (with the assistance of Joseph Smith) wrote the first of eight essays about early Church history. Initially published in the *Messenger and Advocate*, the Mormon newspaper in Kirtland, Ohio, in 1834, an excerpt from Oliver's letter has been canonized as a note to JS-H 1:71.

> These were days never to be forgotten—to sit under the sound of a voice dictated by the inspiration of heaven, awakened the utmost gratitude of this bosom! Day after day I continued, uninterrupted, to write from his mouth, as **he translated with the Urim and Thummim, or, as the Nephites should have said, "Interpreters,"** the history, or record, called "the book of Mormon."[79]

When read in juxtaposition to *Mormonism Unvailed*, the contrast between the narratives is sharp, dramatic, and irreconcilable. On one hand, we have the SITH narrative from *Mormonism Unvailed* and other sources. On the other, we have the narrative from Joseph and Oliver, that Joseph translated the record with the Nephite interpreters, called the Urim and Thummim, that came with the plates.

Some have attempted a faithful reconciliation by proposing that when Joseph and Oliver used the term *Urim and Thummim*, they actually meant both the Nephite interpreters and the seer stone. However, it is evident from the passages in *Mormonism Unvailed* that as early as 1834 the terms referred to distinctly different objects. Subsequent statements from Joseph and Oliver made it clear that the Urim and Thummim Joseph used to translate came with the plates. Even David Whitmer, Martin

---

[78] Intentionally or not, the author missed the points that (i) the U&T that Joseph received was not brought from Jerusalem by Lehi but instead had been used by the Jaredites in America, and (ii) Joseph actually looked at the plates with the spectacles.

[79] https://www.josephsmithpapers.org/paper-summary/history-1834-1836/49. Also found in JS-H, 1:71 footnote.

Harris, and Emma Smith always distinguished the Urim and Thummim from the seer stone.

Nevertheless, David Whitmer insisted that Joseph used SITH to produce the text. Statements from Emma Smith and others arguably corroborate David's claim.

This is where a reframing of the witnesses becomes necessary.

Reframing the witnesses

Old narratives	Reframe
Witnesses later claimed Joseph used SITH exclusively to produce the Book of Mormon	Some of his supporters eventually promoted SITH in an apologetic effort to contradict the other narratives, particularly the Spalding theory.

My reframing of the evidence reconciles the historical evidence through two interpretations of the evidence that I find rational.

First, it is unlikely that the SITH accounts were pure inventions. And it is rational to conclude that David and others were probably telling the truth about what they observed. But witnesses typically conflate what they *observe* with what they *infer* or *assume*.

Witnesses also influence one another, particularly over time. Testimony converges, especially when witnesses have mutual motives. In this case, David, Emma and others had a strong motive to relate the SITH narrative, as we'll see below.

Second, the SITH witnesses forgot to include an important detail. They never said what, exactly, Joseph dictated on the occasions they claimed to observe him using SITH. In other words, there is no "chain of custody" between the SITH statements and the text we have today.

No one said they observed Joseph, with his face in the hat, dictating, say, Lehi's discourse on Adam and Eve. Perhaps that omission was due to forgetfulness, but it leaves us with the obvious problem that, even assuming Joseph was dictating something with his face in a hat, we can't tell if he was dictating the text of the Book of Mormon.

In other words, we can reasonably conclude that whatever Joseph was doing with SITH, it was not translating the Book of Mormon.

As I explained in *A Man that Can Translate*, there is evidence to support the conclusion that Joseph conducted one or more demonstrations in an effort to satisfy the "awful curiosity" of his supporters.[80]

We return to the question of why the SITH witnesses would have insisted on SITH, knowing as they must have that Joseph and Oliver both insisted that Joseph translated the plates with the Urim and Thummim that came with the plates.

In the mid- to late 1800s, the prevailing theory about the origin of the Book of Mormon was the Spalding theory set out in *Mormonism Unvailed*.

The author, E.D. Howe, mocked the SITH narrative as ridiculous. He pointed out that SITH relegated the plates to useless props that no one had actually seen. But because it was common knowledge that Joseph dictated from behind a blanket or screen,[81] Howe proposed an alternative explanation for the Book of Mormon.

The title of the book, *Mormonism Unvailed*, focused on the question of what was behind the "vail" (veil) when Joseph was dictating?

Howe alleged that Joseph was reading from a manuscript that had been written, but never published, by Solomon Spalding. The Spalding theory was widely accepted by critics as a legitimate explanation for the Book of Mormon that avoided the supernatural. When Oliver Cowdery rejoined the Church in 1848, he specifically denied that Sidney Rigdon or Solomon Spalding had written the book. Nevertheless, the Spalding theory prevailed in the popular media through the 19th century.

With this context in mind, it's easy to understand why David Whitmer and Emma Smith, who both sought to support the divinity of the Book of Mormon, would relate SITH. To refute the Spalding theory, it was essential to remove the curtain or veil from the narrative. Relying

---

[80] Zenas Gurley reported "that Joseph had another stone called seers' stone, and peep stone, is quite certain. This stone was frequently exhibited to different ones and helped to assuage their awful curiosity; but the Urim and Thummim never, unless possibly to Oliver Cowdery."

[81] Joseph had been commanded not to show the plates or interpreters to anyone until the translation was complete.

on the demonstration, they developed an apologetic explanation that, in the short term, may have refuted the Spalding theory, but in the long term has caused confusion and led even faithful believers to reject what Joseph and Oliver said all along.[82]

Reframing changes in the D&C

Old narratives	Reframe
Facts. Some early revelations were changed between the 1833 Book of Commandments and the 1835 Doctrine and Covenants, such as inserting the phrase "by the means of the Urim and Thummim" in D&C 10.	
Critical and Faithful. The changes were made to retroactively remove the magical world view and to hide the SITH narrative.	The changes were made to clarify what had once been well understood and to refute the SITH charges.
Critical and Faithful. The changes were made to incorporate the new term "Urim and Thummim" to make the seer stone appear more "biblical."	

When the Book of Commandments was printed in Independence, Missouri, in 1833, Chapter IX read as follows:

NOW, behold I say unto you, that because you delivered up so many writings, which you had power to translate, into the hands of a wicked man, you have lost them, ...[83]

---

[82] For a list of references from LDS General Conference, see https://www.mobom.org/urim-and-thummim-in-lds-general-conference

[83] https://www.josephsmithpapers.org/paper-summary/book-of-commandments-1833/26

The Rational Restoration

The printing press was destroyed on July 20, 1833, along with most of the printed but unbound sheets of the Book of Commandments. Although a few copies were saved, Church leaders could not republish a new edition until 1835, when the compilation was titled Doctrine and Covenants.

Chapter IX in the Book of Commandments was edited and published as Section XXXVI in the Doctrine and Covenants. In modern LDS editions it is Section 10.

The following side-by-side comparison shows the edits.

1833 Book of Commandments	1835 Doctrine and Covenants[84]
NOW, behold I say unto you, that because you delivered up **so many** writings, which you had power to translate, into the hands of a wicked man, you have lost them, and you also lost your gift at the same time, nevertheless it has been restored unto you again	Now, behold I say unto you, that because you delivered up **those** writings which you had power **given unto you** to translate, **by the means of the Urim and Thummim,** into the hands of a wicked man, you have lost them; and you also lost your gift at the same time, **and your mind became darkened**; nevertheless, it is now restored unto you again

Everyone can agree with the fact that these changes were made. People interpret the facts with different assumptions, inferences, and theories.

Believers and critics who assume the SITH narrative infer that the insertion of "Urim and Thummim" in this passage shows an attempt to distance the Restoration from the "magical world view" of a seer stone in a hat. They also infer that the biblical term "Urim and Thummim" was adopted to make the seer stone seem more "biblical." Their theory corroborates their SITH assumption.

---

[84] https://www.josephsmithpapers.org/paper-summary/doctrine-and-covenants-1835/171

Pursuant to the FAITH model, this is not an irrational position. But it is only one of multiple working hypotheses.

The reframing I propose assumes that Joseph did actually use the Nephite interpreters, which Moroni called the Urim and Thummim. With that assumption, I infer that the passage was edited for clarification.

My theory is that when the revelation was given, Joseph understood that "power to translate" meant "power to translate by means of the Urim and Thummim."

After all, the term Urim and Thummim had been in use in 1832, before the Book of Commandments was written, as we'll see in the next section.

Between 1833 and 1835, however, the book *Mormonism Unvailed* had been published, with its assertion that there were two alternative explanations for the translation; i.e., that Joseph dictated words that appeared on the "peep" stone, or words that appeared on the Urim and Thummim. *Mormonism Unvailed* claimed that in either case, Joseph did not refer to the plates.

The first official response to *Mormonism Unvailed* was Oliver Cowdery's Letter I, included in JS-H as a note, in which he affirmed that Joseph translated the record with the Urim and Thummim. Editing the original version of this revelation was another step in clarifying the historical record.

In later years, both Joseph and Oliver again reaffirmed the translation with the Urim and Thummim.

Another example of editing the revelations occurs in D&C 28. The earliest version of the revelation says "no man knoweth where the City shall be built But it shall be given hereafter Behold I say unto you that it shall be among the Lamanites."[85]

The 1833 Book of Commandments published this as "no man knoweth where the city shall be built, but it shall be given hereafter. Behold I say unto you, that it shall be **on the borders by** the

---

[85] https://www.josephsmithpapers.org/paper-summary/revelation-september-1830-b-dc-28/2

Lamanites."[86] It was later edited to add "city of Zion" the way it appears today.

There are several issues in Church history that relate to the Book of Mormon, its setting and origins. Articles on these topics are available at the Museum of the Book of Mormon (MOBOM), mobom.org.

Figure 5 - Church History issues at MOBOM

The links at that site offer references and explanations.

Urim and Thummim in 1832
Urim and Thummim in LDS General Conference
U&T vs Seer Stone in Rough Stone Rolling
Trip to Fayette references
BYU packet on Cumorah
Two departments in the hill Cumorah
Oliver returning to the Church-Reuben Miller journal
Moroni and Nephi clarified
Zelph account

86

Rationality comparison chart - Cumorah
Wentworth letter vs Orson Pratt pamphlet
Translation references
Letter IV in Joseph Smith Papers ("written and deposited" in New York)
Letter VII in Joseph Smith Papers (fact that Cumorah is in New York)
1835 letter by Joseph Smith in the Messenger and Advocate
Cumorah photos
President Ivins on the New York Cumorah
Cumorah's Cave by Cameron Packer
Brigham Young on the New York Cumorah
Narrow and small necks and other geographical terms
Ancient People Joseph Knew
Benjamin Benson letter to Joseph Smith
John Sorenson's Sourcebook Annotated
Origin and rationale of M2C (Mesoamerican/two-Cumorahs theory)
Oliver was truthful except...
Mormonism Unvailed: 1834 to 2023
Gospel Topics Essay on Book of Mormon Translation
Emma Smith's "Last Testimony"
Origin of SITH

The Rational Restoration

Reframing the origins of the Urim and Thummim

Old narratives	Reframe
The term Urim and Thummim was coined by W.W. Phelps in 1833 and Joseph Smith began using it then	The term Urim and Thummim was used by Moroni which explains why Orson Hyde and Samuel Smith described it in Boston in 1832

For many years a consensus among scholars held that Phelps coined the term Urim and Thummim because his 1833 publication was the earliest known reference. Even today, a note in the Joseph Smith Papers, linked to the *Elders' Journal* account, still says, "Extant documents suggest that the biblical term Urim and Thummim was first applied to the interpreters by William W. Phelps in 1833 and that JS adopted the term thereafter."[87]

Several years ago an earlier reference to the term was discovered in an 1832 Boston newspaper. A separate entry in the Joseph Smith Papers, "Glossary: Urim and Thummim," acknowledges this earlier reference. (Why they haven't updated the outdated *Elders' Journal* note is anyone's guess.)

"JS and other church members began referring to the instrument as the Urim and Thummim by 1832. 5"[88]

Before looking at note 5, let's pause and look at the agenda-driven rhetoric in that sentence. The JSP editors claim JS "began" using the term Urim and Thummim "by 1832." But that's not exactly what the historical evidence tells us.

Published accounts can't tell us when JS "began" using the term because we have few accounts (and even fewer verbatim accounts) of what Joseph said between 1823 and 1832. All we can legitimately say is the first known published use of the term was this article from 1832 in

---

[87] https://www.josephsmithpapers.org/paper-summary/questions-and-answers-8-may-1838/2 . Note 5. Accessed September 5, 2023.
[88] https://www.josephsmithpapers.org/topic/urim-and-thummim

103

Boston. But just as the 1832 article contradicted the long-held claim that Phelps coined the term in 1833, an earlier discovery would contradict the claim that JS began using the term in 1832.

Besides, unless Orson Hyde and Samuel Smith coined the term themselves for this interview, they must have heard it from Joseph Smith previously. Samuel could have heard it as early as 1823, actually.

If the JSP editors were not promoting the SITH agenda, they would have factually reported merely that this was the first known published account of the term Urim and Thummim in connection with the translation.

But this is not the only historical evidence. Joseph and Oliver both said that Moroni used the term back in 1823. Scholars can reject their claim, but clarity requires them to do so openly, not by rhetorical tricks the way JSP does here.

Now, let's return to Note 5 from the last quotation above. It gives this citation, which isn't all that helpful because there is no link.

"Questions Proposed to the Mormonite Preachers and Their Answers Obtained before the Whole Assembly at Julien Hall, Sunday Evening, August 5, 1832," *Boston Investigator*, 10 Aug. 1832, [2]

The JSP editors did not provide an excerpt from the content of the article so readers could see it in context. In that article, Samuel Smith and Orson Hyde are quoted in this Q&A session:

Q.-In what manner was the interpretation, or translation made known, and by whom was it written?

A.-It was made known by the spirit of the Lord through the medium of the Urim and Thummim; and was written partly by Oliver Cowdery, and partly by Martin Harris.

Q.-What do you mean by Urim and Thummim?

A.-The same as were used by the prophets of old, which were two crystal stones, placed in bows something in the form of spectacles, which were found with the plates.

Obviously, these answers refute SITH. The missionaries even described the "Urim and Thummim" to avoid confusion.

Nevertheless, the next sentence in the Glossary in the Joseph Smith Papers muddies the water.

"The term was also applied to seer stones JS said he used to translate and to receive some of his early revelations.6"

This sentence is even more misleading. Notice the passive voice "was also applied" which leaves open the question of who, exactly, applied the term this way. There is no record of Joseph Smith saying he used anything other than the Urim and Thummim *that came with the plates* to translate the plates—and several records of Joseph saying precisely that, which are not cited in the Note. Instead, Note 6 cites Brigham Young, Emma Smith and David Whitmer, all of whom clearly distinguished between the Urim and Thummim and the seer stone. That leaves only Wilford Woodruff's ambiguous private journal entry to support this SITH claim.

I took the time to go through this in detail to show how narratives are created and perpetuated by mingling historical facts with assumptions and inferences. The FAITH model helps us separate these elements in the pursuit of clarity, charity and understanding.

Reframing the term "Urim and Thummim"

Old narratives	Reframe
Joseph Smith and Oliver Cowdery used the term Urim and Thummim to apply to both the Nephite interpreters and the seer stone Joseph found in a well	Joseph Smith and Oliver Cowdery used the term Urim and Thummim to apply only to the Nephite interpreters; neither of them said Joseph used the seer stone to translate the text.

In the previous reframing we looked at the way notes in the Joseph Smith Papers, along with the Glossary entry for Urim and Thummim, have been used to promote the narrative that Joseph and Oliver misled everyone by referring to the seer stone as the Urim and Thummim.

We've previously looked at Joseph's explanation in the *Elders' Journal* but it is worth reviewing again. Joseph was answering questions that people were posing daily.

How, and where did you obtain the book of Mormon?

Moroni, the person who deposited the plates, from whence the book of Mormon was translated, in a hill in Manchester, Ontario County, New York, being dead; and raised again therefrom, appeared unto me, and told me where they were, and gave me directions how to obtain them. **I obtained them, and the Urim and Thummim with them, by the means of which, I translated the plates**; and thus came the Book of Mormon. (*Elders' Journal*, July 1838)[89]

This statement is so clear, direct, and unambiguous that it leaves no room for a "seer stone" or "peep stone" in the narrative. Yet the Joseph Smith Papers doesn't refer to Joseph's explanation in its Glossary entry for Urim and Thummim. The Gospel Topics Essay on Book of Mormon Translation doesn't refer to it. Nor does the *Saints* book when it discusses the translation.

Other statements by Joseph and Oliver about the translation of the plates with the Urim and Thummim are likewise missing in these reference materials.

For a detailed discussion of this point see my book *A Man that Can Translate: Joseph Smith and the Nephite Interpreters* and the book I wrote with James Lucas titled *By Means of the Urim and Thummim: Restoring Translation to the Restoration.*

---

[89] https://www.josephsmithpapers.org/paper-summary/elders-journal-july-1838/10

10: Reframing Scripture

Innumerable books about interpreting and applying the Bible have been written, and similar content has been produced about the Book of Mormon. In this section, we will look at a few reframes about interpreting the scriptures, which accommodate multiple working hypotheses.

Reframing Moroni 10

Old narrative	Reframe
The only way to know if the Book of Mormon is true is by a spiritual witness from the Holy Ghost.	The Holy Ghost uses a variety of methods to teach truth, as Moroni explains in subsequent verses.

Most faithful Latter-day Saints affirm that they have a spiritual testimony of the Book of Mormon, pursuant to Moroni 10:4-5.

> 4 And when ye shall receive these things, I would exhort you that ye would ask God, the Eternal Father, in the name of Christ, if these things are not true; and if ye shall ask with a sincere heart, with real intent, having faith in Christ, he will manifest the truth of it unto you, by the power of the Holy Ghost.
> 5 And by the power of the Holy Ghost ye may know the truth of all things. (Moroni 10:4–5)

To those who have felt the spiritual confirmation Moroni described, these verses seem self-evident and difficult to explain. It's like trying to explain the taste of salt. You can't do it verbally. You can only explain it by giving a sample of salt for the other person to taste.

But we've all known people who have read and prayed about the Book of Mormon yet have not received a spiritual witness of its truthfulness. And we all know people in other religious traditions who have received spiritual confirmations of their respective religious beliefs.

This leads us to ask, how does the Holy Ghost manifest the truth to people? Is a spiritual witness the only way to know the truth of all things "by the power of the Holy Ghost?"

Christ explained the vagaries of spiritual matters this way:

> 8 The wind bloweth where it listeth, and thou hearest the sound thereof, but canst not tell whence it cometh, and whither it goeth: so is every one that is born of the Spirit. (John 3:8)

Moroni made a similar point when he wrote that "all these gifts come by the Spirit of Christ; and they come unto every man severally, according as he will."

Perhaps Moroni anticipated questions about how the Holy Ghost manifests truth when he proceeded to explain spiritual gifts.

> there are different ways that these gifts are administered; but it is the same God who worketh all in all; and they are given by the manifestations of the Spirit of God unto men, to profit them.
> 9 For behold, to one is given by the Spirit of God, that he may teach the word of wisdom;
> 10 And to another, that he may teach the word of knowledge by the same Spirit;
> 11 And to another, exceedingly great faith; and to another, the gifts of healing by the same Spirit;
> 12 And again, to another, that he may work mighty miracles;
> 13 And again, to another, that he may prophesy concerning all things;
> 14 And again, to another, the beholding of angels and ministering spirits;
> 15 And again, to another, all kinds of tongues;
> 16 And again, to another, the interpretation of languages and of divers kinds of tongues.
> 17 And all these gifts come by the Spirit of Christ; and they come unto every man severally, according as he will.
> 18 And I would exhort you, my beloved brethren, that ye remember that every good gift cometh of Christ.
> (Moroni 10:8–18)

Those who have the gift of "exceedingly great faith" may accept the Book of Mormon and the Restoration easily and naturally. Others with different gifts may learn truth by the power of the Holy Ghost in other ways. Some people study the Restoration for years, assessing evidence and applying reason, before making a decision to accept or reject it, while others make that decision promptly based on spiritual promptings. This is another reason why we don't judge one another.

Not long after translating Moroni 10 in Harmony, Joseph translated a similar passage in 1 Nephi 10 in Fayette.

> 19 For he that diligently seeketh shall find; and the mysteries of God shall be unfolded unto them, by the power of the Holy Ghost, as well in these times as in times of old, and as well in times of old as in times to come; wherefore, the course of the Lord is one eternal round.
> (1 Nephi 10:19)

Here we see that the Holy Ghost rewards those who "diligently seek" with knowledge of the mysteries of God. 1 Nephi 13 explains that those who "seek to bring forth Zion" will have the gift and power of the Holy Ghost.

> 37 And blessed are they who shall seek to bring forth my Zion at that day, for they shall have the gift and the power of the Holy Ghost; and if they endure unto the end they shall be lifted up at the last day, and shall be saved in the everlasting kingdom of the Lamb;
> (1 Nephi 13:37)

Paul taught that we can "abound in hope through the power of the Holy Ghost.

> 13 Now the God of hope fill you with all joy and peace in believing, that ye may abound in hope, through the power of the Holy Ghost.
> 14 And I myself also am persuaded of you, my brethren, that ye also are full of goodness, filled with all knowledge, able also to admonish one another.
> (Romans 15:13–14)

The phrase "power of the Holy Ghost" appears 31 times in the scriptures: OT (0) NT (1) BM (25) DC (5) PGP (0). Most of those references involve spiritual learning.

But latter-day revelation also emphasizes the importance of learning "by study and by faith." Alluding to Moroni's list of spiritual gifts, one of which is "great faith," the Lord said

> 118 And as all have not faith, seek ye diligently and teach one another words of wisdom; yea, seek ye out of the best books words of wisdom; seek learning, even by study and also by faith. (Doctrine and Covenants 88:118)

The Lord also encouraged study to supplement spiritual learning when he said, "it is my will that you should hasten to translate my scriptures, and to obtain a knowledge of history, and of countries, and of kingdoms, of laws of God and man, and all this for the salvation of Zion." (Doctrine and Covenants 93:53)

Reframing relevance of geography

Old narratives	Reframe
The primary purpose of the Book of Mormon is to testify of Christ, so historicity, including geography, doesn't matter.	The primary purpose of the Book of Mormon is to testify of Christ. Historicity, including geography, is less important. However, it is useful to establish the book's divine authenticity (to use Joseph's words), to understand the context, and to validate what Joseph and other prophets taught.

Faithful believers all recognize that the primary purpose of the Book of Mormon is "to the convincing of the Jew and Gentile that Jesus is the Christ."

Because of disagreements about the origin and setting of the Book of Mormon, in recent years the traditional explanations about these issues has been de-emphasized ("de-correlated"). But for many people, these issues remain relevant.

Hence the reframe.

The Rational Restoration

Historically, believers supported the claims of the book by citing extrinsic evidence of the real-world existence of the people and places the book describes. Chief among these was the hill Cumorah in New York, based on reports that Moroni had identified the hill when he first appeared to Joseph Smith. As Assistant President of the Church, Oliver Cowdery declared the New York Cumorah/Ramah to be a fact.

In the early 1900s, scholars in the Reorganized Church of Jesus Christ of Latter Day Saints proposed that the New York Cumorah was too far from Mesoamerica, where they assumed most of the events took place. They proposed that the "real Cumorah" was in southern Mexico. Hence, the Mesoamerican/two-Cumorahs theory or M2C.

L. E. Hills published a map in 1917 that showed his proposed location.

Figure 6 - M2C map by L. E. Hills

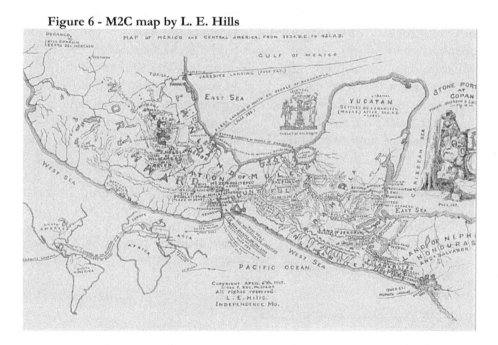

In 1938, Joseph Fielding Smith, then an Apostle and Church Historian, denounced the "two-Cumorahs" theory by observing that

This modernistic theory of necessity, in order to be consistent, must place the waters of Ripliancum and the Hill Cumorah some place within the restricted territory of Central America, notwithstanding the teachings of the Church to the contrary for upwards of 100 years. Because of this theory some members of the Church have become confused and greatly disturbed in their faith in the Book of Mormon.[90]

He and other Church leaders reaffirmed the New York Cumorah in their writings and in General Conference.

In recent decades, LDS scholars have resurrected the Hills M2C theory, elevating it to the de facto official position taught throughout the Church Educational System and Church media.

The Gospel Topics entry on Book of Mormon Geography wisely takes no position on specific settings. Hundreds of archaeological sites potentially fit. But the essay does not address the teachings of the prophets about Cumorah, leaving members to wonder whether the prophets were wrong, as the critics and the M2C scholars claim, or whether the prophets were right all along and we've just ignored them.[91]

Because it is left to each individual to decide how to handle these issues, let's take a moment to discuss whether historicity is relevant.

After he crossed the states of Ohio, Indiana, and Illinois with the rest of the Zion's Camp expedition, Joseph Smith wrote a letter to his wife Emma on June 4, 1834. He wrote,

> The whole of our journey, in the midst of so large a company of social honest men and sincere men, **wandering over the plains of the Nephites**, recounting occasionally the history of the Book of Mormon, roving over **the mounds of that once beloved people** of the Lord, picking up their skulls & their bones, **as a proof of its divine authenticity**.[92]

---

[90] Republished in *Doctrines of Salvation*, Vol. 3 (1956) p. 232, online at https://archive.org/details/Doctrines-of-Salvation-volume-3-joseph-fielding-smith/page/n137/mode/2up?q=Cumorah.

[91] See chapter 13 for a reframe of the Gospel Topics Essays.

[92] https://www.josephsmithpapers.org/paper-summary/letter-to-emma-smith-4-june-1834/2

The Rational Restoration

Later in 1834 the divine authenticity of the Book of Mormon was directly challenged by the book *Mormonism Unvailed*, which claimed Joseph had dictated the text by reading a novel by Solomon Spalding. In response, Oliver Cowdery wrote eight essays about Church history to refute *Mormonism Unvailed* by stating facts about the experiences he and Joseph had.

In the fourth essay, Oliver explained that Moroni had told Joseph that the record "was written and deposited not far from that place,"[93] referring to Joseph's home near Palmyra.

In the seventh essay (Letter VII), Oliver addressed the historicity issue.[94] Excerpts (emphasis in bold):

> I think I am justified in saying that this is the highest hill for some distance round, and I am certain that its appearance, as it rises so suddenly from a plain on the north, must attract the notice of the traveller as he passes by.
> At about one mile west rises another ridge of less height, running parallel with the former, leaving a beautiful vale between. The soil is of the first quality for the country, and under a state of cultivation, which gives a prospect at once imposing, when one reflects on **the fact, that here, between these hills, the entire power and national strength of both the Jaredites and Nephites were destroyed.**
>
> By turning to the 529th and 530th pages of the book of Mormon120 you will read Mormon's account of the last great struggle of his people, **as they were encamped round this hill Cumorah.** (it is printed Camorah, which is an error.) **In this valley fell the remaining strength and pride of a once powerful people, the Nephites**—once so highly favored of the Lord, but at that time in darkness, doomed to suffer extermination by the hand of their barbarous and uncivilized brethren. **From the top of this hill, Mormon**, with a few others, after the battle, gazed with horror upon the mangled remains of those who, the day before, were filled with anxiety, hope or doubt....
>
> **This hill, by the Jaredites, was called Ramah**: by it, or around it pitched the famous army of Coriantumr their tents.

---

[93] https://www.josephsmithpapers.org/paper-summary/history-1834-1836/69
[94] https://www.josephsmithpapers.org/paper-summary/history-1834-1836/90.

Joseph's contemporaries and successors, including member of the First Presidency speaking in General Conference, have reaffirmed the New York Cumorah as stated by Oliver Cowdery when he was the Assistant President of the Church. None of them have discussed locations other than Cumorah, leaving a wide range of possibilities—multiple working hypotheses.

If they were correct about Cumorah, then we have a real-world setting to support the "divine authenticity of the Book of Mormon." Any discussion of Book of Mormon historicity and setting must begin with Cumorah as a "pin in the map."

If they were not correct, then there is nothing linking the new world in the Book of Mormon to any location on earth, apart from speculative interpretations.

Old narrative	Reframe
Even if Joseph and Oliver were wrong about Cumorah, the geography doesn't matter anyway.	Teaching that Joseph and Oliver were wrong undermines their credibility and reliability.

The basic premise of M2C is that Joseph and Oliver, their contemporaries and successors, were all wrong about the New York Cumorah/Ramah. Yet Oliver, with the assistance and endorsement of Joseph Smith, declared it was a fact.

The implications are obvious. Saying Oliver was "mistaken" about what he declared was a fact is a euphemism for calling him a liar. And if he lied about Cumorah, rational observers could conclude that he may have lied about everything.

Papering over this obvious problem by saying Cumorah doesn't matter is not a rational solution. Instead, we should apply the FAITH model and discern facts from assumptions and inferences.

Reframing Cumorah-Identification

Old narratives	Reframe
Faithful: The Hill Cumorah/Ramah is in southern Mexico or another location besides New York. Critical: The Hill Cumorah/Ramah is an imaginary, fictional place.	The Hill Cumorah/Ramah is in western New York, the same hill where Joseph Smith found the plates.

Pursuant to the FAITH model, we first distinguish facts from assumptions and inferences. The relevant facts fall within three basic categories:

(i) Historical documents.

(ii) the text itself.

(iii) extrinsic evidence from archaeology, anthropology, geology, geography, etc.

1. Historical documents include documents created and preserved by Joseph Smith and his contemporaries, including Oliver Cowdery's 1834-5 essays on Church history (particularly Letter VII), Lucy Mack Smith's history, recollections of David Whitmer, Parley P. Pratt and others, articles in various Church publications, and the teachings of the apostles and prophets through the years. Many of these are compiled here: http://www.lettervii.com/p/byu-packet-on-cumorah.html

Of these documents, the most direct and relevant is Letter VII, quoted above.

2. The text of the Book of Mormon describes the setting and surrounding of the land of Cumorah and the hill Cumorah. These descriptions are vague enough to fit in many locations, including the terrain and location of the New York Cumorah.

3. The teachings of the prophets are corroborated by the setting and related archaeology in and around Cumorah. The text describes relatively small groups of people (the largest enumerated Nephite army was only

42,000, assembled after Mormon gathered the people "together in one body" (Mormon 2:7). In Mormon 6:6, Mormon says he and Moroni could see only their respective "ten thousand," a term that normally refers to a military unit and not a specific number of men. The others Mormon refers to were not visible from Cumorah; they may have died during the long, bloody retreat from Bountiful, or they may have been troops killed throughout Mormon's life as a general.

Similarly, the Jaredite battle involved fewer than 10,000 men, based on the narrative in Ether 15:14-29. Imprecise reading of Ether has led to erroneous interpretations.

> ... when Coriantumr had recovered of his wounds, he began to remember the words which Ether had spoken unto him. He saw that there had been slain by the sword already nearly two millions of his people, and he began to sorrow in his heart; yea, there had been slain two millions of mighty men, and also their wives and their children. (Ether 15:1-2)

These "two millions" died long before the battle at Ramah, which commenced over four years later. Coriantumr was reflecting on Ether's prophecy of doom, seeing its fulfillment in the long history of wars documented in the text over 33+ generations. Similarly, in modern times, we say 1,000,000 U.S. military personnel have died in battle, considering those killed during the Civil War, the World Wars, Vietnam, etc.

Two million Jaredite deaths over 33 generations is roughly 60,000 per generation, or around 2,000 per year on average.

Reframing Cumorah-requirements

Old narrative	Reframe
The New York Cumorah doesn't fit any feasible interpretation of the text because (i) there's no narrow neck of land, (ii) the distances are too small, (iii) the land southward and the land northward are proper nouns describing fixed locations, (iv) there are no volcanoes, and (v)	The New York Cumorah fits multiple feasible interpretations of the text because (i) there's no one narrow neck of land, (ii) the Nephites used rivers, and (iii) the land southward and the land northward are relative terms based on the writers' location.

The Rational Restoration

| there could not have been millions of people killed at the hill in New York.. | The text never mentions volcanoes, nor does it describe millions of people being killed at Cumorah/Ramah. |

Proponents of M2C have set out lists of criteria that they claim must be satisfied by any real-world Cumorah. One example is the list found at BMAF.org, the corporate owner of Book of Mormon Central, here:

http://www.bmaf.org/node/414

The criteria are always written to reinforce the Mesoamerican setting, based on the interpretations of the M2C scholars. As such, they are easily dismissed as circular reasoning.

Reframing Cumorah-Repository

Old narratives	Reframe
The repository of Nephite records in the Hill Cumorah is in southern Mexico. OR The Hill Cumorah is an imaginary, fictional place.	The repository of Nephite records in the Hill Cumorah was in western New York, the same hill where Joseph Smith found the plates, but the records are no longer there.

Mormon 6:6 describes the repository of Nephite records:

> 6 And it came to pass that when we had gathered in all our people in one to the land of Cumorah, behold I, Mormon, began to be old; and knowing it to be the last struggle of my people, and having been commanded of the Lord that I should not suffer the records which had been handed down by our fathers, which were sacred, to fall into the hands of the Lamanites, (for the Lamanites would destroy them) therefore I made this record out of the plates of Nephi, **and hid up in the hill Cumorah all the records which had been entrusted to me by the hand of the Lord**, save it were these few plates which I gave unto my son Moroni.

Traditionally, people understood that the repository was in the hill Cumorah Moroni identified as the one in New York where Moroni buried the abridgment. The small plates of Nephi—the Fayette plates—remained there, where Mormon put them, until a divine messenger retrieved them in 1829 and took them to Fayette to be translated. The Harmony plates—the original Book of Mormon that Moroni deposited in the box of stone and cement—were returned by a divine messenger to this repository when Joseph finished translating them in Harmony.

Orson Pratt made this point when he stated,

> When Moroni, about thirty-six years after, made the deposit of the book entrusted to him, he was, without doubt, inspired to select **a department of the hill separate from the great sacred depository of the numerous volumes** hid up by his father.
>
> The particular place in the hill, where Moroni secreted the book, was revealed, by the angel, to the Prophet Joseph Smith, to whom the volume was delivered in September, A.D. 1827. **But the grand repository of all the numerous records of the ancient nations of the western continent, was located in another department of the hill,** and its contents under the charge of holy angels, until the day should come for them to be transferred to the sacred temple of Zion.
>
> The hill Cumorah, with the surrounding vicinity, is distinguished as the great battle-field on which, and near which, two powerful nations were concentrated with all their forces, men, women, and children, and fought till hundreds of thousands on both sides were hewn down, and left to moulder upon the ground.[95]

Orson Pratt had interviewed David Whitmer when David related the account of the messenger taking the abridged plates to Cumorah. David remembered the incident because it was the first time he had heard the word "Cumorah."

Oliver Cowdery made the location of Cumorah clear in his unambiguous Letter VII, which was approved by Joseph Smith and

---

[95] Orson Pratt, "The Hill Cumorah; or the sacred depository of wisdom and understanding," *The Latter-Day Saints' Millennial Star*, July 7, 1866. Online at http://www.lettervii.com/2016/08/the-hill-cumorah-sacred-depository.html.

reprinted multiple times while Joseph was alive and later.[96] Some have claimed that Joseph and Oliver never claimed specific revelation about the location of Cumorah, but that's an irrational requirement when Oliver said he actually entered the repository and saw it for himself.

The existence of the repository in the New York hill is more significant than Moroni's stone box because if the room where Mormon hid all the Nephite records (wagon loads of them) was in New York, then Oliver Cowdery had good reason to write that it was a fact that the final battles also took place there—even if he didn't receive a specific revelation to that effect. And, in that case, Joseph Smith had good reason for endorsing and incorporating Oliver's account.

Cameron Packer wrote an excellent article[97] on the topic that includes ten references to the room of records. The Abstract explains:

> The significance of the Hill Cumorah in the restoration of the gospel goes beyond its identification as the ancient repository of the metal plates known as the Book of Mormon. In the second half of the 19th century, a teaching about a cave in the hill began surfacing in the writings of several leaders of the Church of Jesus Christ of Latter-day Saints. In their view, the hill was not only the place where Joseph Smith received the plates but also their final repository, along with other sacred treasures, after the translation was finished. This article cites ten different accounts, all secondhand, that refer to this cave and what was found there. The author includes a comparison of the accounts that discusses additional records in the cave, God's dominion over Earth's treasure, miraculous dealings of God, and the significance of the presence of the sword of Laban.

In footnote 1, Cameron observes that Orson Pratt had other discussions about Cumorah in New York.

> Orson Pratt often referred to the cave in Cumorah but not with specific reference to Joseph Smith and others entering to return the plates. One of Pratt's accounts is cited in this article. Several of the other references to the

---

[96] A collection of republications is available at http://www.lettervii.com/.
[97] Cameron J. Packer, "Cumorah's Cave," Journal of Book of Mormon Studies 13/1-2 (2004): 50-57, 170-71. Online at http://publications.mi.byu.edu/publications/jbms/13/1/S00006-50be6ae14ef1b5Packer.pdf

cave that are not included in this article are found in Journal of Discourses, 14:330–31; 15:182–83; 16:57; 17:30–31; 17:281; 19:218.
Another source for Pratt's accounts is supposedly the Quorum of the Twelve Minutes, 6 May 1849, but I have not been able to confirm this. Brigham Young's record of that date, however, is interesting to note: "I met with President Willard Richards and the Twelve on the 6th. We spent the time in interesting conversation upon old times, Joseph, **the plates, Mount Cumorah, treasures and records known to be hid in the earth,** the gift of seeing, and how Joseph obtained his first seer stone" (Manuscript History of Brigham Young, 6 May 1849, Church Archives). See also *Journal History of The Church of Jesus Christ of Latter-day Saints*, 6 May 1849.

Orson Pratt made affirmative statements without clearly explaining whether they were speculative or factual. For example, he often spoke of Lehi landing in Chile, even after Joseph Smith edited out Pratt's geography speculation when he wrote the Wentworth letter. However, when he added geography footnotes to the 1879 Book of Mormon, Pratt distinguished between speculative ideas—Lehi's landing in Chile and the location of Zarahemla—and declarative statements of fact, such as the location of Cumorah in New York.

Brigham Young gave the most extensive public comment about the repository on June 17, 1877, at a conference in Farmington. He said

> I lived right in the country where the plates were found from which the Book of Mormon was translated, and I know a great many things pertaining to that country. I believe I will take the liberty to tell you of another circumstance that will be as marvelous as anything can be. This is an incident in the life of Oliver Cowdery, but he did not take the liberty of telling such things in meeting as I take.
>
> I tell these things to you, and I have a motive for doing so. I want to carry them to the ears of my brethren and sisters, and to the children also, that they may grow to an understanding of some things that seem to be entirely hidden from the human family.
>
> **Oliver Cowdery went with the Prophet Joseph when he deposited these plates.** Joseph did not translate all of the plates; there was a portion of them sealed, which you can learn from the Book of Doctrine and Covenants.

The Rational Restoration

When Joseph got the plates, the angel instructed him to carry them back to the hill Cumorah, which he did. Oliver says that when Joseph and Oliver went there, the hill opened, and they walked into a cave, in which there was a large and spacious room. He says he did not think, at the time, whether they had the light of the sun or artificial light; but that it was just as light as day.

They laid the plates on a table; it was a large table that stood in the room. Under this table there was a pile of plates as much as two feet high, and there were altogether in this room **more plates than probably many wagon loads**; they were piled up in the corners and along the walls.

The first time they went there the sword of Laban hung upon the wall; but when they went again it had been taken down and laid upon the table across the gold plates; it was unsheathed, and on it was written these words: "This sword will never be sheathed again until the kingdoms of this world become the kingdom of our God and his Christ."

I tell you this as coming not only from Oliver Cowdery, but others who were familiar with it, and who understood it just as well as we understand coming to this meeting, enjoying the day, and by and by we separate and go away, forgetting most of what is said, but remembering some things.

So is it with other circumstances in life. I relate this to you, and I want you to understand it. **I take this liberty of referring to those things so that they will not be forgotten and lost.**

Carlos Smith was a young man of as much veracity as any young man we had, and **he was a witness to these things.** Samuel Smith saw some things, Hyrum saw a good many things, but Joseph was the leader.

Now, you may think I am unwise in publicly telling these things, thinking perhaps I should preserve them in my own breast; but such is not my mind. **I would like the people called Latter-day Saints to understand some little things with regard to the workings and dealings of the Lord with his people here upon the earth.** I could relate to you a great many more, all of which are familiar to many of our brethren and sisters (emphasis added).[98]

Brigham Young had discussed this repository on previous occasions, but here he decided to make it public. He noted that Oliver didn't talk about this in public, and we have no record that Joseph or the others did, but Brigham was concerned that the knowledge of this room would be forgotten and lost, so he had it put on record in the *Journal of Discourses*.

The repository in Cumorah also helps explain why Mormon chose the Jaredite Ramah for his last stand. It was a rational decision.

Recall that the original repository was in the hill Shim (Mormon 1:3). Later, when the Nephites were fleeing from the Lamanites, Mormon explained:

> And now I, Mormon, seeing that the Lamanites were about to overthrow the land, therefore I did go to the hill Shim, and did take up all the records which Ammaron had hid up unto the Lord. (Mormon 4:23)

Mormon and his armies were on the run. They had no time to construct a new repository somewhere. Logically, he would take the records where he knew the Jaredites had built a secure bunker for their great battle in the hill Ramah. In Mormon 6:6 he explained that he "hid up in the hill Cumorah all the records which had been entrusted to me by the hand of the Lord."

What of the plates today?

When asked where the plates are now, David Whitmer said they were in New York, not in Cumorah, "but not far away from that place." David also said, "when they [the plates] are translated much useful information will be brought to light. But till that day arrives, no Rochester adventurers shall ever see them or the treasures."[99] For a fuller discussion of this point, see my book *Whatever Happened to the Golden Plates?*

---

[98] Available online at http://jod.mrm.org/19/36.
[99] Edward Stevenson, Reminiscences of Joseph the Prophet and the Coming Forth of the Book of Mormon (1877), page 14, online at
https://archive.org/stream/reminiscencesofj00stev#page/n17/mode/2up.

Reframing Cumorah and M2C

Old narratives	Reframe
Because Joseph Smith said the Book of Mormon took place in Central America, and the text describes a limited geography, Cumorah cannot be in New York. There must be two Cumorahs. The one in Mesoamerica is the real Cumorah. The one in New York is the nominal Cumorah, a name applied to the hill by tradition.	Joseph didn't say the Book of Mormon took place in Central America, and the text describes geography in vague terms (like all ancient texts), so any legitimate interpretation must be based on the New York Cumorah (the pin in the map). M2C is inverted logic.

Any rational, faithful interpretation of the Restoration begins with the teachings of the prophets and expands from there.

The most direct statements from Joseph and Oliver regarding the setting of the Book of Mormon teach that Cumorah/Ramah is in New York, that Moroni referred to Cumorah before Joseph obtained the plates, and that the midwestern states are the "plains of the Nephites."

The next tier of statements appears in the articles in the anonymous 1842 *Times and Seasons* articles, attributed to Joseph Smith, that claimed Mayan ruins in Central America were left by Nephites.[100] These articles did not mention Cumorah.

The next tier down are the writings of Joseph's contemporaries, including the Pratt brothers and Benjamin Winchester, who advocated a hemispheric model with the New York Cumorah.

The bottom line here is that there are no prophetic statements that Cumorah is in Mesoamerica. M2C is purely a rationale to support an assumption that Book of Mormon events took place in Mesoamerica.

In a framework based on teachings of the prophets, it is not rational to reject those teachings in favor of speculative interpretations by scholars.

---

[100] See the discussion on reframing the *Times and Seasons* below.

Reframing Crossing to America

Old narratives	Reframe
Faithful: Nephites left the Arabian peninsula and sailed eastward across the Pacific and landed on the west coast of Chile (hemispheric model) or Mesoamerica (M2C model) Critical: The Nephites never crossed any oceans because they are fictional.	Nephites left the Arabian peninsula and sailed west around Africa and across the Atlantic and landed in or near modern-day Florida, probably the panhandle area.

The Book of Mormon explains that Lehi's group left Jerusalem and traveled south until they traveled "nearly eastward" until they arrived at the seashore, which we assume was the coast of the Arabian peninsula. (1 Nephi 17) From there they sailed to the Promised Land.

There are two ways to sail to the western hemisphere: east or west. Those believers who think Lehi sailed east think Lehi landed along the western coast of Central or South America, such as in Chile, Panama, Guatemala, or Baja. Their models are based on such landing sites.

An undated cryptic note written by Frederick G. Williams said Lehi "landed on the continent of South America in Chile thirty degrees south Lattitude," but any link to Joseph Smith is speculative.[101] One of the anonymous 1842 *Times and Seasons* articles claimed Lehi "landed a little south of the isthmus of Darien" which is modern Panama, and again any link to Joseph Smith is speculative.[102]

---

[101] Frederick G. Williams, "Did Lehi Land in Chile?" https://scholarsarchive.byu.edu/cgi/viewcontent.cgi?filename=14&article=1065&context=mi&type=additional

[102] *Times and Seasons*, Vol. 3, No. 22 (15 September 1842): 922, online at http://www.latterdaytruth.org/pdf/100148.pdf

For Lehi, the alternative to sailing east was sailing west, then south along the coast of Africa, around Cape Horn, then north and west across the Atlantic. Prevailing winds and currents would take a sailing ship toward North America, similar to the route Columbus took to the Caribbean and Gulf of Mexico.

The practicality of such a voyage was demonstrated in 2008-2010 and in 2019 by a sailing ship constructed to replicate a Phoenician ship found in the Mediterranean and dated to around 600 B.C.[103] In 2009, a replica of a 600 BC Phoenician ship named *Phoenicia* sailed from Arabia around Africa to demonstrate that the ancient Phoenicians could have circumnavigated Africa, as described in an ancient text. During the voyage in the Atlantic Ocean, currents and wind pushed the ship toward North America. The crew successfully navigated back toward Africa and the Mediterranean.[104]

A second voyage of the *Phoenicia* left Lebanon and crossed the Atlantic to Florida.

The *Phoenicia* ship has demonstrated the plausibility of trans-Atlantic voyages by both Lehi and Mulek, using period technology and real-world conditions.

The ship is being reconstructed for a display to support the historicity of the Book of Mormon.[105]

There are other reasons to infer Lehi sailed west, including the prevailing winds during the time of year he presumably departed from the Arabian Peninsula and an interpretation of Isaiah 18:1 that places the latter-day promised land beyond Africa.[106]

The Williams statement mentioned "thirty degrees south latitude." If that statement was based on something Williams heard, the speaker (whether Joseph or someone else) might have said Lehi landed at thirty degrees latitude and Williams inferred the rest. In North America,

---

[103] https://www.phoeniciansbeforecolumbus.com/
[104] An account of the voyage is available here: https://www.themediterraneantraveller.com/phoenician-ship-expedition/
[105] https://www.phoenicia.rocks/
[106] "Reproducing Lehi's and Mulek's Voyages," https://www.mobom.org/lehi-cross-ocean

modern Tallahassee is at 30 degrees north latitude. This means Lehi may have landed somewhere along the panhandle of Florida. Coincidentally, Jerusalem is at about 30 degrees latitude (31.7 degrees north latitude).

Reframing the setting

Reframes about the teachings of the prophets regarding the New York Cumorah/Ramah and Lehi's route across the oceans do not explain where the Nephites and Lamanites lived.

Old narratives	Reframe
Faithful: Most of the Book of Mormon narrative in the New World took place in Mesoamerica. Critical: The Book of Mormon narrative in the New World took place nowhere because it is fictional.	Most of the Book of Mormon narrative in the New World took place in North America along and east of the Mississippi River.

Proponents of M2C and other settings that reject the New York Cumorah make a good point when they say New York is too far away for the Nephites to travel there only to fight a battle of extinction. In *Mormon's Codex*, page 688, John Sorenson wrote, "

> There remain Latter-day Saints who insist that the final destruction of the Nephites took place in New York, but any such idea is manifestly absurd. Hundreds of thousands of Nephites traipsing across the Mississippi Valley to New York, pursued (why?) by hundreds of thousands of Lamanites, is a scenario worthy only of a witless sci-fi movie, not of history.

Sorenson's rhetoric is rational given his assumption that the Book of Mormon narrative in the New World took place in Mesoamerica. And, given his repudiation of the teachings of the prophets about Cumorah, his Mesoamerican setting is as rational as any of the other multiple working hypotheses. Whether the Nephites would have traveled to New

York from Baja, Mesoamerica, Panama, Chile, or any other site in Latin America, such a journey would be improbable but not impossible.

Recognizing this, people have proposed settings in and around New York, the eastern United States, and the Heartland area (Illinois, Indiana and Ohio).

When I embarked on the investigation that led to my book *Moroni's America*, I took the New York Cumorah as a "pin in the map" given to us by prophets. Then I made a hypothesis that Zarahemla was across from Nauvoo, pursuant to D&C 125. Next I put myself in the position of an earthbound society trying to describe geography.

I was surprised at how well the text described the land, assuming Lehi landed in the panhandle of Florida.

Using *Moroni's America* as a framework for discussion, it's easy to see why the New York Cumorah makes sense.

Figure 7 - Overview of Nephite lands

In this scenario, Lehi landed in Florida along the panhandle or west coast. Nephi and his family and others fled from Laman and Lemuel to the highlands of eastern Tennessee, around Chattanooga. The Nephites lived there until the Lamanites invaded and the Lord led them "down into" the land of Zarahemla. The Tennessee River flows northward, so the Nephites would travel "down" in elevation when they went north to modern-day Illinois—the land of Zarahemla. There they joined with the Mulekites, eventually settling around the city of Zarahemla.

The Book of Mormon describes the Nephite expansion from the land of Zarahemla (along the Upper Mississippi River in what is now Illinois) to the land Bountiful, which I consider to be the area north of the Ohio River in what is now Indiana and Ohio. The Ohio River was a natural border between the Lamanites in the land southward and the Nephites in the land northward.

Mormon explained it this way:

> Now the land south was called Lehi, and the land north was called Mulek, which was after the son of Zedekiah; for the Lord did bring Mulek into the land north, and Lehi into the land south. (Helaman 6:10)

Mulek landed in Iowa, across from Nauvoo, and the Nephites spread throughout the Midwest north of the Ohio River, while Lehi landed in Florida and the Lamanites spread throughout the south, bordered on the north by the Ohio River.

When the final wars started at Zarahemla, the Nephites retreated further and further north and east toward western New York. The Lamanites destroyed the Nephite cities along the way.

Mormon knew the history of the Jaredites and gathered the remainder of his people to the "land of Cumorah" because he "had hope to gain advantage over the Lamanites" there. (Mormon 6:4)

This made sense because the Jaredites had four years to prepare for their final battles. They had built defensive structures on hill tops and, presumably, a bunker in the Hill Cumorah. It was this bunker that Mormon used to secure the Nephite records.

Moroni's America is one of multiple working hypotheses. It reconciles the New York Cumorah with the available extrinsic evidence as well as the descriptions in the text.

Reframing physical evidence

Old narratives	Reframe
Faithful. There is no physical evidence for the Book of Mormon in North America, but there are abundant correspondences in Mesoamerica.	Museums throughout the midwestern USA are full of artifacts that match those described in the text. Hundreds of sites in North America align with the text in terms of location and timing, but because they have been destroyed and because all the Nephite records were in Cumorah, no known written evidence is extant.
Critical. There is no physical evidence for the Book of Mormon anywhere in the world. Attempts to correlate the Book of Mormon to any location so far have been confirmation bias.	Correspondences in Mesoamerica and other parts of the world can be rational because the text is vague enough to support multiple working hypotheses.

The geographical references in the Book of Mormon are vague, as would be expected in any ancient text (including the Bible). Terms such as "a day's journey for a Nephite" (Helaman 4:7) are indeterminate.

Some readers assume that the "land northward" is a proper noun; others assume it is a relative term that changes throughout the text depending on the location of the speaker.

These and other generalities support multiple working hypotheses about the setting of the Book of Mormon. A case can be made for a setting in North America, Mesoamerica, or nearly any place else in the world.

Critics who say there is no physical evidence rely on their own assumptions and inferences. Their position is not irrational, but it is one of many multiple working hypotheses.[107]

---

[107] For more detail, see my book *Between These Hills: A case for the New York Cumorah*.

Reframing volcanoes

Old narratives	Reframe
There are no volcanoes in North America.	There are no volcanoes in the Book of Mormon.

A common rationale for M2C is the claim that the Book of Mormon describes volcanic action, particularly during the destruction leading up to Christ's visit. However, the text never mentions volcanoes, and there are alternative geological explanations for the descriptions in the text, such as the New Madrid earthquakes in Missouri.

Reframing Nephite civilization

Old narratives	Reframe
The size and sophistication of Nephite civilization doesn't match North American archaeology.	The size and sophistication of Nephite civilization described in the text aligns with North American archaeology.

The Book of Mormon, like other ancient texts, is vague enough to allow multiple working hypotheses about the size and sophistication of Nephite civilization.

M2C advocates have interpreted the text so it aligns with archaeological discoveries and culture in Mesoamerica. Advocates of other settings have done the same.

To support M2C, a Book of Mormon horse is a "tapir," a tower is a "pyramid," etc. The population numbers in the text, such as the largest enumerated Lamanite army being 50,000, are expanded to accommodate Mesoamerican population estimates. M2C advocates have rational explanations for their interpretations.

Archaeology tells us that population density in North America was lower than in Mesoamerica. People settled all along the rivers, but not in cities as large as those in Mesoamerica. This is also consistent with the text.

The reframe relies on the teachings of the prophets about the New York Cumorah/Ramah. Alternative settings can be rationalized based on the text and extrinsic evidence, but they directly contradict the teachings of the prophets.

Reframing the Moundbuilder myth

Old narratives	Reframe
Faithful. It is important to separate the Book of Mormon from the Moundbuilder myth that was prevalent in Joseph Smith's day. Critics. Joseph composed the Book of Mormon based on the Moundbuilder myth of a great white race destroyed by dark savages.	The Moundbuilder myth was based on archaeology left by Nephites/Lamanites, but the lack of written evidence makes it impossible to determine the actual history of the ancient North Americans. The Book of Mormon accounts contradicts the Moundbuilder myth.

The Moundbuilder myth arose in the 1800s to explain the existence of extensive ancient earthworks that Native Americans no longer used and could not explain. The myth attributed the earthworks to a lost civilization who were destroyed by, and unrelated to, the Native Americans who inhabited the area when the Europeans arrived on the scene. The myth was debunked when scientists showed living Native Americans are the descendants of the ancient people who built the earthworks (as Joseph Smith said).

Critics find comparisons between the Book of Mormon and the Moundbuilder myths; i.e., the claim that the Nephites were a sophisticated white race who created the earthworks, only to be destroyed by the dark-skinned savage Lamanites.

The reframe explains that these comparisons are superficial. The text rejects the Moundbuilder myth by explaining that there were no racial distinctions, at least after Christ's visit and likely earlier. Oliver Cowdery further distinguished the Moundbuilder myth by explaining that it was not the righteous who were destroyed by the wicked, but two groups of wicked who fought each other.

Joseph Smith explained that "The principal nation of the second race [Lehi's descendants] fell in battle towards the close of the fourth century. The remnant are the Indians that now inhabit this country." *Times and Seasons* III.9:707. This is consistent with the scientists who have determined that the creators of the earthworks were the ancestors of modern Native Americans.

Reframing Zelph

Old narratives	Reframe
Faithful. The Zelph incident involved people who traveled north from Mesoamerica and is confusing because of the various accounts.	The identity of Zelph was revealed to Joseph Smith, archaeological evidence corroborates what Joseph said, and the various accounts emphasize different elements but are consistent with the New York Cumorah.
Critical. Zelph was a fictional invention by Joseph Smith.	

During his lifetime, Joseph Smith identified Hopewell mounds as Nephite/Lamanite and an Adena burial as Jaredite.

As Zion's Camp journeyed from Kirtland to Missouri in 1834, Joseph Smith and his companions crossed the plains of Ohio, Indiana, and Illinois. From the banks of the Mississippi River, Joseph wrote a letter to his wife Emma. He told her that they had been

> wandering over the plains of the Nephites, recounting occasionally the history of the Book of Mormon, roving over the mounds of that once beloved people of the Lord, picking up their skulls and their bones, as a proof of its divine authenticity.[108]

---

[108] https://www.josephsmithpapers.org/paper-summary/letter-to-emma-smith-4-june-1834/2

The Rational Restoration

The connection between the Book of Mormon and the mounds in the midwestern United States was widely recognized among both members and nonmembers. The 1834 book *Mormonism Unvailed* included the first published account of Zelph, the warrior whose bones were dug up in Illinois by members of Zion's Camp.

> A large mound was one day discovered, upon which Gen. Smith ordered an excavation to be made into it ; and about one foot from the top of the ground, the bones of a human skeleton were found, which were carefully laid out upon a board, when Smith made a speech, prophesying or declaring that they were the remains of a celebrated General among the Nephites, mentioning his name and the battle in which he was slain, some 1500 years ago.[109]

Wilford Woodruff and others who were present described the event in their journals.[110] Woodruff wrote,

> While on our travels we visited many of the mounds which were flung up by the ancient inhabitants of this continent probably by the Nephites & Lamanites. We visited one of those Mounds and several of the brethren dug into it and took from it the bones of a man. We visited one of those Mounds: considered to be 300 feet above the level of the Illinois River. Three persons dug into the mound & found a body. Elder Milton Holmes took the arrow out of the back bones that killed Zelph & brought it with some of the bones in to the camp. I visited the same mound with Jesse J. Smith. Who the other persons were that dug in to the mound & found the body I am undecided. Brother Joseph had a vision respecting the person. He said he was a white Lamanite. The curse was taken from him or at least in part. He was killed in battle with an arrow. The arrow was found among his ribs. One of his thigh bones was broken. This was done by a stone flung from a sling in battle years before his death. His name was Zelph.

---

[109] https://archive.org/details/mormonismunvaile00howe/page/158/mode/2up
[110] One brief version is in the Joseph Smith Papers here: https://www.josephsmithpapers.org/paper-summary/history-1838-1856-volume-a-1-23-december-1805-30-august-1834/489 . Other accounts are here: https://josephsmithfoundation.org/account-of-zelph/

Some of his bones were brought into the Camp and the thigh bone which was broken was put into my wagon and I carried it to Missouri. Zelph was a large thick set man and a man of God. **He was a warrior under the great prophet Onandagus that was known from the hill Cumorah or east sea to the Rocky mountains.** The above knowledge Joseph received in a vision.[111]

In the late 1800s, an archaeologist assigned the name Naples Mound #8 to the mound. The mound was scientifically excavated in 1990. "The artifacts found during the excavation confirmed the mound to be a Hopewell burial mound, dating from 100 B.C. to 500 A.D."[112]

Reframing Zarahemla: D&C 125:3

Old narratives	Reframe
D&C 125:3 mentions Zarahemla but does not say it was the site of ancient Zarahemla.	D&C 125:3 says "let the name of Zarahemla be named upon it," evoking Alma 8:7 "Now it was the custom of the people of Nephi to call their lands, and their cities, and their villages, yea, even all their small villages, after the name of him who first possessed them."

We can all read D&C 125:3. The historical evidence, once disputed but now resolved, shows that this site across from Nauvoo, Illinois, was named Zarahemla by this revelation and was not named previously.

Given this passage, people make assumptions and inferences. Obviously, those who believe M2C assume the revelation has no connection to Book of Mormon settings. Those who accept the New York Cumorah/Ramah assume the revelation is connected with Book of

---

[111] Wilford Woodruff Journal, digitized and online at https://catalog.churchofjesuschrist.org/assets?id=14079217-b2a7-4eff-8b53-1be6c1e9bea5&crate=0&index=23

[112] https://en.wikipedia.org/wiki/Naples_Mound_8.

Mormon settings. Specifically, they think the location across from Nauvoo fits the overall geography described in the text.

Pending additional revelation and discoveries, these multiple working hypotheses are both rational.

Reframing Zarahemla: Iowa

Old narratives	Reframe
The site across from Nauvoo doesn't fit descriptions in the text because the Sidon river flows north from the land of Nephi to the city of Zarahemla.	The site across from Nauvoo does fit descriptions in the text because the Sidon river flows north from the land of Nephi (Tennessee) to the land (not city) of Zarahemla (Illinois).

This is another example of the vague text supporting multiple working hypotheses. People make assumptions and inferences that fit their theories to support their overall hypotheses.

Reframing the term Jaredites

The term "Jaredites" is often used to refer to all the immigrants who accompanied Jared and his brother on their journey to the New World. It's a useful generalization in some ways, but it has led to confusion in understanding the text and related extrinsic evidence.

Old narratives	Reframe
The Jaredites became a large nation of all the descendants of Jared, his brother, and their friends.	Ether had abridged the record of his own ancestors; i.e., the "Jaredites." The descendants of the brother of Jared and the "friends" who accompanied Jared and his brother were separate people.

The term "Jaredites" (which appears only once in the scriptures, in Moroni 9:23) connotes descendants of Jared; i.e., the "people of Jared."

The text refers to the "people of Jared" two times.

The Title Page explains that the plates Moroni deposited in the stone box on the hill Cumorah included "an abridgment taken from the Book of Ether also, which is a record of **the people of Jared**." Moroni further explained that, "after having made an end of abridging the account of **the people of Jared**," he didn't expect to write more. (Moroni 1:1).

It makes sense that Ether compiled a record of the people of Jared because they were his people. He was a direct descendant of Jared. (Ether 1:6-33) The Book of Ether is Ether's record of Ether's ancestral line. Ether did not claim to relate the history of the descendants of Jared's brother or the friends who accompanied them.

Thus, the Book of Ether is explicitly *not* a record of all the people who descended from Jared's brother, or the twenty-two friends who accompanied them on a long overland journey before the sea voyage on the barges.

Non-Jaredites. The Jaredites were not the only people who came with Jared.

A record of all the people who came with Jared and his brother would logically have focused more on the brother of Jared who apparently had more of a leadership role, at least in the spiritual sense.

> 40 And it came to pass that the Lord did hear **the brother of Jared**, and had compassion upon him, and said unto him:
> 41 Go to and gather together thy flocks, both male and female, of every kind; and also of the seed of the earth of every kind; and thy families; and **also Jared thy brother and his family; and also thy friends and their families, and the friends of Jared and their families.**
> 42 And when thou hast done this thou shalt go at the head of them down into the valley which is northward. And there will I meet thee, and I will go before thee **into a land which is choice above all the lands of the earth**. (Ether 1:40–42)

Thus, there were four groups: (i) Jared, (ii) his friends, (iii) the brother of Jared, (iv) his friends.

When the brother of Jared "began to be old," he and Jared gathered the people for a census. (Ether 6:19-21) The text relates that Jared had four sons and eight daughters. His brother had twenty-two sons and daughters. They numbered their people. But we read nothing about their friends' descendants, which suggests their friends and their descendants had dispersed.

The text tells us that even after 32-plus generations, right before Ether was born, the people still recognized a distinction between descendants of Jared and descendants of the brother of Jared.

> And it came to pass that there arose another mighty man; and he was a descendant of the brother of Jared.
> (Ether 11:17)

We can reasonably conclude from this detail that the descendants of Jared identified themselves as "Jaredites" while other family lines were outsiders with their own communities and territories.

This reframing is important when we look at Jaredite origins, geography, and population numbers.

Reframing Jaredite civilizations

Old narratives	Reframe
Faithful. The Jaredite civilization numbered in the millions and was completely destroyed at the hill Ramah with Coriantumr as the sole survivor (besides Ether, who wrote about it). Ramah could not be in New York because there is no archaeology to support such vast numbers of ancient people there.	The Book of Ether describes events occurring only "in this north country" around western New York, where Moroni lived when he abridged Ether's record and deposited it in the hill Cumorah. The casualties at Ramah numbered in the thousands, not millions, and is consistent with archaeological evidence in western New York.
Critical. There were never any Jaredites and there is no evidence of any war in which millions of people were killed.	

Many believers have assumed that the Book of Ether describes the total destruction, even the extinction, of all the descendants of Jared, his brother, and their friends who came with them. The reframing of the term "Jaredites" offers a much more limited scope of the Book of Ether.

Right at the outset, Moroni explained that he was writing about only a specific group of people who lived in a specific place.

> And now I, Moroni, proceed to give an account of those ancient inhabitants who were destroyed by the hand of the Lord upon the face of this north country. (Ether 1:1)

What constitutes "*this* north country?" When Moroni first visited Joseph Smith, he

> said this history was written and deposited not far from that place [Joseph's home], and that it was our brother's privilege, if obedient to the commandments of the Lord, to obtain and translate the same by the means of the Urim and Thummim, which were deposited for that purpose with the record.[113]

The Hill Cumorah is "not far" from Joseph's house, being less than three miles away. Because the repository of Nephite records was in the hill Cumorah, we can logically infer that Moroni wrote the Book of Ether in the repository in Cumorah, or at least nearby.

That means that Moroni was referring to western New York when he specified "this north country."

This in turn means that the Book of Ether describes a specific group of people in a relatively small area—the "north country" of modern-day western New York.

We'll discuss the location of the "non-Jaredites" in the next section.

Now, let's look at population numbers.

---

[113] https://www.josephsmithpapers.org/paper-summary/history-1834-1836/68

As we saw above, the Jaredites conducted a census but only listed the children of Jared and his brother. (Ether 6:19-21) Jared had four sons and eight daughters. His brother had twenty-two sons and daughters. Beyond that, the scripture says merely,

> 21 And it came to pass that they did number their people; and after that they had numbered them, they did desire of them the things which they would that they should do before they went down to their graves. (Ether 6:21)

We have no population counts until chapter 15, when Coriantumr remembered what Ether had told him.

> And it came to pass when Coriantumr had recovered of his wounds, he began to remember the words which Ether had spoken unto him.
>
> He saw that there had been slain by the sword already nearly two millions of his people, and he began to sorrow in his heart; yea, there had been slain two millions of mighty men, and also their wives and their children. (Ether 15:1–2)

This passage has led many people—both believers and unbelievers—to infer that two million Jaredites were killed at the final battle of Cumorah.

BYU *Studies* offers a comparison of "The Two Final Battles" involving the Jaredites and the Nephites.[114] The chart below claims 2 million or more Jaredites died at the hill Ramah and around 230,000 Nephites died at the same location, which they called Cumorah.

---

[114] See https://byustudies.byu.edu/further-study-chart/138-the-two-final-battles/. We will discuss the Nephites separately below.

Figure 8 - Two Final Battles - BYU Studies

The Two Final Battles

	Jaredites	Nephites
when	ca. 300 B.C.	385 A.D.
where	hill Ramah	hill Cumorah (hill Ramah)
who	Coriantumr and Shiz	Nephites and Lamanites
how many	2 million or more	around 230,000 Nephites
who gathered	men, wives, children	men, wives, children
outcome	both sides destroyed	Nephites destroyed
Spirit	ceased to strive with	ceased to strive with
prophet	Ether	Mormon
account	Ether 13–15	Mormon 6–7
record	24 gold plates	plates of Mormon
survivor	Coriantumr	Moroni

Critics of the Book of Mormon point to these numbers as both unrealistic and unauthenticated by external evidence. Faithful Latter-day Saints who promote M2C use these large numbers to justify their rejection of the New York Cumorah, claiming there is no evidence in western New York of battles of this size.[115] In both cases, their assumptions about what the text says leads to their respective conclusions.

But what do the scriptures say?

---

[115] E.g., see a compilation of reasons to reject the New York Cumorah here: https://www.fairlatterdaysaints.org/answers/Book_of_Mormon/Geography/New_W orld/Hill_Cumorah#Question:_Are_the_large_population_counts_described_in_the_B ook_of_Mormon_during_the_final_battle_at_the_Hill_Cumorah_accurate.3F

When Coriantumr remembered what Ether had told him and saw that two millions of his people had been slain, this was more than four years before the final battle at the hill Ramah.

After his reminiscence, Coriantumr wrote to Shiz, hoping to spare his people. Instead, the people on both sides became angry and found another battle. Coriantumr fled to the waters of Ripliancum. There "they fought an exceedingly sore battle" and Coriantumr was wounded again, but his armies prevailed and the armies of Shiz fled southward. Only after that did the army of Coriantumr pitch his tents by the hill Ramah.

Then they spent four years gathering their people. (Ether 15:14)

The text supports two inferences regarding millions of people.

(i) Coriantumr could have been reflecting on the death of "two millions" of his people during the conflicts during his lifetime leading up to the time of his reflection.

(ii) Alternatively, Coriantumr could have been thinking of the accumulated deaths of his people during their recorded history.

The latter inference makes more sense to me because the record of the Jaredites consists of a series of civil wars. For example, in Chapter 8, Jared rebelled against his father, gave battle and imprisoned his father, only to have Jared's siblings kill Jared's army. (Ether 8:2-6)

Ether listed over 30 generations from the original Jared. Three times he wrote someone was "a descendant" of an ancestor, suggesting there could have been more generations involved.

A generation is normally 30-40 years, but any given generation could be shorter or longer in time. The common interpretation of Enos, for example, is that Jacob was his father, making Enos Lehi's grandson. Enos wrote around 420 B.C.—about 180 years after Lehi left Jerusalem.

Regardless of how much time elapsed during the 30+ generations of the Jaredites, the death of two million people (or more, if wives and children were counted separately) is not surprising. It amounts to around 67,000 per generation. If a generation is around 35 years on average, that means about 2,000 people/year dying in conflicts. Such a number would leave little, if any, evidence beyond the burial mounds we find throughout the midwestern and eastern U.S.

What about the final Jaredite battle at Cumorah?

The 8-day Jaredite battle at Cumorah could not have involved more than a few thousand, as we see from the count of the actual number killed on the last two days. (Ether 15:15-32)

Even after four years, Coriantumr could gather only a relatively few people to Cumorah. They fought for five days without enumerating the casualties, but at the end of the sixth day, there were only 121 people left. The next day, there were only 59 left. Over the next two days, everyone was killed except Coriantumr and Shiz.

If we assume, based on the numbers Ether gave us, that half the people were killed each day, we can calculate backward and derive the figure of about 7,744 on the first day of battle—total, including both sides.

It turns out that Oliver Cowdery addressed this point in 1835 and came to the same conclusion.

In Letter VII, Oliver explained that Mormon foresaw the approaching destruction and its parallel to the Jaredite destruction in the same place. Speaking from Mormon's perspective, and after describing the mile-wide valley west of the Hill Cumorah, Oliver wrote:

> "In this vale lie commingled, in one mass of ruin **the ashes of thousands**, and in this vale was destined to consume the fair forms and vigerous systems of tens of thousands of the human race—blood mixed with blood, flesh with flesh, bones with bones and dust with dust!"[116]

Oliver, writing from the perspective of Mormon's prophetic understanding, described the remains of the Jaredites as "the ashes of thousands." Not millions, but thousands. Not even tens of thousands, which was Oliver's term to describe those who would be killed in the yet future final battle of the Nephites.

Just thousands.

In the early 1800s, students were taught to count in ones, tens, hundreds, thousands, tens of thousands, and hundreds of thousands. This correlates to the Roman Numeral system. Both the Book of

---

[116] http://www.josephsmithpapers.org/paper-summary/history-1834-1836/92

Mormon and the Doctrine and Covenants use the phrase "tens of thousands," even though the phrase does not appear in the Bible.

> And in one year were **thousands** and **tens of thousands** of souls sent to the eternal world, that they might reap their rewards according to their works, whether they were good or whether they were bad, to reap eternal happiness or eternal misery, according to the spirit which they listed to obey, whether it be a good spirit or a bad one. (Alma 3:26)

For Oliver to write "thousands" instead of "tens of thousands" suggests the number was lower than ten thousand, and certainly lower than twenty thousand.

An interpretation of the text that has fewer than ten thousand Jaredites being killed at Ramah, and other deaths in the thousands (but not millions) over the course of Jaredite history, is easily compatible with the archaeological evidence in western New York.

Aside from the archaeological discoveries, Heber C. Kimball, who lived in western New York, joined the Church in 1832, and became a Counselor in the First Presidency, made this observation.

> In the towns of Bloomfield, Victor, Manchester, and in the regions round about, there were hills upon the tops of which were entrenchments and fortifications, and in them were human bones, axes, tomahawks, points of arrows, beads and pipes, which were frequently found; and it was a common occurrence in the country to plow up axes, which I have done many times myself.
>
> I have visited the fortifications on the tops of those hills frequently, and the one near Bloomfield I have crossed hundreds of times, which is on the bluff of Honeyoye River, and the outlet of Honeyoye Lake....
>
> The hill Cumorah is a high hill for that country, and had the appearance of a fortification or entrenchment around it. In the State of New York, probably there are hundreds of these fortifications which are now visible, and I have seen them in many other parts of the United States.[117]

---

[117] Orson F. Whitney, *Life of Heber C. Kimball* (1888), p. 41, online at https://www.google.com/books/edition/Life_of_Heber_C_Kimball/jdkRAAAAIAAJ

Reframing Asian DNA

The discovery of DNA and related technology demonstrated that most Native Americans have Asian ancestry. This prompted a reassessment of traditional views about a hemispheric setting for the Book of Mormon, particularly among Latter-day Saints who believed all the Native Americans descended from Lehi. But close reading of the text and the explanations from Joseph and Oliver show that the DNA evidence is consistent with the text.

Old narratives	Reframe
Faithful. DNA evidence can neither prove nor disprove the Book of Mormon narrative because we don't have the DNA from Jared's group to begin with, we don't know what route Jared took to come to America, and population bottlenecks and dilution erase most evidence of ancestry from DNA except for direct lines. **Critical.** DNA disproves the Book of Mormon because all indigenous people in the Americas came from Asia.	The Book of Mormon Jaredites migrated to America from Asia, consistent with the DNA evidence. Names in the text indicate that Jaredite peoples mixed with Zarahemla's peoples.

DNA and Jaredites. DNA evidence indicates that most indigenous people in the Americas have East Asian ancestry, presumably because they crossed over the frozen Bering Strait thousands of years ago.

That evidence does not contradict the Book of Mormon, however. Instead, it is what we could expect.

The Rational Restoration

The Book of Mormon explains that the Jaredites left "the great tower" (presumably the tower of Babel in modern Iraq or a Sumerian tower, around 2200 B.C.) and spent an unspecified time journeying across land and bodies of water "into the wilderness, yea, into that quarter where there never had man been." (Ether 2:5) They arrived at a seashore where they stayed for four years. (Ether 2:13) Hugh Nibley,[118] among others, inferred that they crossed central Asia and reached the coast of what is now China, which makes sense to me. They could have traveled in the area that later came to be known as the Silk Road from Iraq to the northeastern coast of China. Although they traversed an uninhabited area, naturally we would expect them to encounter other tribes or civilizations at various points along the way. There would be plenty of opportunity for intermarriage with people having Asian DNA.

The Gospel Topics Essay on Book of Mormon and DNA Studies notes that

> a 2014 study indicates that as much as one-third of Native American DNA may have originated anciently in Europe or West Asia. From this evidence, scientists conclude that some Europeans or West Asians migrated eastward across Asia, mixing with a group that eventually migrated to the Americas millennia before the events described in the Book of Mormon.[119]

That is consistent with the eastward migration of the Jaredites, except for one thing: timing.

The phrase "millennia before" Book of Mormon events refers to the study cited in the essay that focused on the genome of "an approximately 24,000-year-old individual."[120] This is one of several citations in the essay that are based on evolutionary theories that conclude modern humans

---

[118] E.g., see Nibley's *The World of the Jaredites*, p. 190, and his series in the *Improvement Era* in 1951-2, such as the November 1951 issue, online here: https://catalog.churchofjesuschrist.org/assets?id=3df6b264-bacd-4420-a7c6-bb0ef6e0d8ba&crate=0&index=0

[119] The essay claims that "DNA studies cannot be used decisively to either affirm or reject the historical authenticity of the Book of Mormon." See https://www.churchofjesuschrist.org/study/manual/gospel-topics-essays/book-of-mormon-and-dna-studies?lang=eng.

[120] *Nature* 505 (2014): 87-91, https://www.nature.com/articles/nature12736.

appeared over 100,000 years ago. That time frame directly contradicts D&C 77:6, which affirms the biblical timeline ("seven thousand years of [earth's] continuance, or its temporal existence"). The Book of Mormon and Pearl of Great Price affirm the creation of Adam as described in the Bible.

The discrepancy has led to discussions of "pre-Adamites" with Adam and Eve being a "special creation." Some people reject the scriptural timeline, while others reject the scientific timeline. Others claim the scientific timeline is an estimate based on erroneous assumptions. A discussion of the discrepancies between scriptural and scientific time frames is beyond the scope of this book. Like the question of Book of Mormon geography, both sides of the equation contain unknown variables that future discoveries and/or revelation may resolve.

In my view, the narrative in the Book of Ether is congruent with the scientific narrative of the DNA origins of indigenous people in the Western Hemisphere, apart from the time frames.

Jared, his brother, their friends, and all their families embarked in ships (barges) and arrived in the Promised Land after 344 days at sea. (Ether 6:11) By comparison, it took about a year for debris to drift from Japan to Canada after the 2011 tsunami.[121] As I discussed in *Moroni's America*, a First Nations tribe in British Columbia, Canada, has an origin story that relates their ancestors came in tight ships illuminated by shining pearls.

If the Jaredites crossed the North Pacific from China to Canada, we would expect their Asian DNA to show up the way it has.

One researcher has discovered evidence that the people crossed by boat from northern Asia to North America and migrated both northward into what is now northwestern Canada and Alaska and southward into what is now the United States and Latin America.[122]

Assuming as I do that the Jaredites landed in British Columbia, how did Asian DNA expand throughout Latin America?

---

[121] See https://www.theguardian.com/world/2012/may/02/motorcycle-japanese-tsunami-reaches-canada#

[122] See https://www.smithsonianmag.com/science-nature/how-humans-came-to-americas-180973739/. This article presents the same dating issues as all DNA/archaeological studies.

Other migrations. One answer is that the Jaredites were not the only people who migrated from Asia to the Western Hemisphere. They may have come before or after other groups.

Joseph Smith explained it this way:

> In this important and interesting book the history of ancient America is unfolded, from its first settlement by a colony that came from the tower of Babel, at the confusion of languages to the beginning of the fifth century of the Christian era. We are informed by these records that America in ancient times has been inhabited by two distinct races of people. The first were called Jaredites and came directly from the tower of Babel. ... The Jaredites were destroyed about the time that the Israelites came from Jerusalem, who succeeded them in the inheritance of the country.[123]

Notice that Joseph did not define "America" here. Scholars have debated the meaning he intended. Some say he meant the country in which he lived—the United States of America—because that's how people referred to the country in the 1840s. I agree with that view, but I also recognize that some people say Joseph meant all of North America, while others claim he meant all of the Western Hemisphere—the continents of North and South America. The last word of the quotation—"country"—corroborates my interpretation, and later in the letter Joseph distinguished between "continent" and "country" when he wrote, "penetrated every **continent**, visited every clime, swept every **country**." But you can reach whatever conclusion you want.

Two important points stand out. First, Joseph did not say these were the *only* two races or groups of people who inhabited America. Others could have come before or after the Jaredites. True, Joseph wrote "from its first settlement by a colony that came from the tower of Babel," but he was describing the Book of Mormon; i.e., the first settlement mentioned in the Book of Mormon, not the first settlement ever.

Second, Joseph said Lehi's people succeeded the Jaredites "in the inheritance of the country." In my view, this limits the scope of the territory occupied by the "Jaredites" and says nothing about the others

---

[123] The Wentworth letter. https://www.josephsmithpapers.org/paper-summary/church-history-1-march-1842/2#8180497476075025433

who crossed the sea with Jared who lived outside "the country." This leads to the second explanation for the spread of Asian DNA throughout the Americas.

Non-Jaredites. The Jaredites were not the only people who came with Jared.

The Book of Ether is a record of Ether's ancestors who directly descended from Jared. Ether listed over 30 generations of his ancestors, a direct line back to Jared. The term "Jaredites" (which appears only once in the scriptures, in Moroni 9:23) itself connotes descendants of Jared. Thus, the Book of Ether is explicitly *not* a record of all the people who descended from Jared's brother, or the twenty-two friends who accompanied them on a long overland journey before the sea voyage on the barges.

When the brother of Jared "began to be old," he and Jared gathered the people for a census. (Ether 6:19-21) The report itemizes their children but does not mention their friends, which suggests their friends and their descendants had dispersed.

Moroni explained the limited scope of the Book of Ether. "I, Moroni, proceed to give an account of those ancient inhabitants who were destroyed by the hand of the Lord upon the face of **this north country.**" (Ether 1:1)

The term "this" indicates Moroni was referring to the place where he lived when he engraved the Book of Ether. Recall, Moroni told Joseph that the record was "written and deposited" not far from Joseph's home near Palmyra.

The term "north country" limits the scope of the record; i.e., there were inhabitants elsewhere who were not involved with the destruction.

This leads me to infer that the friends of Jared and his brother likely spread to different areas, primarily south of the land occupied by the Jaredites. Their descendants could have produced or participated in the Olmec civilization, for example.

Conclusion. The Book of Ether describes a migration from western Asia to the western hemisphere that could account, at least in part, for the presence of Asian DNA among indigenous people. Moroni's limited the scope of the destruction of the Jaredites to "this north country," suggesting that descendants of non-Jaredites who arrived with Jared inhabited other areas, which is also consistent with the archaeological record.

Reframing "the Americas"

Old narratives	Reframe
Although the Book of Mormon text never mentions a setting in the New World, Joseph and others explained the events took place in the Americas, even though they were wrong about the New York Cumorah.	The same people who taught an American setting taught the New York Cumorah, so it is irrational to accept the American setting but reject the New York Cumorah. "The Americas" is a non-historical term used by modern scholars to blur the historical record.

For more detail on this reframe, see chapter 16: All/Some/None on Book of Mormon Geography.

Reframing Book of Mormon Language

Old narratives	Reframe
The Book of Mormon uses Early Modern English and resolves doctrinal disputes from the 1600s OR The Book of Mormon is a 19th century creation that plagiarizes existing books and resolves doctrinal disputes of Joseph Smith's era	The Book of Mormon is a 19th century translation of an ancient text that fits squarely within the Christian tradition.

For more detail on this reframe, see chapter 17: All/Some/None on Book of Mormon Translation.

Reframing the purpose of the Book of Mormon

Old narratives	Reframe
The Book of Mormon is a missionary tool for the Church of Jesus Christ of Latter-day Saints because if it's true, then Joseph Smith is a prophet and so are his successors.	The Book of Mormon is a tool to convince people that Jesus is the Christ, regardless of whether people join any church or accept any other doctrine.

The Title Page of the Book of Mormon, which Joseph said is a literal translation from the last leaf of the plates, spells out the purpose of the Book of Mormon.

> Wherefore, it is an abridgment of the record of the people of Nephi, and also of the Lamanites—Written to the Lamanites, who are a remnant of the house of Israel; and also to Jew and Gentile—Written by way of commandment, and also by the spirit of prophecy and of revelation—Written and sealed up, and hid up unto the Lord, that they might not be destroyed—To come forth by the gift and power of God unto the interpretation thereof—Sealed by the hand of Moroni, and hid up unto the Lord, to come forth in due time by way of the Gentile—The interpretation thereof by the gift of God.
> An abridgment taken from the Book of Ether also, which is a record of the people of Jared, who were scattered at the time the Lord confounded the language of the people, when they were building a tower to get to heaven— **Which is to show unto the remnant of the house of Israel what great things the Lord hath done for their fathers; and that they may know the covenants of the Lord, that they are not cast off forever—And also to the convincing of the Jew and Gentile that Jesus is the Christ, the Eternal God, manifesting himself unto all nations**—And now, if there are faults they are the mistakes of men; wherefore, condemn not the things of God, that ye may be found spotless at the judgment-seat of Christ.
> (Title Page, 1–2)

Nothing in the Title Page says the book is intended to persuade anyone to join any church.

The Rational Restoration

It's reasonable to infer that by helping people "know the covenants of the Lord" they would desire to enter those covenants, which would mean accepting Christ through covenant.

But people can also accept the Book of Mormon and be convinced that Jesus is the Christ while rationally adhering to their own traditions.

Reframing Joseph's knowledge

Old narratives	Reframe
Joseph Smith knew nothing about Book of Mormon geography, but he eventually adopted a false narrative about the New York Cumorah that originated with unknown early Latter-day Saints	Joseph Smith learned from Moroni that the hill where the plates were deposited was called Cumorah anciently and was the same hill the Jaredites called Ramah

For more detail on this reframe, see chapter 16: All/Some/None on Book of Mormon Geography.

Reframing Cumorah teachings

Old narratives	Reframe
Lucy Mack Smith, Oliver Cowdery, Martin Harris, David Whitmer, Brigham Young, Wilford Woodruff, Heber C. Kimball, and other Church leaders, including members of the First Presidency speaking in General Conference, all promoted a false narrative about Cumorah based on their own incorrect opinions.	Lucy Mack Smith, Oliver Cowdery, Martin Harris, David Whitmer, Brigham Young, Wilford Woodruff, Heber C. Kimball, and other Church leaders, including members of the First Presidency speaking in General Conference, related a correct narrative about Cumorah based on what Moroni told Joseph and what Joseph and Oliver personally experienced.

For more detail on this reframe, see chapter 16: All/Some/None on Book of Mormon Geography.

Reframing the hemispheric model

Old narratives	Reframe
The Pratt brothers, Benjamin Winchester, William Smith, and others connected the Book of Mormon with ancient ruins in Central America because Joseph Smith believed and taught that.	The Pratt brothers, Benjamin Winchester, William Smith, and others connected the Book of Mormon with ancient ruins in Central America for apologetic reasons. Joseph never said or implied that he agreed; in fact, he contradicted what Orson Pratt wrote.

One of the longest published articles "signed" by Joseph Smith (published over his name) is the Wentworth letter, published as "Church History" in the *Times and Seasons* on March 1, 1842. The Historical Introduction to the letter in the Joseph Smith Papers explains that:

> No manuscript copy has been located, and it is not known how much of the text JS originally wrote or dictated. In several places the historical narrative parallels other accounts JS produced between 1832 and 1838 or echoes wording from Orson Pratt's 1840 tract *A[n] Interesting Account of Several Remarkable Visions*.[124]

A side-by-side comparison[125] of the Wentworth letter with Orson Pratt's 1840 tract shows the changes Joseph made. Orson wrote several pages describing his hemispheric theory about Book of Mormon events, including Lehi landing in Chile and the Nephites building ships near the Isthmus of Darien.

Joseph replaced all of Orson Pratt's speculation about a hemispheric model with his short statement that "the remnant are the Indians that now inhabit this country." This is consistent with D&C 28, 30 and 32

---

[124] https://www.josephsmithpapers.org/paper-summary/church-history-1-march-1842/1#historical-intro

[125] https://www.mobom.org/wentworth-orson-pratt

which directed Oliver Cowdery and his companions to "go unto the Lamanites and preach my gospel unto them." (Doctrine and Covenants 28:8) The missionaries preached to the Native Americans (Indians) living in New York, Ohio, and Missouri.

Reframing the Times and Seasons

Old narratives	Reframe
Faithful: Joseph Smith learned about Book of Mormon geography from a popular book about Central America written by Stephens and Catherwood. Critical: Joseph Smith built a fictional narrative about Book of Mormon geography based on a popular book about Central America written by Stephens and Catherwood	Wilford Woodruff, Benjamin Winchester and others were enthusiastic about the Stephens and Catherwood book, which described ruins dating after Book of Mormon time frames, but Joseph Smith didn't pay attention to them. In the Wentworth letter, he corrected Orson Pratt's hemispheric model by clarifying that the descendants of Lehi were the Indians that lived in what was then the United States

This is an important reframe because these articles are the basis for the focus on Mesoamerica, which led to the Mesoamerican/two-Cumorahs theory.

Two issues of the *Times and Seasons*, 15 September and 1 October 1842, contain three articles that connect the Book of Mormon with the books by Stephens and Catherwood titled *Incidents of Travel in Central America*.

The three articles contain about 900 words of editorial content spread among 5,400 words of extracts from the Book of Mormon and the Stephens books.

The Stephens books arrived in Nauvoo in October 1841 when Wilford Woodruff brought them. They were a gift from John Bernhisel, who was corresponding with Joseph Smith about purchasing land in

Nauvoo. Bernhisel lived in New York and acquired the books about the time Benjamin Winchester visited him there.

On his journey to Nauvoo, Woodruff read through the books and recorded in his journal that he enjoyed them very much. He also recorded that he wrote a letter to Bernhisel in November, but that letter is not extant.

As part of his dictated ongoing correspondence with Bernhisel, a letter purportedly from Joseph thanked Bernhisel for the Stephens books and praised the books in words similar to what Woodruff wrote. Because Joseph did not write or sign the letter, it is unknown whether he dictated it or asked someone to send a thank-you note.

Ever since, people have assumed that Joseph wrote the note and had read Stephens two volumes, despite no one recording such activity in Joseph's journal or any other document.

In my view, the evidence indicates that Woodruff drafted or related the thank you note to John Taylor, who penned the letter and added a comment about the real estate transactions.

Ten months later, the articles quoting from the Stephens books appeared in the *Times and Seasons*.

Because Joseph Smith was the nominal editor of the paper during this time, it has long been assumed that he composed, or at least edited, these articles. That assumption fed the narratives of the M2C advocates as well as the critics, as shown in the table above.

In 2013, Matthew Roper, Paul J. Fields, and Atul Nepal published an article titled "Joseph Smith, the Times and Seasons, and Central American Ruins" that purported to apply stylometric (wordprint) analysis to the 900 words. They considered only three candidates, Joseph Smith, John Taylor, and Wilford Woodruff, and used unspecified writing samples from these three to compare with the 900 words. Although the 900 words varied significantly from the three candidates, they were closest in style to Joseph Smith, which led the authors to conclude that Joseph wrote the articles.

The problems with the analysis are many and fundamental, starting with opacity about the writing samples they used for their database and the software they employed. I discussed this in *The Lost City of Zarahemla*. The second edition of that book incorporates the comments and criticisms generated by the first edition. Two additional books, *Brought to*

Light and *The Editors: Joseph, Don Carlos, and William Smith* go into even more detail about the *Times and Seasons*.

People have a range of opinions about the authorship of these 900 words. In my view, 900 words is an insufficient sample to determine unambiguously who wrote the editorial comments, but the narrative and language closely resembles what Benjamin Winchester was writing contemporaneously, and what William Smith claimed subsequently.

It remains possible that, despite the Wentworth letter and the lack of evidence to corroborate Joseph's authorship of the 900 words, Joseph did speculate about the ruins in Central America.

But at the same time, everyone agrees that Joseph wrote the letter that now appears as D&C 128, including verse 20 that reaffirms the New York Cumorah. Thus, even if Joseph wrote about Central America, he never wavered from the New York Cumorah.

Reframing Joseph as Editor

Old narratives	Reframe
Joseph Smith was listed as publisher, editor, and printer of the *Times and Seasons* from March to October of 1842; therefore, he wrote, edited or approved of everything published within its pages during this time	Although Joseph was listed as publisher, editor, and printer of the *Times and Seasons* from March to October of 1842, no one believes that he actually operated the printing press. He was the nominal printer. Likewise, no journal entries or recorded observations describe Joseph editing articles for the *Times and Seasons*. He was merely the nominal editor (in name only).

The boilerplate at the end of each issue of the *Times and Seasons* from March 15 through June 15 read:

The Times and Seasons, IS EDITED BY Joseph Smith.
Printed and published about the first and fifteenth of every month, on the corner of Water and Bain Streets, Nauvoo, Hancock County, Illinois, by JOSEPH SMITH. (Times and Seasons III.9:718 ¶21)

From July 1 through October 1, the boilerplate read:

The Times and Seasons, Is edited, printed and published about the first and fifteenth of every month, on the corner of Water and Bain Streets, Nauvoo, Hancock County, Illinois, by JOSEPH SMITH (Times and Seasons III.17:846 ¶28)

There is no historical evidence, apart from this boilerplate, that Joseph Smith ever edited or printed the *Times and Seasons*. Yet there is abundant historical evidence of his other activities during this time period. Wilford Woodruff observed that Joseph was so busy he didn't have time to even sign documents that were prepared for his signature.

Under the circumstances, it strains credulity to infer that Joseph was actually operating the printing press or spending hours editing articles for the Times and Seasons. There is evidence that Wilford Woodruff worked in the printing shop. Joseph's brother William used the same press and printing shop to publish the *Wasp* newspaper. On some occasions the two papers published the same or similar material.

All of this indicates it is more likely that someone other than Joseph Smith was actually printing and editing the *Times and Seasons*, despite what the boilerplate says.

Reframing Joseph as author in the Times and Seasons

Old narratives	Reframe
Joseph Smith was responsible for the entire content of the *Times and Seasons* from March to October of 1842 because he said he was responsible.	Joseph Smith was responsible only for the few articles he personally signed, such as the Wentworth letter, and he learned the content of the *Times and Seasons* only after reading the printed newspaper.

The March 15, 1842, *Times and Seasons* begins with this notice:

TO SUBSCRIBERS.

The Rational Restoration

> This paper commences my editorial career, I alone stand for it, and shall do for all papers having my signature henceforward. I am not responsible for the publication, or arrangement of the former paper; the matter did not come under my supervision.
> JOSEPH SMITH. (*Times and Seasons* III.9:710 ¶7–8)

On its face, the statement seems to make Joseph responsible for the content of every paper that has his signature on it.

1. The first obvious problem: the statement is prospective. It was never repeated. As such, it is aspirational, looking forward, not factual. Good intentions for the future are not evidence of what actually transpired.

2. The majority of the statement is a disavowal of previous issues. After Joseph's brother Don Carlos died in August 1841 (Don Carlos had edited and published the *Times and Seasons* until his death), problems arose with the management and content. Benjamin Winchester, who lived in Philadelphia, had published his own newspaper, the *Gospel Reflector*, in 1841. The paper was unsuccessful financially. When he learned that Don Carlos had died, Winchester wrote a letter to Joseph suggesting that he could replace him as publisher. The *Times and Seasons* had republished many of Winchester's articles anonymously, so it was a natural fit.

Winchester moved to Nauvoo and began working at the paper. On October 31st, 1841, Wilford Woodruff reported that "Joseph severely reproved Benjamin Winchester for getting out of his place & doing wrong." Joseph's history reports that

> Attended a Council with the Twelve Apostles. Benjamin Winchester being present, complained that he had been neglected and misrepresented by the Elders, and manifested a contentious spirit. <1242> I gave him a severe reproof telling him of his folly and vanity and shewing him that the principles which he suffered to control him, would lead him to destruction. I counselled him to change his course— govern his dispositions, and quit his talebearing and slandering his brethren.[126]

---

[126] https://www.josephsmithpapers.org/paper-summary/history-1838-1856-volume-c-1-addenda/19

Nevertheless, Winchester worked at the *Times and Seasons* until the Quorum of the Twelve dismissed him in January 1842.

Problems at the *Times and Seasons* persisted. For the details, see *The Lost City of Zarahemla*, 2d Edition (2016). The point is, Joseph had plenty of reasons to disavow the previous newspaper and assume responsibility to maintain the credibility of the newspaper.

3. Even after March 15, 1842, when Joseph assumed responsibility, there were several specific instances in which Joseph was unaware of the contents of the paper until after it was published. This suggests that while he accepted responsibility in a general sense, he was not directly involved enough to know the contents that were being written, edited, typeset and printed by others.

4. Assuming responsibility itself is a vague term. Does it mean he vouched for the veracity of the contents? Does it mean he agreed with everything published in the paper? Or does it mean that he assumed the burden of responsibility to alleviate the burdens on the staff? There are articles in the *Times and Seasons* during this period that contradict one another as well.

5. The phrase "all papers having my signature" is unclear. Does it refer to the boilerplate at the end of every issue, or to articles which he separately signed, such as the Wentworth letter?

Reframing Joseph as author generally

Old narratives	Reframe
Articles in the *Times and Seasons* about Central America were written and published by Joseph Smith.	Articles in the *Times and Seasons* about Central America were written by Benjamin Winchester and/or others such as William Smith or W.W. Phelps.

Joseph Smith was well-known for disliking the writing process. He dictated the Book of Mormon, the revelations, his correspondence, and other official business. He also delegated writing projects to his scribes, including his own history (excerpts from which are found in Joseph Smith—History in the Pearl of Great Price).

Oliver Cowdery, not Joseph Smith, wrote the first detailed history of the church in eight essays published as letters in the Messenger and Advocate. Joseph had his scribes copy the essays into his own journal as part of his life story. He later approved their republication in the *Gospel Reflector* and *Times and Seasons*.

The Joseph Smith Papers has collected all known documents in Joseph Smith's handwriting, here: https://www.josephsmithpapers.org/site/documents-in-joseph-smiths-handwriting

These consist mostly of brief journal entries and letters. None are speculative articles about history or archaeology that analyze books or current events. For Joseph to write the articles in the *Times and Seasons* about Central America would be out of character.

Worse, the civilizations featured in the Stephens and Catherwood book have been dated by modern archaeologists. They date to periods later than 400 AD. This means they could not be Book of Mormon ruins. If Joseph wrote these articles, he misled the Church and the world.

On the other hand, if Winchester, Phelps, or someone else wrote the articles, they would have had no first-hand knowledge of the actual setting of the Book of Mormon, so their speculation is immaterial.

Reframing William Smith

Old narratives	Reframe
Joseph's brother William Smith published the *Wasp* twice monthly from the same printing office as the *Times and Seasons* but had nothing to do with the *Times and Seasons*, even though the two papers sometimes published the same material.	Joseph's brother William Smith published the *Wasp* twice monthly from the same printing office as the *Times and Seasons* and produced content for both newspapers. William solicited content from Benjamin Winchester.

Here, little discussion is necessary. The historical record offers abundant evidence that William was involved with both the *Wasp* and the *Times and Seasons*. William was a close friend of Benjamin Winchester as well. William not only published the *Wasp*, but he went on to publish *The Prophet* newspaper in New York City, where he directly solicited contributions from Winchester for *The Prophet*.

Summary. When we reframe the Book of Mormon as an inspired translation of an ancient record that contained "a history of the aborigines of this country"[127] that was "written and deposited not far from" Joseph's home near Palmyra, New York, we have a rational explanation for all the events in Church history related to the origin and setting of the Book of Mormon.

We don't have to ignore or reject what Joseph and his contemporaries taught about the translation with the Nephite interpreters known as the Urim and Thummim. We don't have to ignore or reject what they taught about Cumorah/Ramah in western New York.

We can readily identify extrinsic evidence that corroborates both the translation and the setting of the Book of Mormon.

In so doing, we lower barriers to acceptance of this book as another Testament of Jesus Christ.

---

[127] https://www.josephsmithpapers.org/paper-summary/history-1834-1836/68

11: Reframing Mortality

A Window into Eternity

Before leaving his apartment, the sergeant taped the blade of a knife to the palm side of his forearm. A thick steak knife from his kitchen drawer. With the handle near his wrist. Where it was easy to grab.

He pulled his shirt on. The sleeve was tight, but not too tight. Leave the wrist unbuttoned, he told himself. And keep the arm straight. Don't bend the elbow. The sharpened tip of the knife was mere millimeters from his brachial artery.

He got in his old BMW and drove to his defense lawyer's office.

Turning the wheel, thinking about the tradeoff between years in prison and the threats made by his co-conspirators if he squealed, he momentarily forgot about the knife and bent his elbow.

The tip poked the skin.

He thought about squeezing it more, slicing the artery, ending his troubles by bleeding out along the side of the road.

But first he had a job to do.

———

My client entered my outer office and demanded to see me. My paralegal replied that he'd need to make an appointment.

I heard the discussion, opened the door, and invited him in.

I leaned against my desk and invited him to sit by the coffee table in the center of my office.

He declined.

He paced in front of my window, back and forth, repeating things he'd said before.

I took a seat by the table and said I'd postpone the hearing.

He began circling the room.

I reached for the phone as he stepped behind me.

I felt him pound my back, knocking me over onto my Persian carpet. I rolled over. He reached down, straining to grab my neck with outstretched fingers. I held him off, but my legs went numb.

Then, for a moment—an instant—I was elsewhere.

It may be a cliché that your life flashes before you when you die, but I discovered it's a reality.[128] It's incomprehensible, really. It may seem impossible given the situation—after all, I was struggling to stay alive with a knife in my spine and my assailant trying to strangle me—but in that instant, I reviewed my entire life. I felt an incredible peace, as though there was nothing to fear, no reason to be concerned at all.

But then my secretary opened the door and screamed.

Mortality rushed back in. I stared into the murderous intensity in my client's eyes that bore down on me. My arms instinctively thwarted his grasping hands, but I sensed my body was weakening.

The carpet beneath me was squishy. Something was terribly wrong.

A friend burst into the room and grabbed the assailant. Immediate relief. But I felt nothing from the waist down. People told me not to move. Help was on its way.

The paramedics told me not to move because the knife was still stuck in my back. In my spine, actually, it turned out.

They put me, sideways, on a stretcher. I turned to see a thick pool of my own blood in the center of my Persian rug.

Despite the commotion, my brief glimpse of eternity led me to this realization:

The hardest thing about mortality is how real it seems.

Such a change in perspective can be described as "reframing."

In this book, we've discussed several reframes that may change your outlook on life dramatically.

---

[128] For an example of the scientific basis for this phenomenon, see https://www.smithsonianmag.com/smart-news/brain-scans-suggest-life-flashes-before-our-eyes-upon-death-180979647/

The Rational Restoration

When my life flashed before me, it was retrospective. After all, we can't "remember the future," at least, not most of the time.

I've wondered how long it would have taken me to describe the details of that experience, assuming I even could have. To do so would be impossible.

My background put me at the confluence of multiple streams of influences. My father's father was an Irish Catholic. His mother descended from Mormon pioneers. My mother's parents descended from non-Mormon immigrants from Sweden. Thus, only one of my grandparents was Mormon.

Growing up, my father attended Church sporadically, but he also had a collection of pipes that he enjoyed smoking. My parents had two boys, me and my younger brother, before they divorced when I was seven. My mother married an old family friend who had four children. They had a child together, my step-brother who was murdered when he was twenty-five years old.

My father married an active Latter-day Saint who also had four children. He jettisoned the pipes and became fully active in the Church, serving in numerous leadership positions.

My parents shared custody, so my brother and I grew up in both families. When we lived with our father, we were part of an active LDS family with all the trimmings: Family Home Evening, regular church and temple attendance, Home Teaching, youth activities, etc. Because I was living with our mother's family when I was eight, I wasn't baptized until I was nine, which qualifies as a "convert baptism."

When we lived with our mother, our family was vaguely Christian but only my brother and I attended any church—the LDS church. My mom encouraged us to attend because she thought it was a good influence, even though she didn't believe in it. My step-brother in that family eventually became an anti-Mormon Christian activist, part of the Campus Crusade for Christ. He would tell me all the reasons why "Mormons" were wrong. When I was on my mission, he wrote to me, addressing me as "Younger Jonathan Neville" to emphasize that I was hardly an "Elder" in any sense of the word.

My mom found inspiration in a variety of sources, including Edgar Cayce. She believed in reincarnation.

Although in retrospect, it was a complex childhood, at the time it seemed normal to us. We lived in California, Washington, Nevada, Tennessee, the Philippines, and Germany. We would live for a year with our Mormon family, then a year with our nonreligious family, then back again with the Mormons. Living in different families, all of whom were wonderful, taught me from a young age that people can live in love and harmony even when they have different—completely different—religious and political beliefs.

When I was nineteen, I served for two years in the France Paris mission. That was my first in-depth encounter with orthodoxy. Catholics would tell us they already had a religion and they weren't interested in another one. A common saying was, "In France we have one religion and a thousand kinds of cheese. In America, you have a thousand religions and one kind of cheese."

We had modest success—I baptized two people, but some of my fellow missionaries not only never baptized anyone, they didn't even *see* a baptism during their mission. I've visited France many times since then. One of my converts remained in the Church, the other left, and the branch where I served as Branch President in the 1970s closed down in 2019 (before covid). Despite a modest nominal growth in France, and despite the spectacular 100 million Euro temple in Paris, the Church in France is pretty much where it was in the 1970s: sporadic attendance at branches and wards that haven't changed much in over 40 years.

For various reasons I've lived in Europe for eight years, in the Philippines, in China, and in Africa (Mauritius). I've lived in New York, Illinois, Tennessee, Arizona, Nevada, Utah, Washington state, California, and now in Oregon. I've visited over 60 countries and every continent (including the Chilean base in Antarctica). We've attended church and temples around the world, in many languages. We have friends and business associates of many nationalities, languages, and religions, including former Latter-day Saints.

One common theme among everyone I've known or know of is, as Thomas Jefferson wrote, the pursuit of happiness.

Most people around the world seek for the ideal society we call Zion. But as Joseph explained long ago, they don't know where to find it.

And we're not telling them.

I'm not sure we Latter-day Saints know where to find it ourselves.

For Thy Good

Why didn't the Spirit warn me that my client had a knife literally up his sleeve? People get spiritual impressions and warnings all the time. We don't always notice, and we don't always heed them even when we do notice, and it's not always easy to distinguish them from ordinary fears and insecurity (and common sense), but many people relate their experiences with spiritual warnings.

And in a way, the Spirit did warn me. The night before. But that's another story.

One of Joseph Smith's revelations explained why God doesn't protect us from everything.

> all these things shall give thee experience, and shall be for thy good.
> (Doctrine and Covenants 122:7)

This is basic Christian doctrine. To a non-believer, this approach to the challenges of life might appear irrational. An after-the-fact rationalization. Maybe even a state of denial.

But to a believer, it is perfectly rational to understand the vicissitudes of mortality as beneficial life experiences that bring us closer to God and refine us.

Paul wrote about it.

> we glory in tribulations also: knowing that tribulation worketh patience;
> 4 And patience, experience; and experience, hope:
> 5 And hope maketh not ashamed; because the love of God is shed abroad in our hearts by the Holy Ghost which is given unto us.
> (Romans 5:3–5)

> 35 Who shall separate us from the love of Christ? *shall* tribulation, or distress, or persecution, or famine, or nakedness, or peril, or sword?
> 36 As it is written, For thy sake we are killed all the day long; we are accounted as sheep for the slaughter.
> 37 Nay, in all these things we are more than conquerors through him that loved us.

38 For I am persuaded, that neither death, nor life, nor angels, nor principalities, nor powers, nor things present, nor things to come,
39 Nor height, nor depth, nor any other creature, shall be able to separate us from the love of God, which is in Christ Jesus our Lord.
(Romans 8:35–39)

The latter-day scriptures add insight:

1 Verily I say unto you, concerning your brethren who have been afflicted, and persecuted, and cast out from the land of their inheritance—
2 I, the Lord, have suffered the affliction to come upon them, wherewith they have been afflicted, in consequence of their transgressions;
3 Yet I will own them, and they shall be mine in that day when I shall come to make up my jewels.
4 Therefore, they must needs be chastened and tried, even as Abraham, who was commanded to offer up his only son.
5 For all those who will not endure chastening, but deny me, cannot be sanctified. (Doctrine and Covenants 101:1–5)

Aside from the intellectually rational aspect of handling life's challenges, my own lived experience corroborates the veracity of these and related scriptures. Like me, many people who have near-death experiences report the existence of another reality. Like me, any Latter-day Saints can relate experiences in the temples and other settings where the veil is thin.

Reframing how God operates

Old narratives	Reframe
The narrative of the Restoration is irrational because God wouldn't do things this way.	The narrative of the Restoration is rational when we reframe the irrational narratives.

I like to think of the Restoration as a proxy for all the arguments about God that start with "God wouldn't do…"
Looking at the world from God's perspective is impossible, of course; we aren't God. But we can imagine how a rational God would deal with mortals.

The Rational Restoration

For one thing, God would understand human psychology and physiology. He would understand the right brain/left brain dichotomy, the influence of hormones and chemical imbalances, the effect of fatigue, injury, disease, worry, stress, the interaction between thinking and emotions, and all the rest.

This is basic Christian doctrine, taught in the Book of Mormon this way:

> 11 And he shall go forth, suffering pains and afflictions and temptations of every kind; and this that the word might be fulfilled which saith he will take upon him the pains and the sicknesses of his people.
> 12 And he will take upon him death, that he may loose the bands of death which bind his people; and he will take upon him their infirmities, that his bowels may be filled with mercy, according to the flesh, that he may know according to the flesh how to succor his people according to their infirmities. (Alma 7:11–12)

A parallel theme is the notion that "the natural man is an enemy to God, and has been from the fall of Adam." (Mosiah 3:19)

Juxtaposed with human frailty, we have the universal human aspiration for "life, liberty, and the pursuit of happiness," all with the hope and expectation that we can make the world a better place and, eventually, achieve an ideal society that enables every person to achieve full potential.

With all these factors, the Christian narrative of creation, fall and atonement is rational. But so is the narrative of a falling away and a Restoration.

We previously saw how Jonathan Edwards articulated Christian expectations for the "prosperity of the church, in its most glorious state on earth in the latter days." He showed how the Restoration would start small and spread out until it filled the earth.

That is a rational process, given human psychology and all the other factors involved.

That's why, while arguments against God can be rational, a global reframe regarding God can also be rational.

Reframing sin

Old narratives	Reframe
Sin is disobedience to God.	Sin is missing the purpose of mortality; i.e., pursuing perfection.

The Greek word translated as "sin" is transliterated as "hamartia."[129] It connotes the idea of a forfeiture for missing the target or mark, as in archery. It can mean an error of understanding as well as an evil deed.

If we assume mortality is a state of probation, a time for testing and for learning about our own values, priorities, aspirations, etc., then "sin" is anything that misses those targets.

The LDS Gospel Topics page defines sin this way:

> To commit sin is to willfully disobey God's commandments or to fail to act righteously despite a knowledge of the truth (see James 4:17).
>
> The Lord has said that He "cannot look upon sin with the least degree of allowance" (Doctrine and Covenants 1:31). Sin results in the withdrawal of the Holy Ghost. It makes the one who sins unable to dwell in the presence of Heavenly Father, for "no unclean thing can dwell with God" (1 Nephi 10:21).
>
> Other than Jesus Christ, each person who has ever lived on earth has broken commandments or failed to act according to knowledge of the truth. The Apostle John taught: "If we say that we have no sin, we deceive ourselves, and the truth is not in us. If we confess our sins, [Jesus Christ] is faithful and just to forgive us our sins, and to cleanse us from all unrighteousness" (1 John 1:8–9). Through the Atonement of Jesus Christ, each person can repent and be forgiven of these sins.[130]

The reframe doesn't change the scriptural definition or meaning of "sin" but it articulates it as a rational approach to life. It's another way of understanding God's commandments as being for our own good.

---

[129] https://biblehub.com/greek/266.htm
[130] https://www.churchofjesuschrist.org/study/manual/gospel-topics/sin?lang=eng

The Rational Restoration

Reframing the creation

Old narratives	Reframe
Science is wrong because the Bible and other scriptures say Adam and Eve lived 6,000 years ago. OR Religion is wrong because evidence shows the earth is 4.3 billion years old and the first humans evolved 250,000 years ago	Science has shown that life is a complex code that could not be random. The Restoration is rationale regardless of the actual age of the earth.

The debate between evolution and creationism has raged for years, with scientists and polemicists on all sides. It's not always a debate about God; religious people have different interpretations of the scriptures and different levels of acceptance of science.

It's another classic example of how the FAITH model can lead to clarity, charity and understanding. Everyone looks at the identical facts, makes assumptions, draws inferences, and applies theories to reconcile everything rationally. They end up with multiple working hypotheses for people to choose from. One compromise hypothesis accepts adaptive evolution while rejecting materialistic evolution as the explanation for the original creation.

The reframe accepts science for both evolution and creationism, pending additional information from science or revelation. The reframe doesn't assume static knowledge and recognizes that the more we learn about science, the less likely it seems that nondirected, random evolution can explain the world around us (irreducible complexity, etc.). Physicists and philosophers debate whether we are living in a simulation.

The reframe also recognizes that these debates, so far, haven't solved for clarity, charity, and understanding. But they can and should.

In *Darwin's Doubt*, Stephen C. Meyer makes a case for intelligent design that relies on physics and mathematics. On p. 173 he cites evolutionary biologists Jack King and Thomas Jukes who wrote that

"Natural selection is the editor, rather than the composer, of the genetic message."[131]

Another excerpt from Meyer's book sets out one of the basic quandaries that scientists are still working on.

> Although the theory of intelligent design infers that an intelligent cause played a role in shaping life's history, it does not say how the intelligent cause affected matter. Nor does it have to do so.
> There is a logical reason we cannot without further information determine the mechanism or means by which the intelligent agent responsible for life transmitted its design to matter. We can infer an intelligent cause from certain features of the physical world, because intelligence is known to be a necessary cause, the only known cause, of those features. That allows us to infer intelligence retrospectively as a cause by observing its distinctive effects....
> At present no one has any idea how our thoughts—the decisions and choices that occur in our conscious minds—affect our material brains, nerves, and muscles, going on to instantiate our will in the material world of objects. However, we know that is exactly what our thoughts do. We have no mechanistic explanation for the mystery of consciousness, nor what is called the "mind-body problem"—the enigma of how thought affects the material state of our brains, bodies, and the world that we affect with them. Yet there is no doubt that we can—as the result of events in our conscious minds called decisions or choices—"will into existence" information-rich arrangements of matter or otherwise affect material states in the world.[132]

Another aspect of the creation that adds rationality to the overall plan of salvation (aka the work of redemption) is the concept of pre-mortal existence. Many people sense, intuitively, that their existence as individuals did not commence at birth on earth. Biblical and Latter-day scriptures explain that our spirits existed before mortality and that after death we *return* to God's presence. Awareness of our pre-mortal existence gives us a broader perspective on mortality; i.e., "all these things shall give thee experience, and shall be for thy good." (D&C 122:7).

---

[131] Citing King and Jukes, "Non-Darwinian Evolution," 788.
[132] *Darwin's Doubt*, 396-7.

12: Critics and Apologists

From the outset, the Restoration generated opposition and support. Critics and apologists (defenders) battled in public meetings, through publications, and in person. Wherever the Church was established, Joseph Smith set up newspapers to counter the critical newspapers of the day. The "strife of words and a contest about opinions" that Joseph observed among Christian denominations extended to the Restoration.

It's an ongoing contest of reframes.

In the early days, debates focused on interpretations of the Bible. Most people in America and England were Christians. They considered the Bible authoritative, so naturally early missionaries preached from the Bible to "prove" the Restoration, while critics advocated interpretations of the Bible that contradicted the Restoration.[133]

In modern times, fewer people consider the Bible authoritative or even know (or care) what it says. Consequently, secular critics who focus on Church history and social issues have become more prominent, particularly on social media. LDS apologists have responded, but in some cases agree with the critics on interpretations of Church history.

Two approaches to critics have been pursued: (i) "heed them not" and (ii) "have an answer."

(i) Of those pointing the finger of scorn, Nephi said "we heeded them not. These are the words of my father: For as many as heeded them, had fallen away." (1 Nephi 8:33–34)

(ii) Paul encouraged the Saints to "be ready always to give an answer to every man that asketh you a reason of the hope that is in you." (1 Peter 3:15)

Both approaches are rational, depending on the circumstances.

In this chapter, we will look at some of the primary critics and apologists. People have a tendency to choose a team and stick with it. As

---

[133] There were Christian "Restoration" movements before and after 1830, many of which continue to the present. They based their doctrine and authority on the Bible and thus oppose the non-biblical addition of new scripture, revelation, and prophets—especially when the "Mormons" offer new interpretations of the Bible.

we discussed at the outset, we all have busy, complicated lives. We rely on others (farmers, doctors, lawyers, plumbers, teachers, etc.) to handle aspects of life we don't have the time or ability to do for ourselves.

But no one else can live our lives for us. In matters of faith and worldview, we owe it to ourselves to make informed decisions.

When the Restoration commenced with the translation of the Book of Mormon, it attracted immediate criticism. The first published article about the Book of Mormon was "Golden Bible," published in August 1829 in the *Palmyra Freeman*. The author, Jonathan Hadley, wrote that

> "The greatest piece of superstition that has ever come within the sphere of our knowledge is one which has for sometime past and still occupies the attention of a few superstitious and bigoted individuals of this quarter... The subject was almost invariably treated as it should have been -- with *contempt*.

Writing in 1842, Hadley looked back on his role:

Soon after the translation was completed, I was one day waited upon by Harris, and offered the printing of the Book of Mormon. This was in the summer of 1829, at which time I was carrying on the printing business at Palmyra. Harris owned a good farm in that town, and offered to mortgage it to secure the expense of printing. Though he was a subscriber to my paper, and had frequently "labored" to convert me to the Mormon faith, I was so sceptical as to utterly refuse to have any "part or lot" in the imposition, telling him at the same time, that if he proceeded with the publication, I should feel it my duty, as the conductor of a faithful public journal, to expose him and the whole Mormon gang. He took the work, however, to the other office in the village, and it was soon put to press. It was then I wrote and published an article, which you may recollect, headed "THE GOLDEN BIBLE," giving a history of the humbug up to that time. This article was extensively copied, it having been the first ever published about the Mormons.[134]

---

[134] See a discussion about Hadley here: http://www.ldshistoricalnarratives.com/2023/08/the-jonathan-hadley-account-and-sith.html

The Rational Restoration

Hadley's 1829 article was widely republished and contributed to the animosity the early Saints encountered in New York, Ohio, Missouri, and Illinois. Joseph Smith responded in the Preface to the 1830 edition of the Book of Mormon when he complained that "many false reports have been circulated respecting the following work." On March 7, 1831, Joseph again addressed the problem of fake news in the media. Then, as now, the media's business model incentivized them to attract readers with sensational stories.

> At this age of the church many false reports, lies, and foolish stories were published in the newspapers, and circulated in every direction, to prevent people from investigating the work, or embracing the faith. A great earthquake in China, which destroyed from one to two hundred thousand inhabitants, was burlesqued in some papers, as "Mormonism in China." But to the joy of the saints who had to struggle against every thing that prejudice and wickedness could invent, I received [D&C 45].[135]

In 1835, the book *Mormonism Unvailed* intensified the opposition. That book speculated that Joseph and Oliver had not even used the plates for the translation, that Joseph had read a manuscript written by Solomon Spaulding, and that the Restoration was a "delusion" and example of "the depths of folly, degradation and superstition, to which human nature can be carried."[136]

Partly in response to *Mormonism Unvailed*, Oliver Cowdery (with the assistance of Joseph Smith) wrote the eight essays on Church history that were published in the *Messenger and Advocate*, copied into Joseph's own journal, and republished in the *Gospel Reflector, Millennial Star, Times and Seasons, The Prophet*, and the *Improvement Era*.

The debates between critics and apologists continue today.

---

[135] History, 1838–1856, volume A-1, p. 104, online at https://www.josephsmithpapers.org/paper-summary/history-1838-1856-volume-a-1-23-december-1805-30-august-1834/110

[136] https://archive.org/details/mormonismunvaile00howe/page/n21/mode/2up

Reframing The Faith Crisis Study

Several events led up to the shift in Church history away from traditional teachings, but the historical record suggests one of the most significant was the Faith Crisis study of 2013 and the impetus it gave to modern critics. While ostensibly a private, good-faith effort to help the Church understand and assist members who were having a faith crisis, the report laid the groundwork for undermining the message of the Restoration by creating a false narrative about Church history; i.e., the claim that the Church had hidden "the truth" about Church history.

Faith Crisis study	
Old narratives	Reframe
The Faith Crisis Report is a good-faith effort to help the Church understand, and assist members who are in the midst of, the epidemic of faith crises caused by the Church having hidden "the truth" about Church history.	The Faith Crisis Report explained why some people lose their faith, but attributed the faith crisis epidemic to a false narrative that the Church had hidden "the truth" about Church history.

In 2012, John Dehlin, Greg Prince and Travis Stratford prepared a report titled Understanding Mormon Disbelief.[137] It included analysis of responses from 3,086 respondents who had once been active believing members of the Church of Jesus Christ of Latter-day Saints but were no longer. The respondents reported the top four factors that contributed to disbelief.

(i) I ceased to believe in the church's doctrine/theology (74%)
(ii) I studied church history and lost my belief (70%)
(iii) I lost faith in Joseph Smith (70%)
(iv) I lost faith in the Book of Mormon (65%)

---

[137] Online at https://faenrandir.github.io/a_careful_examination/2013-faith-crisis-study/.

The Rational Restoration

In 2013 they compiled a report titled "LDS Personal Faith Crisis" that defined a "faith crisis" as

> a state of intense emotional and spiritual distress resulting from the discovery of Church history facts that do not align with the traditional LDS narrative. This distress results in members losing faith in some or all foundational truth claims of the LDS Church and in the Church itself.[138]

The group prepared a supplemental "Faith Crisis Chronicles" consisting of selected responses from over 1,500 participants.[139] The documents were delivered to President Dieter F. Uchtdorf, then Second Counselor in the First Presidency, and other leaders.

In the conclusion of the Faith Crisis study, on page 125, the authors listed four items under "Our Challenge."

> 1. Faith Crisis is a viral challenge affecting individuals, families and ward communities worldwide.
> 2. Today, Faith Crisis is being driven primarily by uncorrelated content propagated by social media.
> 3. The "Mormon Moment" will continue the presentation of uncorrelated information to our membership.
> 4. Unless bold measures are taken to treat those in Faith Crisis and to mitigate the challenge for future generations, significantly more LDS families will become impaired and the future success of the Church will be put at risk.

There are several indicia of an underlying agenda in this list. The claim that Faith Crisis is driven by "uncorrelated content propagated by social media" is a fallacy because "uncorrelated content" can be faith-affirming as well as faith-denying. And "correlated content" can be problematic as well.

One of the authors of this study, John Dehlin, went on to host a podcast called "Mormon Stories" that consists of interviews focused on

---

[138] Page 10, https://faenrandir.github.io/a_careful_examination/documents/faith_crisis_study/Faith_Crisis_R28e.pdf

[139] https://faenrandir.github.io/a_careful_examination/documents/faith_crisis_study/Faith_Crisis_Accounts_R3.pdf

"uncorrelated content" critical of the Church. The Faith Crisis study thus laid the groundwork for Dehlin's podcast. Rather than "mitigating the challenge for future generations," the report provided an outline for exactly how to undermine faith and impair LDS families.

On page 126, the authors propose a method of "breaking the cycle of disaffection" that is replete with their faith-denying rhetoric. The first paragraph worries about future generations "shocked by gaps" that the authors themselves invented.

The second paragraph claims that if "we cannot" give them "good reasons to stay," we risk losing the participation of members having a faith crisis. Dehlin's podcast repeatedly insists that the Church cannot give members good reasons to stay because, according to Dehlin, the Church has lied about its history.

The final paragraph urges struggling members to "share concerns" with others. While that is reasonable in theory, in practice (as shown by his podcast) Dehlin encourages disaffected members to share Dehlin's narrative with other faithful Latter-day Saints.

> 1) Mitigating Faith Crisis for Future Generations
> Mitigating Faith Crisis for future generations is possible but will require bold steps. The key is to ensure future generations no longer become **shocked by gaps between our official LDS narrative and our uncorrelated history**.
>
> 2) Treating Those Currently in Faith Crisis
> Addressing the pain and suffering of members currently in Faith Crisis—and encouraging them to remain faithful and active—is **the more difficult challenge**. However, many of those in Faith Crisis are looking for reasons to stay. Our challenge is to **give them good reasons to stay**. If we cannot, we risk losing their participation.
>
> The first and key point-of-recovery is when **the active member shares concerns** with family, friends, and leaders. Instead of treating that person harshly, our membership—and our leaders—must learn to treat him or her with empathy, compassion, and unconditional love. These struggling members must be embraced to make clear they are wanted and needed (doubts and all)

The Rational Restoration

Next, the report offered suggestions for how to "close the history gap" based on Dehlin's theory that "the history currently taught" is different from the "factual history." The implication: that the history currently taught is not based on facts. But that itself is a false implication.

The first step is the "insight."

> Insight
> The gap between the history currently taught and factual history is—in certain instances—highly differentiated.

It is true that there are multiple accounts of events in early LDS history from a variety of perspectives. This is typical of most historical events.

However, the report simply chooses one set of faith-denying accounts and attaches the label "factual" to them while rejecting the contrary accounts upon which the traditional narrative relied.

Based on the report's "insight," the authors propose a strategy to "inoculate" members by changing the traditional narrative to align more closely with the faith-denying narrative.

> Strategy
> Inoculate current membership and future generations by closing the gap between our historical narrative and factual history.

Finally, the report offers five "possible tactics" to accomplish the inoculation strategy.

The inoculation metaphor is apt because with any inoculation, the initial medical question is whether the shot we administer is inoculating or infecting.

Again, we have the rhetoric implying that traditional Church history is not taught "openly and honestly," that Church materials need to "more accurately depict Church history," and that official position papers should be published.

> Possible Tactics
> · Have a member of the First Presidency deliver a major address to all CES leadership and staff that makes clear the urgent obligation of CES to teach Church history openly and honestly (within a faith- based context).

177

· In an expeditious manner, update CES and other Church manuals and curricula to more accurately depict Church history. Collaborate with respected, non-Church employed historians to add credibility.
· Openly publish official position papers on difficult historical / doctrinal topics. If known answers are inconclusive, concede uncertainty and advance multiple 'viable' answers, including those that may be uncomfortable for the Church.
· Strategically identify difficult issues already being highlighted in the Church's Joseph Smith Papers.
· Place Church history back into the adult curriculum (Relief Society and Priesthood) and provide members a framework for better understanding complicated Church history

Coincidentally or not, on December 6, 2013, the Church published the first of the "Gospel Topics Essays," which we'll discuss below.

The Grievance grifters

Even before the Book of Mormon was published, a cottage industry arose among critics who complained that the "gang of Mormons"[140] were promoting the "greatest piece of superstition."

In recent years, the Internet has enabled a broader variety of critics. Some, usually Christian evangelicals, continue to focus on Bible-bashing, but secular critics emphasize grievances expressed by current and former Latter-day Saints.

These sophisticated "grievance grifters" understand that there is a never-ending stream of people who have legitimate resentments, annoyances, and complaints in all walks of life. Encouraging and amplifying these grievances has become a profitable endeavor in society generally and in the Latter-day Saint community specifically, especially on social media.

We respect the experience and perspective of people who have grievances even when our experience is much different. A rational

---

[140] The quotation is from Jonathan Hadley, who wrote the first "anti-Mormon" article. For an overview of the critics, see https://www.churchofjesuschrist.org/study/history/topics/critics-of-the-book-of-mormon?lang=eng

The Rational Restoration

perspective recognizes that given human nature, difficulties inevitably arise, particularly in a large organization.

There are over 30,000 units in the Church, each one led by a lay minister (Bishop or Branch President), usually assisted by counselors. Each unit has lay leaders of other organizations (including but not limited to Relief Society, Elders Quorum, Primary, Sunday School, Young Men and Young Women). Any one of these leaders, as well as the people they work with, can give or take offense at any moment.

When compared to any comparable set of organizations, particularly voluntary associations with no compensation involved, it is astonishing how well these Church organizations function. Most of the time, Latter-day Saints work well together. They recognize that everyone makes mistakes and that people are doing their best to contribute positively in an effort to reach shared objectives in the pursuit of Zion.

Nevertheless, we all realize that human nature being what it is, grievances arise. In most cases, problems are worked out amicably. But sometimes individuals cannot let them go.

The Church's course on Emotional Resilience, discussed in Chapter 7, offers solutions for handling personal interactions.

Eckhart Tolle writes about the impact of reactivity and grievances.

> There are many people who are always waiting for the next thing to react against, to feel annoyed or disturbed about—and it never takes long before they find it. "This is an outrage," they say. "How dare you...." "I resent this." They are addicted to upset and anger as others are to a drug. Through reacting against this or that they assert and strengthen their feeling of self.
>
> A long-standing resentment is called a grievance. To carry a grievance is to be in a permanent state of "against," and that is why grievances constitute a significant part of many people's ego. ...
>
> One strong grievance is enough to contaminate large areas of your life and keep you in the grip of the ego.[141]

---

[141] Eckhart Tolle, *A New Earth: Awakening to Your Life's Purpose* (Plume 2005): 65.

Obviously, sometimes an event is so egregious that intervention is appropriate and necessary, including legal intervention. Sometimes the impact is so severe that professional counseling is needed. Helping out in these situations, as productive as it is, gives cover for the grievance grifters who profit from the complaining coalition.

Reframing Mormon Stories

Mormon Stories is a website and YouTube channel that has 167,000 subscribers. MormonStories.org explains its background and purpose:

> Founded in 2005, Mormon Stories podcast is the longest running and most popular Mormon-themed podcast. Hosted by Dr. John Dehlin (Clinical/Counseling Psychology), Mormon Stories podcast seeks to understand, explore, challenge, and improve the Mormon experience through stories. Some of the primary objectives of Mormon Stories podcast include:
>
> Providing support to Mormons who are transitioning away from either orthodox Mormonism, or from Mormonism altogether, with a particular emphasis on:
> - Minimizing the anxiety, depression, and occasional suicidality that can accompany a transition away from religious orthodoxy.
> - Reducing the number of unnecessary divorces attributable to Mormon faith crises.
> - Creating a community of support for liberal/progressive and post-Mormons.
> - Building greater awareness regarding accurate LDS/Mormon church history, doctrine, and theology
> – so that both active, believing Mormons and investigators of the church can make informed decisions regarding their investment in, and engagement with the church.
>
> Identifying opportunities for growth/improvement within the LDS church, and within broader Mormon culture.[142]

---

[142] https://www.mormonstories.org/about/

Mormon Stories hosts regular podcasts that attract hundreds of thousands of views with titles such as "The Dark Side of a Mormon Mission," "Mormon Influencer Reads the CES Letter," "The Dark Side of Young Mormon Marriage," and "Mormon Missionary's Parents Leave Church."

The Mormonstories.org website lists dozens of resources about "Mormon Truth Claims," "Navigating a Mormon Faith Crisis," and "Mormon-Themed Podcasts/Youtube Channels."

Whatever the original intentions of John Dehlin—and in the spirit of clarity, charity, and understanding he deserves the benefit of the doubt—his organization has evolved to portraying a highly critical, intolerant, and selectively unrepresentative caricature of the Restoration.

One of Dehlin's stated objectives is to help people to "make informed decisions regarding their investment in, and engagement with the church." The lack of balance on his show obviously contradicts that objective.

The financial demands and rewards of social media continue the long-time media rule of "if it bleeds it leads." Dehlin's headlines reveal what his audience wants to see. Which is fine, of course. People can believe whatever they want.

Dehlin has said that the top three resources that generate a faith crisis among Latter-day Saints are the Gospel Topics Essays (discussed in Chapter 13), *Rough Stone Rolling* (discussed in Chapter 15), and *No Man Knows My History*.

Those seeking clarity, charity and understanding can apply the FAITH model to what Dehlin teaches and then make their own informed decisions.

Reframing the CES Letter

In his original letter to a CES director, Jeremy Runnels wrote, "You may have new information and/or a new perspective that I may not have heard or considered before. This is why I'm genuinely interested in what your answers and thoughts are to these issues."[143]

---

[143] https://read.cesletter.org/introduction/

That CES director apparently never responded to Jeremy's letter, so Jeremy made his letter public. Since then, various LDS apologists have responded, such as FAIR (https://www.fairlatterdaysaints.org/), which provided formal, detailed discussions of the issues Jeremy raised.

The problem: the apologetic responses offered little new information or perspectives that Jeremy had not heard or considered before.

Jeremy has pointed out the logical and factual fallacies that permeate the responses so far. He has collected them here: https://cesletter.org/debunkings/.

Apologists who agree with the premises of the critics compound the problems raised by the critics. On the all/some/none spectrum, many of the apologists are in the "some" category while the CES Letter is in the "none" category

For example, most of the CES Letter's objections to the Book of Mormon are based on the premise that Joseph didn't translate the plates but instead read words off a stone. The LDS apologists agree with that narrative, making their responses unpersuasive.

For more on the CES Letter, https://cesanswers.blogspot.com/.

LDS Critics	
Old narratives	Reframe
Mormon Stories, CES Letter, and other critics simply want to help active, believing Latter-day Saints and investigators of the church to make informed decisions regarding their investment in, and engagement with the church.	Mormon Stories, CES Letter, and other critics base their objections on the faithful M2C and SITH narratives that elevate scholars above the prophets. They reject faithful narratives that corroborate the prophets about the origin and setting of the Book of Mormon.

Reframing apologists

The introduction to this chapter briefly discussed the back-and-forth debates between critics and apologists in the early days of the Church.

Joseph Smith and Oliver Cowdery were directly involved, but they left most of the debating to others, particularly the Pratt brothers (Orson and Parley P.), Benjamin Winchester, William Smith, John Taylor, and other authors.

Apologetics continued through the 1800s and 1900s with Church leaders such as B. H. Roberts, James E. Talmage, and John A. Widtsoe writing books and articles.

Gradually, apologetics shifted more toward academics, primarily staff at BYU but also independent scholars.[144]

In 1979, John W. (Jack) Welch, a lawyer in California, formed The Foundation for Ancient Research and Mormon Studies (FARMS) to promote faithful scholarship.[145] FARMS published a limited geography model (M2C) for the Book of Mormon based on the work of John Sorenson. Eventually it was absorbed by the Neal A. Maxwell Institute at BYU. Two of its principals, Dan Peterson and Jack Welch, moved on to form separate organizations (The Interpreter Foundation and Book of Mormon Central, respectively).

Meanwhile, in 1997, another group of Latter-day Saints formed an organization now called FAIR (Faithful Answers, Informed Response).[146] They adopted the M2C model for Book of Mormon setting and the SITH explanation for the origin of the Book of Mormon.

Reframing the Interpreter

The Interpreter Foundation was founded in 2012 by Daniel Peterson as a sort of sequel to FARMS. Like FAIR, the editorial board adopted the M2C and SITH models. The organization produced a feature movie, *Witnesses*, that depicts SITH.

The Interpreter Foundation's name is ironic because their editorial position rejects Joseph Smith as using the Urim and Thummim to

---

[144] See: https://en.wikipedia.org/wiki/Category:Mormon_apologists
[145] See https://en.wikipedia.org/wiki/Foundation_for_Ancient_Research_and_Mormon_Studies and https://www.templestudy.com/2012/06/25/rise-fall-farms/
[146] https://www.fairlatterdaysaints.org/

translate the plates. The name suggests an assumption of authority as the "interpreter" for ordinary Latter-day Saints.

The organization publishes scholarly articles weekly and produces a regular radio show/podcast. The people involved with the Interpreter are all thoughtful, faithful scholars and fine people, but in my view they are intolerant of alternative faithful perspectives. I've published a blog on their work.[147]

Reframing Book of Mormon Central

Book of Mormon Central (BMC) is a non-profit subsidiary of the Book of Mormon Archaeological Foundation (BMAF.org). BMC was founded by Jack Welch and began operating in May 2015. It has raised and spent millions of dollars to create extensive websites and social media presence.

BMC, FAIR, and the Interpreter have interlocking staff and a united front when it comes to promoting SITH and M2C.

BMC has expanded its presence with several websites under its umbrella, including Scripture Central. But with respect to the origin and setting of the Book of Mormon, it strictly enforces the views of its editorial board; i.e., SITH is the origin and M2C is the setting.

This is evident in the logo BMC used until 2023, which uses a Mayan glyph to represent the Book of Mormon. They embedded M2C right in their logo.

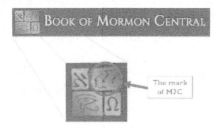

This is the same logo that FARMS (which promoted M2C for decades) used before the principals left to form the Interpreter Foundation and Book of Mormon Central.

---

[147] https://interpreterpeerreviews.blogspot.com/

In early 2023, Book of Mormon Central changed its logo to a more generic starburst, but it has not changed its editorial insistence on only one acceptable interpretation of the Book of Mormon setting.

Although retired from BMC's main site, one of BMC's umbrella websites, "Seminary Central," has retained the M2C logo to indoctrinate young Latter-day Saints.

The organization makes M2C explicit in its Spanish-language site, where they teach Spanish-speaking readers about a specific Mesoamerican (M2C) setting without informing them what Church leaders have said about Cumorah.

https://geografia.centralldm.es/

BMC does not make this website available in English, so most English-speaking Latter-day Saints don't realize what BMC is doing.

Like most of the Joseph Smith Papers, Oliver Cowdery's eight essays on Church history have never been officially translated into Spanish (or any other language). This means Letter VII has never been officially translated into Spanish—except for the translation of my book on Letter VII.[148]

Once I shared the Spanish version of Letter VII with a former Stake President from Guatemala. He was shocked and angry that he had never been told what the prophets have taught about Cumorah. His fellow Saints from Spanish-speaking countries will feel the same once they realize how they have been manipulated by BMC.

BMC has tremendous potential to unite Latter-day Saints in the pursuit of clarity, charity and understanding. The BMC staff are top-notch scholars, faithful Latter-day Saints, and good people.

Unfortunately, as of this writing the organization has chosen instead to allow only one interpretation of the origin (SITH) and setting (M2C) of the Book of Mormon.

LDS Apologists	
Old narratives	Reframe
FAIR, Interpreter, and Book of Mormon Central are faithful, scholarly organizations that defend the Gospel and the Church.	FAIR, Interpreter, and Book of Mormon Central are advocacy groups for M2C and SITH which elevate scholars above the prophets. They reject faithful narratives that corroborate the prophets about the origin and setting of the Book of Mormon.

---

[148] The illustrated book that explains Letter VII is available in Spanish in Kindle, here: https://www.amazon.com.mx/Lemures-Camaleones-y-Planchas-Oro-ebook/dp/B09LB65HSH/

13: Reframing the Gospel Topics Essays

People often ask what I think about the Gospel Topics Essays.

The introduction to the essays perfectly expresses my approach to Church history, doctrine and practices. "The Church places great emphasis on knowledge and on the importance of being well informed about Church history, doctrine, and practices."

I encourage people to be well informed so they can make informed decisions. As President Nelson has said, "Good inspiration is based upon good information."

My position is simple.

The Gospel Topics Essays are useful resources that point to reliable sources. They have not been canonized. They have been revised in the past and can be revised and improved at any moment. I point out errors and omissions in the essays because I'm hopeful that the essays will continue to be improved, particularly by including the relevant and reliable sources from the Joseph Smith Papers that have so far been omitted.

I agree with and embrace what President Russell M. Ballard said about the essays being important. I *encourage* people to read and study the essays because they contain useful references to reliable sources.

But nowhere have Church leaders stated, suggested, or implied that these essays were ever intended to replace the scriptures, the teachings of the prophets, or authentic historical documents.

A memo dated Sept. 9 from the church's "Priesthood Department" to "General Authorities; Area Seventies; Stake, Mission, and District Presidents; Bishops and Branch Presidents" explains the purpose of — and audience for — the essays.

> The purpose of the Gospel Topics section is to provide accurate and transparent information on church history and doctrine within the framework of faith... When church members have questions regarding [LDS] history and doctrine, possibly arising when detractors spread

misinformation and doubt, you may want to direct their attention to these resources.

Leaders should emphasize that "prayer, regular study of the scriptures and the teachings of the living prophets, the exercise of faith, and humility are fundamental to receiving inspired answers to sincere questions."

Nevertheless, some people inside and outside the Church refer to the essays as though they have been canonized.

I encourage people to read the essays partly because the introduction to those essays perfectly expresses my objection to those who insist on their own private theories about Church history and related topics.

Old narratives	Reframe
The Gospel Topics Essays constitute Church doctrine	The Gospel Topics Essays are anonymous and do not replace the scriptures or the teachings of the prophets.

Old narratives	Reframe
The Gospel Topics Essays represent official Church doctrine and cannot be questioned	The Gospel Topics Essays were written by anonymous scholars and were intended as a resource for study and consideration, but are subject to change at any time without notice and do not replace the standard works or teachings of Church leaders

Old narratives	Reframe
The Church has hired scholars to guide members in matters of Church history and scriptural interpretation, and to maintain and enforce orthodoxy.	The Church has hired scholars to do scholarly research and encourages members to make their own informed decisions.

The introduction[149] to the essays quotes D&C 88:118 and explains that "Seeking 'out of the best books' does not mean seeking only one set of opinions, but it does require us to distinguish between reliable sources and unreliable sources."

Contrary to that guidance, some scholars (both faithful and critical) insist on "only one set of opinions" that consists of the consensus among those scholars. I don't object that they promote different interpretations than I do. That's fine with me. I fully endorse the concept of multiple working hypotheses. My problem with these faithful scholars is the same as my problem with the critics; both groups deprive people of good information through censorship and sophistry purely to promote their respective agendas.

In other words, they don't see clarity, charity and understanding.

———

To reiterate, it is also important to recognize that the Gospel Topics Essays have been revised in the past and can be revised and improved at any moment.

I point out errors and omissions in the essays because I'm hopeful that the essays will continue to be improved, particularly by including the reliable sources from the Joseph Smith Papers that have so far been omitted.

One example is the Gospel Topics entry on Book of Mormon geography.

Gospel Topics entry on Book of Mormon Geography

After it was first published in January 2019, I made some suggestions (in **bold** below) on 4 February 2019. About three weeks later, the entry was revised, as shown in the following table. This example shows the Gospel Topics Essays are subject to improvement at any time.

———

[149] https://www.churchofjesuschrist.org/study/manual/gospel-topics-essays/essays?lang=eng

Original (Jan 2019)	My comments (4 Feb 2019)	Revised (27 Feb 2019)
Book of Mormon Geography Overview	Book of Mormon Geography Overview	Book of Mormon Geography Overview
The Church takes no position on the specific geographic location of Book of Mormon events in the ancient Americas. Church members are asked not to teach theories about Book of Mormon geography in Church settings but to focus instead on the Book of Mormon's teachings and testimony of Jesus Christ and His gospel.	**Apart from the Hill Cumorah in western New York,** the Church takes no position… Comment: Church leaders, including members of the First Presidency and Quorum of the Twelve, have consistently and persistently taught that the Hill Cumorah referred to in Mormon 6 is the same hill in western New York from which Joseph Smith, Jr., obtained the ancient Nephite records that he translated into the Book of Mormon. To date, no member of either of these quorums has ever officially questioned or repudiated the teachings of his predecessors.	[overview deleted] The Church takes no position on the specific geographic location of Book of Mormon events in the ancient Americas. Church members are asked not to teach theories about Book of Mormon geography in Church settings but to focus instead on the Book of Mormon's teachings and testimony of Jesus Christ and His gospel. [no change]
The Book of Mormon includes a history of an ancient people who migrated from the Near East to the Americas. This history contains information about the places they lived, including descriptions of	The Book of Mormon includes a history of an ancient people who migrated from the Near East to the Americas. This history contains information about the places they lived, including descriptions of	The Book of Mormon includes a history of an ancient people who migrated from the Near East to the Americas. This history contains information about the places they lived, including descriptions of

landforms, natural features, and the distances and cardinal directions between important points. The internal consistency of these descriptions is one of the striking features of the Book of Mormon.	landforms, natural features, and the distances and cardinal directions between important points. The internal consistency of these descriptions is one of the striking features of the Book of Mormon. Explanation: No change suggested because neither Joseph Smith nor Oliver Cowdery left a clear statement about where Lehi landed.	landforms, natural features, and the distances and cardinal directions between important points. The internal consistency of these descriptions is one of the striking features of the Book of Mormon. [no change]
Since the publication of the Book of Mormon in 1830, members and leaders of The Church of Jesus Christ of Latter-day Saints have expressed numerous opinions about the specific locations of the events discussed in the book.	**Leaders of The Church of Jesus Christ of Latter-day Saints have consistently taught that the Hill Cumorah referred to in Mormon 6 is in western New York.** **The New York Cumorah was declared to be a fact in an important essay written by Oliver Cowdery, as Assistant President of the Church, with the assistance of Joseph Smith. Published in 1835 as "Letter VII" in the *Messenger and Advocate* and republished in other Church newspapers, Letter VII was also copied into Joseph's personal his-**	Since the publication of the Book of Mormon in 1830, members and leaders of The Church of Jesus Christ of Latter-day Saints have expressed numerous opinions about the specific locations of the events discussed in the book. [no change]

	tory, where it can be read today in the **Joseph Smith Papers.** <u>https://www.josephsmithpapers.org/paper-summary/history-1834-1836/90</u> **Regarding the specific locations of other events discussed in the book, however, members and leaders have expressed numerous opinions.** <u>Explanation</u>: Church leaders have made a clear distinction between formal, published teachings about the New York Cumorah, which have never varied, and expressions about other locations, which have been private and/or speculative.	
Some believe that the history depicted in the Book of Mormon occurred in North America, while others believe that it occurred in Central America or South America. Although Church members continue to discuss such theories today, the Church takes no position	Some believe that the history depicted in the Book of Mormon occurred in North America, while others believe that it occurred in Central America or South America. Although Church members continue to discuss such theories today, the Church takes no position	Some believe that the history depicted in the Book of Mormon — **with the exception of the events in the Near East**—occurred in North America, while others believe that it occurred in Central America or South America. Although Church members continue to discuss

on the geography of the Book of Mormon except that the events it describes took place in the Americas.	on the geography of the Book of Mormon except that the events it describes took place in the Americas **and that the Hill Cumorah is in western New York.** Explanation: It is critical to keep the two separate elements distinct.	such theories today, the Church's only position is that the events the Book of Mormon describes took place in the ancient Americas. [This changes the former statement of "no position except" to "only position is." The term "Americas" is a recent development. The Church History Department uses it to replace what the historical documents actually say. Moroni and Joseph Smith both referred to the aborigines in "this country," but that causes problems for M2C, so instead we always see "Americas" instead. The same tactic was used in the *Saints* book to write Cumorah out of Church history.]
The Prophet Joseph Smith himself accepted what he felt was evidence of Book of Mormon civilizations in both North America and Central America. While traveling with Zion's Camp in 1834, Joseph wrote to his wife Emma that they were "wandering over the plains of the Nephites,	**The Prophet Joseph Smith himself personally linked locations in North America with the Book of Mormon.** While traveling with Zion's Camp in 1834, Joseph wrote to his wife Emma that they were "wandering over the plains of the Nephites, recounting occasionally the history of the Book	The Prophet Joseph Smith himself accepted what he felt was evidence of Book of Mormon civilizations in both North America and Central America. While traveling with Zion's Camp in 1834, Joseph wrote to his wife Emma that they were "wandering over the plains of the Nephites,

recounting occasionally the history of the Book of Mormon, roving over the mounds of that once beloved people of the Lord, picking up their skulls and their bones, as a proof of its divine authenticity."1 In 1842, the Church newspaper *Times and Seasons* published articles under Joseph Smith's editorship that identified the ruins of ancient native civilizations in Mexico and Central America as further evidence of the Book of Mormon's historicity.2 Note 2: "Traits of the Mosaic History, Found among the Azteca Nation," *Times and Seasons*, June 15, 1842, 818–20; see also "American Antiquities," *Times and Seasons*, July 15, 1842, 858–60. Although it is not clear how involved Joseph Smith was in writing these editorials, he never refuted them.	of Mormon, roving over the mounds of that once beloved people of the Lord, picking up their skulls and their bones, as a proof of its divine authenticity."1 **Others, contemporary with Joseph Smith, suggested other locations. In 1842, the Church newspaper *Times and Seasons* published anonymous articles that identified the ruins of ancient native civilizations in Mexico and Central America as further evidence of the Book of Mormon's historicity.2** **Unlike the anonymous editorials, Joseph Smith signed an article titled "Church History," published in the March 1842 *Times and Seasons*, commonly referred to as the Wentworth letter. In this article, Joseph adapted the contents of a pamphlet written by Elder Orson Pratt, a member of the Quorum of the Twelve. Pratt had speculated at length about evidence**	recounting occasionally the history of the Book of Mormon, roving over the mounds of that once beloved people of the Lord, picking up their skulls and their bones, as a proof of its divine authenticity."1 In 1842, the Church newspaper *Times and Seasons* published articles under Joseph Smith's editorship that identified the ruins of ancient native civilizations in Mexico and Central America as further evidence of the Book of Mormon's historicity.2 Note 2: "Traits of the Mosaic History, Found among the Azteca Nation," *Times and Seasons*, June 15, 1842, 818–20; see also "American Antiquities," *Times and Seasons*, July 15, 1842, 858–60. Although it is not clear how involved Joseph Smith was in writing these editorials, he never refuted them. [No change; i.e., the essay retains the misleading opening sentence which the rest of the essay debunks.]

for the Book of Mormon in Central America.

Joseph replaced Pratt's speculation with the simple statement that "The remnant are the Indians that live in this country."3

In October 1842, the *Times and Seasons* published a letter written and signed by Joseph Smith and sent to the editor for publication.

Now canonized as D&C 128:20, the letter included this: "And again, what do we hear? Glad tidings from Cumorah! Moroni, an angel from heaven, declaring the fulfilment of the prophets—the book to be revealed."

Note 2: "Traits of the Mosaic History, Found among the Azteca Nation," Times and Seasons, June 15, 1842, 818–20; see also "American Antiquities," *Times and Seasons*, July 15, 1842, 858–60. **Although Joseph Smith was listed as the nominal editor of**

	the *Times and Seasons* at the time, he never explicitly approved of or rejected these editorials. Note 3: "Church History," Times and Seasons, March 1, 1842, republished in the Joseph Smith Papers with Historical Background notes here: https://www.josephsmithpapers.org/paper-summary/church-history-1-march-1842/1 <u>Explanation</u>: The proposed changes are necessary to clarify the historical facts and distinguish between fact and inference.	
Anthony W. Ivins, a Counselor in the First Presidency, stated: "There has never been anything yet set forth that definitely settles that question [of Book of Mormon geography]. So the Church says we are just waiting until we discover the truth."3	**President Anthony W. Ivins, a Counselor in the First Presidency, made clear the distinction between the known location of Cumorah in New York and the uncertain locations of other Book of Mormon geography in two General Conference addresses. In April 1928, shortly after the Church purchased the hill Cumorah in New York,**	The Ivins quote was deleted instead of put in context.

	President Ivins described that hill and stated: "We know that all of these records, all the sacred records of the Nephite people, were deposited by Mormon in that hill." 4

The following year, President Ivins stated: "There has never been anything yet set forth that definitely settles that question **[of the location of Zarahemla and other sites].** So the Church says we are just waiting until we discover the truth."**5**

Note 4. Anthony W. Ivins, in Conference Report, Apr. 1928, 16.

Note 5. (same as original note 3)
<u>Explanation</u>: The original version of the essay omitted the context of President Ivins' statements. The revisions provide the full context for clarity and accuracy. | |
| The Church urges local leaders and members not to advocate theories of Book of Mormon geography in official | The Church urges local leaders and members not to advocate theories of Book of Mormon geography in official | The Church does not take a position on the specific geographic locations of Book of Mormon events in the ancient Americas. |

Church settings.	Church settings. **Such advocacy includes illustrations, artwork, media, and exhibits on web pages including churchofjesuschrist.org and in Church buildings, publications, visitors centers, etc.** Explanation: The original version of the essay implied that visual depictions were authorized, while advocacy was not.	President M. Russell Ballard, Acting President of the Quorum of the Twelve Apostles, reminded members that "the Book of Mormon is not a textbook on topography. Speculation on the geography of the Book of Mormon may mislead instead of enlighten; such a study can be a distraction from its divine purpose." Comment. This paragraph basically restates the original paragraph about "the Church's only position," using the term "Americas." President Ballard's quotation replaces President Ivins' but the authors forgot to provide a footnote. It is undoubtedly true that speculation on geography can be a distraction, but it is also a distraction to ignore or, worse, reject the teachings of past prophets.
		Individuals may have their own opinions regarding Book of Mormon geography and other such matters about which the Lord has not

	spoken.

Comment. This new sentence raises the question, how do we know when the Lord has spoken? We understand that the Lord speaks through his prophets, every one of whom has affirmed the New York Cumorah when they have addressed the topic. This sentence could mean that individuals may have their own opinions about geography other than the New York Cumorah. If the sentence is intended to repudiate the teachings of past prophets, that should be made clear. |
| | However, the First Presidency and Quorum of the Twelve Apostles urge leaders and members not to advocate those personal theories in any setting or manner that would imply either prophetic or Church support for those theories.

[Comment. Presumably this sentence does not repudiate the clear teachings of past prophets about Cumorah but instead is focused on |

		non-Cumorah theories.]
		All parties should strive to avoid contention on these matters. [Comment. There's no reason to contend about any of this. Everyone involved should have equal access to the relevant facts derive their own interpretations as multiple working hypotheses.]
Speaking of the book's history and geography, President Russell M. Nelson taught: "Interesting as these matters may be, study of the Book of Mormon is most rewarding when one focuses on its primary purpose—to testify of Jesus Christ. By comparison, all other issues are incidental."<u>4</u>	[no change suggested]	[no change]

I realize that Book of Mormon geography can generate strong feelings that detract from the message of Christ. But when we seek clarity, charity and understanding, the topic encourages readers to see all the evidence of the divine authenticity of the record—just as Joseph Smith observed when he crossed "the plains of the Nephites" in Ohio, Indiana and Illinois.

Gospel Topics Essay on Book of Mormon Translation

This essay is found at this web page: https://www.churchofjesuschrist.org/manual/gospel-topics-essays/book-of-mormon-translation?lang=eng

The essay thoughtfully tackles an issue that has no readily apparent resolution. As you read the essay, however, you will notice that although it quotes many observers and commentators, it never quotes what Joseph Smith and Oliver Cowdery taught about the Urim and Thummim.

Not even once.

The essay does include a few quotations from Joseph and Oliver, but it edits those quotations to *omit* their references to the term *Urim and Thummim*.

This is a strange editorial decision for an essay that is intended to educate people about this important topic.

Although the essay has undergone undocumented changes over time, the online version has not changed since at least December 2019 and it makes speculative assumptions that lead to speculative conclusions. The essay omits important facts. It does not acknowledge, let alone discuss, alternative interpretations of the known facts.

I included a similar review is in the appendix of the second edition of my book *A Man that Can Translate: Joseph Smith and the Nephite Interpreters*. In the book I propose a revised essay.

Except as indicated, all footnotes to the essay are original. My annotations are in brackets and **bold** typeface.

Book of Mormon Translation

Essay	Comment
Joseph Smith said that the Book of Mormon was "the most correct of any Book on earth & the keystone of our religion & a man would get nearer to God by abiding by its precepts than by	It's good to see the original source cited here. As indicated in the footnote, this is a quotation from Wilford Woodruff's summary of a day's teaching, not a direct quotation

any other Book."[1]	of something Joseph said. Woodruff did not put the sentence in quotation marks, as he often did when recording a direct quotation. Nevertheless, Church historians converted it into a first-person quotation in History of the Church and other publications. I hope this is a first step toward correcting the misquotation that appears still today in the Introduction to the Book of Mormon[2] in every copy.
The Book of Mormon came into the world through a series of miraculous events. Much can be known about the coming forth of the English text of the Book of Mormon through a careful study of statements made by Joseph Smith, his scribes, and others closely associated with the translation of the Book of Mormon.	Note: Although this paragraph suggests a careful study of Joseph Smith's statements, the essay actually omits every one of Joseph's statements in which he used the term *Urim and Thummim*.
"By the Gift and Power of God"	
Joseph Smith reported that on the evening of September 21, 1823, while he prayed in the upper room of his parents' small log home in Palmyra, New York, an angel who called himself Moroni appeared and told Joseph that "God had a work for [you] to do."[3]	The quotation is from what is now Joseph Smith—History 1:33. That verse identifies the angel as Moroni. The original version was published in the *Times and Seasons* on 15 April 1842.[4] There, the angel who visited was identified as Nephi. Lucy Mack Smith's history quoted the *Times and Seasons*, also identifying the angel as Nephi.[5] Some have wondered why the compilers of this history would have identified the angel as "Nephi" and why Joseph, supposedly the active editor of the *Times and Seasons* when this account was published, would not

	have "corrected" the identification. One reason could be that Joseph was merely the nominal editor; i.e., someone else was the actual editor. (That's what I think the evidence shows.) Another could be that the compilers knew Joseph interacted with both Moroni and Nephi and weren't sure which one appeared in 1823.

Brigham Young taught that Joseph had interactions with Nephi (one of the unnamed three Nephites from 3 Nephi 28) as well as with Moroni.

One such incident can be pieced together from the historical record. Before leaving Harmony in May/June 1829, Joseph gave the plates to a divine messenger he later identified as "one of the Nephites." The same messenger later showed the Fayette plates to Mary Whitmer. She said he identified himself as Brother Nephi.

The essay's footnote discusses the identity of the angel, citing a note in the Joseph Smith Papers that in turn quotes President Oliver Cowdery's 1835 Letter IV as authority for the identity of the angel as Moroni. |
| He informed Joseph that "there was a book deposited, written upon gold plates, giving an account of the former inhabitants of this continent, and the source from whence they sprang." | The quotation is from Joseph Smith—History 1:33 |
| The book could be found in a hill not far from the Smith family farm. | This is an uncredited paraphrase of President Cowdery's 1835 Letter IV, in which Moroni tells Joseph "this history was written and deposited <u>not</u> |

	far from that place [Joseph's home near Palmyra]." Letter IV gives additional details from this visit that relate to the translation, but these details are omitted in this essay. The angel "proceeded and gave a general account of the promises made to the fathers, and also gave a history of the aborigenes of this country, and said they were literal descendants of Abraham…. He said this history was written and deposited not far from that place [Joseph's home near Palmyra], and that it was our brother's privilege, if obedient to the commandments of the Lord, to obtain and translate the same by the means of the Urim and Thummim, which were deposited for that purpose with the record.[6]
This was no ordinary history, for it contained "the fullness of the everlasting Gospel as delivered by the Savior."[7]	This is another quotation from Joseph Smith—History 1:34. Oddly, the next verse, 35, is never quoted or cited in the essay. That verse explains what accompanied the plates: "Also, that there were two stones in silver bows—and these stones, fastened to a breastplate, constituted what is called the Urim and Thummim—deposited with the plates; and the possession and use of these stones were what constituted "seers" in ancient or former times; and that God had prepared them for the purpose of translating the book."
The angel charged Joseph Smith to translate the book from the ancient language in which it was written.	While true, this sentence is a misleading setup for the thesis of the essay because it omits Moroni's explanation that Joseph would translate the plates by means of the

	Urim and Thummim that came with the plates. The Urim and Thummim was specifically prepared for a seer to translate the unknown language.
The young man, however, had very little formal education and was incapable of writing a book on his own, let alone translating an ancient book written from an unknown language, known in the Book of Mormon as "reformed Egyptian."[8]	Joseph's formal education was limited to three years, but he knew the many Biblical passages Moroni quoted well enough to discern that Moroni had quoted some exactly and changed the wording in other passages. Joseph was also "intimately familiar" with Christian doctrines and writings.
Joseph's wife Emma insisted that, at the time of translation, Joseph "could neither write nor dictate a coherent and well-worded letter, let alone dictat[e] a book like the Book of Mormon."[9]	Emma purportedly related this statement to her son, Joseph Smith III, in 1879. The account was published after her death. Emma never publicly acknowledged the statement. We discussed it in Chapter 4. The full statement is in Appendix 4.
Joseph received the plates in September 1827 and the following spring, in Harmony, Pennsylvania, began translating them in earnest, with Emma and his friend Martin Harris serving as his main scribes.	It's not clear exactly when Emma served as a scribe, but according to her "Last Testimony" she wrote while Joseph stared at a stone in a hat, and she said he did that only after the 116 pages were lost. Joseph said she wrote for him after he received back the Urim and Thummim and the plates after the 116 pages were lost. See quotations below.
The resulting English transcription, known as the Book of Lehi and referred to by Joseph Smith as written on 116 pages, was subsequently lost or stolen. As a result, Joseph Smith was rebuked by the Lord and lost the ability to translate for a short time.[10]	The essay doesn't explain what "lost the ability to translate" means, but Lucy Mack Smith explained that Joseph had to give up the Urim and Thummim after losing the 116 pages. Later, Joseph told her that "on the 22d of September [1828], I had the joy and satisfaction of again receiving the Urim and Thummim; and have commenced translating again, and Emma writes for me; but the angel

	said that the Lord would send me a scribe, and I trust his promise will be verified. He also seemed pleased with me, when he gave me back the Urim and Thummim; and he told me that the Lord loved me, for my faithfulness and humility. "Soon after I received them I inquired of the Lord, and obtained the following revelation": "Now, behold I say unto you, that, because <you> delivered up those writings, which you had power given you to translate, by the means of the Urim and Thummim into the hands of a wicked man, you have lost them; and you also lost your gift at the same time, and your mind became darkened;"[11] Notice how the Urim and Thummim was directly linked to Joseph's ability to translate throughout this incident. The essay explains none of this; it merely says Joseph "lost the ability to translate for a short time."
Joseph began translating again in 1829, and almost all of the present Book of Mormon text was translated during a three-month period between April and June of that year.	This contradicts Emma's "Last Testimony," which states "In writing for your father I frequently wrote day after day, often sitting at the table close by him, he sitting with his face buried in his hat, with the stone in it, and dictating hour after hour with nothing between us." Separately, Emma said that "Now the first that my husband translated was translated by the use of the Urim and Thummim, and that was the part that Martin

The Rational Restoration

His chief scribe during these months was Oliver Cowdery, a schoolteacher from Vermont who learned about the Book of Mormon while boarding with Joseph's parents in Palmyra. Called by God in a vision, Cowdery traveled to Harmony to meet Joseph Smith and investigate further. Of his experience as scribe, Cowdery wrote, "These were days never to be forgotten—to sit under the sound of a voice dictated by the *inspiration* of heaven."[12]

Harris lost, after that he used a small stone, not exactly, black, but was rather a dark color."

This quotation is from President Cowdery's Letter I, now canonized as a footnote to Joseph Smith – History 1:71.[13] The essay terminates the quotation just before the following sentence that directly pertains to the translation:

"Day after day I continued, uninterrupted, to write from his mouth, as he translated with the Urim and Thummim, or, as the Nephites would have said, 'Interpreters,' the history or record called 'The Book of Mormon.'"

Oliver said the entire text was translated with the Urim and Thummim. This is consistent with Letter IV, quoted above, in which Moroni told Joseph he would "translate the same by the means of the Urim and Thummim, which were deposited for that purpose with the record." Oliver does not mention any seer stone or hat.

The essay omits other relevant passages from Joseph Smith—History. Besides JS-H 1:35 (quoted above), the essay omits these verses:

JS-H 1:42 Again, he told me, that when I got those plates of which he had spoken—for the time that they should be obtained was not yet fulfilled—I should not show them to

207

	any person; neither the breastplate with the Urim and Thummim; only to those to whom I should be commanded to show them; if I did I should be destroyed. JS-H 1:62 By this timely aid was I enabled to reach the place of my destination in Pennsylvania; and immediately after my arrival there I commenced copying the characters off the plates. I copied a considerable number of them, and by means of the Urim and Thummim I translated some of them, which I did between the time I arrived at the house of my wife's father, in the month of December, and the February following.
The manuscript that Joseph Smith dictated to Oliver Cowdery and others is known today as the original manuscript, about 28 percent of which still survives.[14] This manuscript corroborates Joseph Smith's statements that the manuscript was written within a short time frame and that it was dictated from another language. For example, it includes errors that suggest the scribe heard words incorrectly rather than misread words copied from another manuscript.[15]	Actually, there are relatively few misheard words, which suggests that Joseph and Oliver were working in relatively quiet conditions, free from distractions.

No comment on the following section of the essay.

In addition, some grammatical constructions that are more characteristic of Near Eastern languages than English appear in the original manuscript, suggesting that the base language of the translation was not English.[16]

Unlike most dictated drafts, the original manuscript was considered by Joseph Smith to be, in substance, a final product. To assist in the publication of the book, Oliver Cowdery made a handwritten copy of the original manuscript.

The Rational Restoration

This copy is known today as the printer's manuscript. Because Joseph Smith did not call for punctuation, such as periods, commas, or question marks as he dictated, such marks are not in the original manuscript. The typesetter later inserted punctuation marks when he prepared the text for the printer.[17] With the exceptions of punctuation, formatting, other elements of typesetting, and minor adjustments required to correct copying and scribal errors, the dictation copy became the text of the first printed edition of the book.[18]

Translation Instruments

Many accounts in the Bible show that God transmitted revelations to His prophets in a variety of ways. Elijah learned that God spoke not to him through the wind or fire or earthquake but through a "still small voice."[19] Paul and other early apostles sometimes communicated with angels and, on occasion, with the Lord Jesus Christ.[20] At other times, revelation came in the form of dreams or visions, such as the revelation to Peter to preach the gospel to the Gentiles, or through sacred objects like the Urim and Thummim.[21]

Joseph Smith stands out among God's prophets, because he was called to render into his own language an entire volume of scripture amounting to more than 500 printed pages, containing doctrine that would deepen and expand the theological understanding of millions of people. For this monumental task, God prepared additional, practical help in the form of physical instruments.

Joseph Smith and his scribes wrote of two instruments used in translating the Book of Mormon.	This is a misleading sentence. First, Joseph never wrote of any instrument other than the Urim and Thummim. Second, Oliver Cowdery, his main scribe for all but a few pages of the Book of Mormon we have today, never wrote of any instrument other than the Urim and Thummim. Presumably the sentence refers to Martin Harris and Emma Smith, neither of whom said Joseph used the Urim and Thummim to translate the text we have today. But neither of them acted as scribes for the text we have today, either.
According to witnesses of the translation, when Joseph looked into	This sentence assumes facts not in evidence. The only person who looked

the instruments, the words of scripture appeared in English.	into the instruments was Joseph Smith. We have no record of a direct statement by Joseph about what he saw or how he used the instruments, except that he used them to translate. No witness claimed that Joseph told them what he saw. Their statements reflect inference, assumption, and conjecture. Furthermore, these witnesses could not have seen the actual translation because Joseph was forbidden to show them either the plates or the Urim and Thummim. Instead, the evidence suggests they merely observed a demonstration. All of their statements are consistent with having observed a demonstration, not the actual translation of the plates.]
One instrument, called in the Book of Mormon the "interpreters," is better known to Latter-day Saints today as the "Urim and Thummim." Joseph found the interpreters buried in the hill with the plates.[22]	Joseph himself referred to the Nephite interpreters as the "Urim and Thummim," as is plain throughout Joseph Smith—History and his other accounts of Moroni's visit.
Those who saw the interpreters described them as a clear pair of stones bound together with a metal rim. The Book of Mormon referred to this instrument, together with its breastplate, as a device "kept and preserved by the hand of the Lord" and "handed down from generation to generation, for the purpose of interpreting languages."[23]	this is the only instrument that Oliver and Joseph ever said that Joseph used during the translation. As indicated in the footnote, some scholars assume it was W.W. Phelps who coined the term "Urim and Thummim" for the interpreters because Phelps' article in the 1833 *Evening and Morning Star* is the earliest extant published account that uses that term. However, Phelps' article is also consistent with prior use

of the term, whether verbal or printed; i.e., Phelps was providing an explanation of the term for readers who were familiar with the Bible. **Besides,** the first known use of the term *Urim and Thummim* to refer to the Nephite interpreters was reported on August 5, 1832, when Orson Hyde and Samuel Smith told an audience in Boston that the translation "was made known by the spirit of the Lord through the medium of the Urim and Thummim."[24] Of course, Orson and Samuel undoubtedly heard that from someone else—presumably Joseph or Oliver.

Letter IV portrays Moroni telling Joseph that it was his privilege "to obtain and translate the same by the means of the Urim and Thummim, which were deposited for that purpose with the record." When Oliver wrote these letters, he explained he was using original documents then in their possession. He could have referred to the notebook he kept during the translation process, in which he recorded the things Joseph told him. In other words, it could have been Moroni, not W.W. Phelps, who first identified the interpreters as the Urim and Thummim.

The footnote observes that Joseph "most often used the term "Urim and Thummim," but does not explain that we have no record of Joseph ever using the term seer stone in connection with the translation.

The other instrument, which Joseph Smith discovered in the ground years before he retrieved the gold plates, was a small oval stone, or "seer stone."[25] As a young man during the 1820s, Joseph Smith, like others in his day, used a seer stone to look for lost objects and buried treasure.[26] As Joseph grew to understand his prophetic calling, he learned that he could use this stone for the higher purpose of translating scripture.[27]	The last sentence is pure speculation, portrayed here as fact. There are no historical records in which Joseph says or implies anything like this.
Apparently for convenience, Joseph often translated with the single seer stone rather than the two stones bound together to form the interpreters.	This is also pure speculation, portrayed as fact. Neither Joseph nor Oliver ever said he used one seer stone to translate the text. As I explain in Chapter 4, others observed Joseph dictating words, but none of them reported what the words were. None quoted Joseph saying he was translating the plates during these occasions. These accounts are consistent with people who observed a demonstration and inferred it was the actual translation. But they also said Joseph did not use the Urim and Thummim or the plates, so by their own admission, they did not observe what Joseph and Oliver described about the actual translation.
These two instruments—the interpreters and the seer stone—were apparently interchangeable and worked in much the same way such that, in the course of time, Joseph Smith and his associates often used the term "Urim and Thummim" to refer to the single stone as well as the interpreters.[28]	Although the essay claims Joseph and his associates "often" used the term to refer to a seer stone, the footnote gives only one example, and that example doesn't support the claim. On December 27, 1841, Wilford Woodruff recorded in his journal "The Twelve or a part of them spent the day with Joseph the seer + he

unfolded unto them many glorious things of the kingdom of God the privileges + blessings of the priesthood + I had the privilege of seeing for the first time in my day the URIM & THUMMIM."[29]

Woodruff does not describe the object, leaving historians to *surmise* he was referring to the seer stone so many people reported seeing Joseph use years previously.

If Woodruff was referring to the seer stone that many people had already seen, he doesn't explain why it was such a privilege.

On February 19, 1842, Woodruff recorded in his journal that "the Lord is Blessing Joseph with Power to reveal the mysteries of the kingdom of God; to translate through the Urim and Thummim Ancient records."

Lucy Mack Smith wrote that "Joseph kept the Urim and Thummim constantly about his person." She was writing about an event that occurred in 1827, shortly after Joseph obtained the plates, but it's also possible that Joseph still had the Urim and Thummim in Nauvoo, having retained them when he delivered the plates. In Joseph Smith—History 1:60, he says nothing about delivering the Urim and Thummim to the messenger.

Years later, Heber C. Kimball declared in General Conference that Brigham

	Young had the Urim and Thummim. Some say this referred to a seer stone, which is possible. But it is also congruent with Woodruff's journal entry to infer that what Woodruff saw and what Brigham Young possessed was the Urim and Thummim that Joseph obtained with the plates.
	All of Joseph's contemporaries and successors in Church leadership taught that Joseph translated the plates with the Urim and Thummim. None said or implied that he used a seer stone instead.
In ancient times, Israelite priests used the Urim and Thummim to assist in receiving divine communications. Although commentators differ on the nature of the instrument, several ancient sources state that the instrument involved stones that lit up or were divinely illumined.[30] Latter-day Saints later understood the term "Urim and Thummim" to refer exclusively to the interpreters.	It's true that Joseph's contemporaries and successors all understood the term this way. The historical evidence gives them good justification for doing so.
Joseph Smith and others, however, seem to have understood the term more as a descriptive category of instruments for obtaining divine revelations and less as the name of a specific instrument.	"Seem to have understood" is mindreading—and unsupportable historical revisionism. While it is possible that later usage developed this way, such as in D&C 130:8-10, that usage was in 1843.
	In 1834, there was no confusion about the two terms. The book *Mormonism Unvailed*, published in October 1834, spelled out the two distinct and alternative explanations for the translation. One involved a seer or "peep" stone in a hat. The other

	involved the Urim and Thummim.
	In response to *Mormonism Unvailed*, Oliver Cowdery and Joseph Smith declared unequivocally that Joseph used the Urim and Thummim. They published Letter I (now the footnote to Joseph Smith—History 1:71 that we discussed above) in October 1834. Letter 1 makes the connection explicit: "he translated with the Urim and Thummim, or, as the Nephites would have said, 'Interpreters,' the history or record called "The Book of Mormon'."
	Thereafter, Joseph and Oliver consistently taught that Joseph used the Urim and Thummim. All of Joseph's contemporaries and successors did likewise.
	There are no known instances in which Joseph or Oliver used the term Urim and Thummim to refer to anything Joseph used for the translation of the Book of Mormon except the instrument Moroni put in the stone box.
Some people have balked at this claim of physical instruments used in the divine translation process, but such aids to facilitate the communication of God's power and inspiration are consistent with accounts in scripture. In addition to the Urim and Thummim, the Bible mentions other physical instruments used to access God's power: the rod of Aaron, a brass serpent, holy anointing oils,	The first statement quoted here establishes Joseph's claim that he actually translated the ancient records. The last statement quoted here does not explicitly refer to the translation. While "the coming forth of the book of Mormon" *could* include the manner of translation, it does not appear to have been understood that way by those present at the meeting. David Whitmer and Martin Harris were both

the Ark of the Covenant, and even dirt from the ground mixed with saliva to heal the eyes of a blind man.[31]	present, and both went on to discuss details about the translation. If Joseph meant "it is not intended to tell the world all the particulars *of the translation* of the Book of Mormon," then these two men violated Joseph's instructions. There is no record of anyone stating that Joseph told them not to talk about the mechanics of the translation.
The Mechanics of Translation	
In the preface to the 1830 edition of the Book of Mormon, Joseph Smith wrote: "I would inform you that I translated [the book], by the gift and power of God." When pressed for specifics about the process of translation, Joseph repeated on several occasions that it had been done "by the gift and power of God"[32] and once added, "It was not intended to tell the world all the particulars of the coming forth of the book of Mormon."[33]	
	The "coming forth of the Book of Mormon" involved more than the translation. It involved the education of Joseph Smith by divine messengers including Moroni and others (including Nephi). It involved details about the plates, the breastplate, and the interpreters. It may have referred to the details of the two sets of plates and the depository of Nephite records and other artifacts in the Hill Cumorah, a topic that we would not expect Joseph to make public because of all the treasure seekers in the area.
Nevertheless, the scribes and others who observed the translation left numerous accounts that give insight into the process.	This statement assumes these witnesses saw the actual translation instead of merely a demonstration of the concept. Oliver Cowdery was the only scribe for the current text, and he always said Joseph used the Urim and Thummim to translate.
Some accounts indicate that Joseph studied the characters on the plates. Most of the accounts speak of Joseph's use of the Urim and Thummim (either the interpreters or the seer stone), and many accounts refer to his use of a single stone.	This analysis conflates the accounts. Joseph and Oliver consistently said that Joseph translated with the Urim and Thummim that Moroni put in the stone box. Neither ever said or implied that Joseph used a seer stone. Other observers who mentioned the seer stone in the hat may or may not

	have observed the translation. They did not record what words they heard Joseph dictate, so we can't tell what parts, if any, of the text they witnessed being translated.
	Dan Vogel, a critic of Joseph Smith, agrees with the anonymous authors of this essay.
	"Eyewitness testimony confirms that Joseph Smith translated the Book of Mormon in the same manner that he once hunted for buried treasure: that is, with his brown-colored seer stone placed in the crown of his white top hat and his face snug to its brim. Rather than seeing treasures in the bowels of the earth, Smith claimed he saw luminous words on the stone, which he read to a scribe. In this manner the entire Book of Mormon as we have it came into existence. This fact conflicts with Joseph Smith's official history, which claims that he used magic spectacles—which he euphemistically called Urim and Thummim—attached to a breastplate." [34]
	I agree with Vogel that the stone-in-the-hat narrative conflicts with the official history—as well as every other statement made by Joseph and Oliver.
	But I disagree with Vogel—and this Gospel Topics Essay—when they claim the other witnesses observed Joseph translating the Book of Mormon.
According to these accounts, Joseph	Here again, the essay assumes the

placed either the interpreters or the seer stone in a hat, pressed his face into the hat to block out extraneous light, and read aloud the English words that appeared on the instrument.[35]

witnesses were describing the actual translation of the Book of Mormon instead of a demonstration. Witnesses who claimed Joseph read aloud English words failed to record those words so we cannot tell if they consisted of the text of the Book of Mormon. As part of the demonstration, Joseph could have spoken memorized scriptural passages or sermons—or even portions of the text that he had previously translated. None of the witnesses claimed to have observed either the plates or the Urim and Thummim that Joseph had been commanded not to show to anyone.

The essay's footnote claims two Apostles have written accounts of the translation process, but each involve isolated quotations from the historical record, not rejections of what Joseph and Oliver taught about the Urim and Thummim.

Elder Maxwell wrote, "The Prophet Joseph alone knew the full process, and he was deliberately reluctant to describe details. We take passing notice of the words of David Whitmer, Joseph Knight, and Martin Harris, who were observers, not translators.... Oliver Cowdery is reported to have testified in court that the Urim and Thummim enabled Joseph 'to read in English, the reformed Egyptian characters, which were engraved on the plates.'"[36]

This statement by Oliver is consistent

	with everything else he taught; i.e., that Joseph translated the characters with the Urim and Thummim.
	Many years before becoming President of the Church, Elder Russell M. Nelson wrote, "The details of this miraculous method of translation are still not fully known. Yet we do have a few precious insights." He then quoted David Whitmer and Emma Smith without further comment.
	These statements may be "precious insights," but the question remains: insights into what? Neither David nor Emma served as scribes for the text of the Book of Mormon we have today.
The process as described brings to mind a passage from the Book of Mormon that speaks of God preparing "a stone, which shall shine forth in darkness unto light."[37]	The passage in Alma (37:21-25) refers twice to "interpreters," but that was a change made in the 1920 edition. Earlier editions, including the original 1830 edition, used the term "directors" instead. That suggests a meaning different from the "interpreters" mentioned in Ether 4:5 and Mosiah 8 and 28, to which Oliver Cowdery referred in Letter 1 ("the Urim and Thummim, or, as the Nephites would have said, 'Interpreters'").
	The witness accounts don't describe the time of day when they observed the proceeding, but if Joseph used a hat, day after day, he presumably worked during the day. One wonders why he didn't simply work at night, when a stone that would present English words that "shine forth in darkness unto light" would operate

	more effectively.

Perhaps the scriptural phrase doesn't refer to shining words appearing on a stone.

Consider the other instances of the phrase "shine forth" in the scriptures. "Thou shalt shine forth" (Job 11:17). "Thou that dwellest between the cherubims, shine forth" (Psalms 80:1). "Then shall the righteous shine forth as the sun" (Matthew 13:43). "The King of heaven shall very soon shine forth among all the children of men" (Alma 5:50). "Then shall the righteous shine forth in the kingdom of God" (Alma 40:25). "It shall be brought out of the earth, and it shall shine forth out of darkness" (Mormon 8:16). "Prepare them [stones] that they may shine forth in darkness" (Ether 3:4). "Thy church may… shine forth" (D&C 109:73. "Arise and shine forth…" (D&C 115:5).

The teachings of the Book of Mormon "shine forth" regardless of the method of translation. |
| The scribes who assisted with the translation unquestionably believed that Joseph translated by divine power. Joseph's wife Emma explained that she "frequently wrote day after day" at a small table in their house in Harmony, Pennsylvania. She described Joseph "sitting with his face buried in his hat, with the stone in it, and dictating hour after hour with nothing between us."[38] | Emma's 1879 account does not specify when she acted as scribe. Other than claiming to write "day after day," she never specified when she wrote or what portion of the text she recorded. She may have written during Joseph's early attempts to translate before Martin Harris arrived, but that contradicts a letter she wrote in 1870, in which she stated, "Now the first that my husband translated was |

translated by the use of the Urim and Thummim, and that was the part that Martin Harris lost, after that he used a small stone, not exactly, black, but was rather a dark color."

Based on her description above, this means she must have acted act as scribe after Martin lost the 116 pages. Emma's handwriting does not appear on the extant Original Manuscript, although we only have about 28% of it.

Oliver Cowdery said he wrote the entire manuscript, save a few pages only. There are a few pages from the Fayette translation in the handwriting of a Whitmer brother and an unknown scribe.

Lucy Mack Smith said Joseph told her that on September 22, 1828, "I had the joy and satisfaction of again receiving the Urim and Thummim; and have commenced translating again, and Emma writes for me; but the angel said that the Lord would send me a scribe." Of course, this conflicts with Emma's 1870 letter because she said he did not use the Urim and Thummim after he lost the 116 pages.

Emma's claim that she wrote "day after day" raises the question of why Joseph needed Martin Harris or Oliver Cowdery to act as scribes. It is understandable that Emma would want a break, of course. Or perhaps

	her pregnancy in 1828 disrupted her ability to write. But according to the accounts we have, the translation could not proceed until these men showed up. Joseph said Oliver was an answer to his prayer for help. Lucy Mack Smith wrote in her history that while Joseph and Oliver were working in Harmony, Joseph applied the Urim and Thummim to his eyes and looked on the plates. Again, this contradicts Emma's 1879 Final Testimony.
According to Emma, the plates "often lay on the table without any attempt at concealment, wrapped in a small linen table cloth."	This statement has been taken to mean Joseph never used the plates *during the translation*, but that's not what it says. If Joseph *often* left the plates on the table without concealment (other than the cloth), that means at other times he *did* conceal them. The statement is consistent with Joseph sometimes concealing the plates when he wasn't using them, but often not bothering to conceal them. In other words, this statement is consistent with what Lucy Mack Smith said about Joseph looking upon the plates with the Urim and Thummim.
When asked if Joseph had dictated from the Bible or from a manuscript he had prepared earlier, Emma flatly denied those possibilities: "He had neither manuscript nor book to read from." Emma told her son Joseph Smith III, "The Book of Mormon is of divine authenticity—I have not the slightest doubt of it. I am satisfied that no man could have dictated the	After he would say "Written," Martin claimed that "if correctly written that sentence would disappear and another appear in its place, but if not written correctly it remained until corrected, so that the translation was just as it was engraven on the plates, precisely in the language then used." The reference to the engravings on the

writing of the manuscripts unless he was inspired; for, when acting as his scribe, your father would dictate to me for hour after hour; and when returning after meals, or after interruptions, he would at once begin where he had left off, without either seeing the manuscript or having any portion of it read to him."[39]	plates is consistent with the language of D&C 10. Martin's statement seems to imply a literal translation, but Joseph said only that the Title Page was a literal translation. Martin never claimed to have seen what Joseph saw when he translated. He also didn't claim that Joseph told him what saw. Instead, Martin apparently made this claim based on his own inference of what occurred.
Another scribe, Martin Harris sat across the table from Joseph Smith and wrote down the words Joseph dictated. Harris later related that as Joseph used the seer stone to translate, sentences appeared. Joseph read those sentences aloud, and after penning the words, Harris would say, "Written."	This statement has led some to conclude that the translation was "tightly controlled," but we do not have the 116 pages to see if there were misspellings and other errors of the type present in the Original Manuscript. Martin wrote the 116 pages, so the process may have been different for the translation we have today.
An associate who interviewed Harris recorded him saying that Joseph "possessed a seer stone, by which he was enabled to translate as well as from the Urim and Thummim, and for convenience he then used the seer stone."[40]	The essay's footnote here points out that Martin Harris recognized the distinction between the Urim and Thummim (the Nephite interpreters) and the seer stone. Like his contemporaries, Martin didn't use the term to apply to both. Of course, Martin's statement here contradicts Emma's statement that Joseph used the stone after the 116 pages were lost.
The principal scribe, Oliver Cowdery, testified under oath in 1831 that Joseph Smith "found with the plates, from which he translated his book, two transparent stones, resembling	This is consistent with every statement by Joseph and Oliver about the translation, although it contradicts the stone-in-a-hat narrative.

glass, set in silver bows. That by looking through these, he was able to read in English, the reformed Egyptian characters, which were engraved on the plates."[41]	
In the fall of 1830, Cowdery visited Union Village, Ohio, and spoke about the translation of the Book of Mormon. Soon thereafter, a village resident reported that the translation was accomplished by means of "two transparent stones in the form of spectacles thro which the translator looked on the engraving."[42]	This report has Joseph looking on the engraving instead of having the plates resting nearby under a cloth. This is consistent with what Lucy Mack Smith wrote about how Joseph translated the plates. The phrase "two transparent stones" is the description always given of the Nephite interpreters.
Conclusion Joseph Smith consistently testified that he translated the Book of Mormon by the "gift and power of God." His scribes shared that testimony. The angel who brought news of an ancient record on metal plates buried in a hillside and the divine instruments prepared especially for Joseph Smith to translate were all part of what Joseph and his scribes viewed as the miracle of translation. When he sat down in 1832 to write his own history for the first time, he began by promising to include "an account of his marvelous experience."[43] The translation of the Book of Mormon was truly marvelous.	Even in the conclusion, the essay omits what Joseph said about the Urim and Thummim.
The truth of the Book of Mormon and its divine source can be known today. God invites each of us to read the book, remember the mercies of the Lord and ponder them in our hearts, "and ask God, the Eternal	

Father, in the name of Christ, if these things are not true." God promises that "if ye shall ask with a sincere heart, with real intent, having faith in Christ, he will manifest the truth of it unto you, by the power of the Holy Ghost."[44]

[1] Wilford Woodruff journal, Nov. 28, 1841, Church History Library, Salt Lake City., https://www.josephsmithpapers.org/paper-summary/remarks-28-november-1841/1.

[2] https://www.churchofjesuschrist.org/study/scriptures/bofm/introduction?lang=eng

[3] On the identity of the angel, see Karen Lynn Davidson, David J. Whittaker, Mark Ashurst-McGee, and Richard L. Jenson, eds., *Histories, Volume 1: Joseph Smith Histories, 1832–1844*, vol. 1 of the Histories series of The Joseph Smith Papers, edited by Dean C. Jessee, Ronald K. Esplin, and Richard Lyman Bushman (Salt Lake City: Church Historian's Press, 2012), 223 n 56.

[4] Online at https://www.josephsmithpapers.org/paper-summary/times-and-seasons-15-april-1842/3

[5] Online at https://www.josephsmithpapers.org/paper-summary/lucy-mack-smith-history-1845/86

[6] Letter IV, online at https://www.josephsmithpapers.org/paper-summary/history-1834-1836/68

[7] Davidson et al., *Joseph Smith Histories*, 223; punctuation regularized; Joseph Smith, "Church History," *Times and Seasons* 3 (March 1, 1842): 706-7. See also Joseph Smith—History 1:33–34.

[8] Mormon 9:32. See also 1 Nephi 1:2.

[9] "Last Testimony of Sister Emma," *Saints' Herald* 26 (Oct. 1, 1879), 290.

[10] Joseph Smith History, 1838–ca. 1841, 8–11 (draft 2), in Karen Lynn Davidson, David J. Whittaker, Mark Ashurst-McGee, and

Richard L. Jenson, eds., *Histories, Volume 1: Joseph Smith Histories, 1832–1844,* vol. 1 of the Histories series of *The Joseph Smith Papers,* edited by Dean C. Jessee, Ronald K. Esplin, and Richard Lyman Bushman (Salt Lake City: Church Historian's Press, 2012), 252–3; available at josephsmithpapers.org; Doctrine and Covenants 3:5–15.

[11] D&C 10:1-2; Lucy Mack Smith, History, 1845, online at https://www.josephsmithpapers.org/paper-summary/lucy-mack-smith-history-1845/143

[12] Joseph Smith History, ca. summer 1832, in *Joseph Smith Histories,* 16; Oliver Cowdery to William W. Phelps, Sept. 7, 1834, in *Messenger and Advocate* 1 (Oct. 1834): 14; italics in original.

[13] The essay's footnote refers to the obscure *Messenger and Advocate*, but Joseph had his scribes copy Oliver's letters into is personal history, which is available online here: https://www.josephsmithpapers.org/paper-summary/history-1834-1836/49

[14] Most of the manuscript disintegrated or became otherwise unreadable due to water damage between 1841 and 1882, as a result of being placed in the cornerstone of the Nauvoo House in Nauvoo, Illinois. Most of the surviving pages were later archived in the historian's office of The Church of Jesus Christ of Latter-day Saints in Salt Lake City. The extant original manuscript has been published in *The Original Manuscript of the Book of Mormon: Typographical Facsimile of the Extant Text,* ed. Royal Skousen (Provo, UT: Foundation for Ancient Research and Mormon Studies, 2001). A complete copy of this original, known as the printer's manuscript, was made by Oliver Cowdery and two other scribes between August 1829 and early 1830. It was used to set the type for most of the printing in Palmyra. The printer's manuscript is published in *The Printer's Manuscript of the Book of Mormon: Typological Facsimile of the Entire Text in Two Parts,* ed. Royal Skousen (Provo, UT: Foundation for Ancient Research and Mormon Studies, 2001). Both the printer's manuscript and the original manuscript will be published in future volumes of *The Joseph Smith Papers.* (Dean C. Jessee, "The Original Book of Mormon Manuscript," *BYU Studies* 10, no. 3 [Spring 1970]: 261–72; Royal Skousen, "Piecing Together the Original Manuscript," *BYU Today* 46, no. 3 [May 1992]: 18–24.)

[15] For example, when Joseph translated the text that is now in 1 Nephi 13:29, the scribe wrote "&" in one place where he should have written

"an." At 1 Nephi 17:48, the scribe wrote "weed" where he should have written "reed." (See Royal Skousen, "Translating the Book of Mormon: Evidence from the Original Manuscript," in Noel B. Reynolds, ed., *Book of Mormon Authorship Revisited: The Evidence for Ancient Origins* [Provo, UT: Foundation for Ancient Research and Mormon Studies, 1997], 67; see also Grant Hardy, "Introduction," in *The Book of Mormon: The Earliest Text*, ed. Royal Skousen [New Haven: Yale University Press, 2009], xv–xix.)

[16] John A. Tvedtnes, "Hebraisms in the Book of Mormon" and "Names of People: Book of Mormon," in Geoffrey Kahn, ed., *Encyclopedia of Hebrew Language and Linguistics* (Brill Online, 2013); M. Deloy Pack, "Hebraisms," in *Book of Mormon Reference Companion,* ed. Dennis L. Largey (Salt Lake City: Deseret Book, 2003), 321–25; John A. Tvedtnes, "The Hebrew Background of the Book of Mormon," in John L. Sorenson and Melvin J. Thorne, eds., *Rediscovering the Book of Mormon* (Salt Lake City and Provo, UT: Deseret Book and Foundation for Ancient Research and Mormon Studies, 1991), 77–91; Donald W. Parry, "Hebraisms and Other Ancient Peculiarities in the Book of Mormon," in Donald W. Parry and others, eds., *Echoes and Evidences of the Book of Mormon* (Provo, UT: Foundation for Ancient Research and Mormon Studies, 2002), 155–89.

[17] On the role of the typesetter John Gilbert, see Royal Skousen, "John Gilbert's 1892 Account of the 1830 Printing of the Book of Mormon," in Stephen D. Ricks and others, eds., *The Disciple as Witness: Essays on Latter-day Saint History and Doctrine in Honor of Richard Lloyd Anderson* (Provo, UT: Foundation for Ancient Research and Mormon Studies, 2000), 383–405.

[18] Some grammatical constructions that sound odd to English speakers were edited out of later editions of the Book of Mormon by Joseph Smith or others in order to render the translation into more standard current English. See Richard E. Turley Jr. and William W. Slaughter, *How We Got the Book of Mormon* (Salt Lake City: Deseret Book, 2011), 44–45. Approximately five-sixth of the 1830 first edition of the Book of Mormon was typeset from the printer's manuscript. The other one-sixth was typeset from the original manuscript. (Royal Skousen, "Editor's Preface," in *The Book of Mormon: The Earliest Text,* xxx.)

[19] 1 Kings 19:11–12.

[20] Acts 9:1–8; 12:7–9.

[21] Acts 11:4–17; 16:9–10; Exodus 28:30; Leviticus 8:8; Numbers 21:9.

[22] Michael Hubbard MacKay, Gerrit J. Dirkmaat, Grand Underwood, Robert J. Woodford, and William G. Hartley, eds., *Documents, Volume 1: July 1828–June 1831*, vol. 1 of the Documents series of *The Joseph Smith Papers*, edited by Dean C. Jessee, Ronald K. Esplin, Richard Lyman Bushman, and Matthew J. Grow (Salt Lake City: Church Historian's Press, 2013), xxix.

[23] Mosiah 28:14-15, 20; see also Mosiah 8:13, 19; and Ether 4:5. Joseph Smith seems to have used the terms "interpreters" and "spectacles" interchangeably during the early years of the Church. Nancy Towle, an itinerant Methodist preacher, recounted Joseph Smith telling her about "a pair of 'interpreters,' (as he called them,) that resembled spectacles, by looking into which, he could *read* a writing engraven upon the plates, though to himself, in a tongue unknown." (Nancy Towle, *Vicissitudes Illustrated in the Experience of Nancy Towle, in Europe and America* [Charleston: James L. Burges, 1832], 138-39.) Joseph's 1832 history referred to "spectacles." (Joseph Smith History, ca. summer 1832, in *Joseph Smith Histories*, 16.) In January 1833, the Latter-day Saint newspaper *The Evening and the Morning Star*, edited by William W. Phelps, equated "spectacles" and "interpreters" with the term "Urim and Thummim": the Book of Mormon "was translated by the gift and power of God, by an unlearned man, through the aid of a pair of Interpreters, or spectacles— (known, perhaps, in ancient days as Teraphim, or Urim and Thummim)." ("The Book of Mormon," *The Evening and the Morning Star*, January 1833, [2].) By 1835 Joseph Smith most often used the term "Urim and Thummim" when speaking of translation and rarely, if ever, used the terms "interpreters" or "spectacles." (Joseph Smith, Journal, Nov. 9-11, 1835, in *Journals: Volume 1: 1832-1839*, 89; Joseph Smith, History, 1834-1836, in Davidson et al., *Histories, Volume 1*, 116; John W. Welch, "The Miraculous Translation of the Book of Mormon," in John W. Welch, ed., with Erick B. Carlson, *Opening the Heavens: Accounts of Divine Manifestations, 1820–1844* [Provo, UT, and Salt Lake City: Brigham Young University Press and Deseret Book, 2005], 123-28.)

[24] "Questions Proposed to the Mormonite Preachers and Their Answers Obtained Before the Whole Assembly at Julian Hall, Sunday Evening, August 5, 1832," *Boston Investigator* Vol. II, No. 20 (August 10, 1832). Online at http://www.sidneyrigdon.com/dbroadhu/NE/miscne01.htm

[25] Joseph Smith probably possessed more than one seer stone; he appears to have found one of the stones while digging for a well around 1822. (Richard L. Bushman, *Joseph Smith and the Beginnings of Mormonism* [Urbana: University of Illinois Press, 1984], 69–70.)

[26] According to Martin Harris, an angel commanded Joseph Smith to stop these activities, which he did by 1826. (See Bushman, *Joseph Smith and the Beginnings of Mormonism*, 64–76; and Richard Lloyd Anderson, "The Mature Joseph Smith and Treasure Searching," *BYU Studies* 24, no. 4 [Fall 1984]: 489–560.) Joseph did not hide his well-known early involvement in treasure seeking. In 1838, he published responses to questions frequently asked of him. "Was not Jo Smith a money digger," one question read. "Yes," Joseph answered, "but it was never a very profitable job to him, as he only got fourteen dollars a month for it." (Selections from *Elders' Journal*, July 1838, 43, available at josephsmithpapers.org.) For the broader cultural context, see Alan Taylor, "The Early Republic's Supernatural Economy: Treasure Seeking in the American Northeast, 1780–1830," *American Quarterly* 38, no. 1 (Spring 1986): 6–33.

[27] Mark Ashurst-McGee, "A Pathway to Prophethood: Joseph Smith Junior as Rodsman, Village Seer, and Judeo-Christian Prophet," (Master's Thesis, Utah State University, 2000).

[28] For example, when Joseph Smith showed a seer stone to Wilford Woodruff in late 1841, Woodruff recorded in his journal: "I had the privilege of seeing for the first time in my day the URIM & THUMMIM." (Wilford Woodruff journal, Dec. 27, 1841, Church History Library, Salt Lake City.) See also Doctrine and Covenants 130:10.

[29] The journal is online at https://catalog.lds.org/assets/28b53d73-2ba2-418b-8ef7-dafcc935bee3/0/125

[30] Cornelius Van Dam, *The Urim and Thummim: A Means of Revelation in Ancient Israel* (Winona Lake, IN: Eisenbrauns, 1997), 9–26.

[31] Exodus 7:9-12; 30:25; 40:9; Leviticus 8:10-12; Numbers 21:9; Joshua 3:6-8; John 9:6.

[32] Preface to the Book of Mormon, 1830 edition.

[33] Minutes, Church conference, Orange, OH, Oct. 25–26, 1831, in Minute Book 2, Church History Library, Salt Lake City, available at josephsmithpapers.org; Welch, "Miraculous Translation,",121–9.

[34] http://www.mormonthink.com/essays-bom-translation.htm

[35] Virtually all of the accounts of the translation process are reproduced in Welch, "Miraculous Translation." Two accounts of the translation process, including the use of a seer stone, have been written by members of the Quorum of the Twelve Apostles and published in Church magazines. Historians have also written about the seer stone in Church publications, both in the *Ensign* and in *The Joseph Smith Papers*. (See Neal A. Maxwell, "'By the Gift and Power of God,'" *Ensign*, Jan. 1997, 36–41; Russell M. Nelson, "A Treasured Testament," *Ensign*, July 1993, 61–63; Richard Lloyd Anderson, "'By the Gift and Power of God,'" *Ensign*, Sept. 1977, 78–85; and *Documents, Volume 1: July 1828–June 1831*, xxix–xxxii.)

[36] https://www.churchofjesuschrist.org/study/ensign/1997/01/by-the-gift-and-power-of-god?lang=eng

[37] Alma 37:23-24.

[38] "Last Testimony of Sister Emma," *Saints' Herald* 26 (Oct. 1, 1879), 289–90. Some outside reports describe the spectacles being placed in the hat during the translation process. A Palmyra newspaper published the earliest known account of the translation in August 1829: Jonathan Hadley, a Palmyra printer who may have spoken with Joseph Smith about translation, claimed that the plates were found with a "huge pair of Spectacles," and that "by placing the Spectacles in a hat, and looking into it, Smith could (he said so, at least,) interpret these characters." ("Golden Bible," *Palmyra Freeman,* Aug. 11, 1829, [2].) In the winter of 1831, a Shaker in Union Village, Ohio, spoke of "two transparent stones in the form of spectacles" through which the translator "looked on the engraving & afterwards put his face into a hat & the interpretation then flowed into his mind." (Christian Goodwillie, "Shaker Richard McNemar: The Earliest Book of Mormon Reviewer," *Journal of Mormon History* 37, no. 2 [Spring 2011]: 143.)

[39] "Last Testimony of Sister Emma," 289–90.

[40] "One of the Three Witnesses," *Deseret Evening News,* Dec. 13, 1881, 4. Here Martin Harris uses the term "Urim and Thummim" to refer to the interpreters found with the plates.

[41] A. W. B., "Mormonites," *Evangelical Magazine and Gospel Advocate* 2 (Apr. 19, 1831): 120.

[42] Goodwillie, "Shaker Richard McNemar," 143. For additional accounts of translation by one of the Three Witnesses, see *David Whitmer*

Interviews: A Restoration Witness, ed. Lyndon W. Cook (Orem, UT: Grandin Book, 1991).

[43] Joseph Smith History, ca. Summer 1832, 1, in *Histories, Volume 1, 1832–1844,* 10; available at josephsmithpapers.org. Spelling modernized.

[44] Moroni 10:3–5.

14: Reframing *Saints*, volume 1

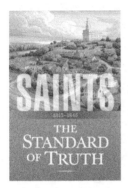

Church history is complicated, so it's useful to have a condensed narrative published in multiple languages. The *Saints* books could—and should—have provided a common narrative based on the facts as documented in the Joseph Smith Papers and elsewhere.

Unfortunately, the *Saints* books omit relevant, material historical facts and distort the narrative in some specific ways, apparently to accommodate the SITH and M2C narratives.

The *Saints* books were intended to provide readers with an accurate "narrative present," meaning they were supposed to relate the events of the Restoration from the perspective of the people who lived those events. In most respects, they do so. But in other respects, the "narrative present" has been altered to accommodate modern theories about the origin and setting of the Book of Mormon.

We realize *Saints* is a summary, not an encyclopedia. But a summary that contains false narratives and obvious omissions doesn't lead to clarity, charity and understanding. In this chapter, we discuss how the editors manipulated Church history, then offer suggestions to make *Saints* more historically accurate and useful.

We can read *Saints*, volume 1, two ways.[150]

1. Read (or listen to) the narrative and just accept the editors' spin on Church history.

3. Read the citations (references) and learn the actual history.

---

[150] Link to .pdf version: https://www.churchofjesuschrist.org/bc/content/ldsorg/media-library/ebook-pdf/Saints-v1-English-PD60001624.pdf?lang=eng.
Link to online version: https://www.churchofjesuschrist.org/study/history/saints-v1/06-the-gift-and-power-of-god?lang=eng

This wouldn't be a problem if the editors had decided to accurately present the historical events from the perspective of the people involved; i.e., if they had presented an accurate "historical narrative present." Instead, they chose to promote modern ideas about Cumorah and the translation of the Book of Mormon.

Consequently, passive readers ("lazy learners") will simply assume the narrative accurately reflects the original sources and will not take the time to read the references.

People listening to an audio version of *Saints* will never hear the references.

For non-English speakers it's a bigger problem. Few of the references have been translated into other languages. I've checked the foreign-language editions of *Saints* and they cite English-only references, particularly the Joseph Smith Papers and *Rough Stone Rolling*, which (so far as I know) has never been translated into another language. (For comments on *Rough Stone Rolling*, see the next chapter.)

A good example is in Chapter 3. Look at the sentence in *Saints*, and then look at the cited reference in the footnote. You'll see the two are quite different. Nothing in Lucy's account states, suggests, or implies that "Joseph's gift for using the stone impressed family members, who saw it as a sign of divine favor." Quite the opposite, actually.

Note that the reference to Alma 37:23 is gratuitous except for the editors' effort to set up the SITH narrative later in the book.

Saints, volume 1, Chapter 3, page 21	References: Lucy Mack Smith and Alma
"Joseph's gift for using the stone impressed family members, who saw it as a sign of divine favor." 4	4. Lucy Mack Smith, History, 1845, 95; see also Alma 37:23. Lucy Mack Smith's account: A short time before the house was completed, a man by the name of Josiah Stoal came from Chenango County, New York, to get Joseph to assist him in digging for a silver mine. He came for Joseph from having heard that he was in possession of certain means, by which he could discern things, that could not

> be seen by the natural eye. Joseph endeavored to divert him from his vain project; but he was inflexible, and offered high wages to such as would dig for him; and was still very anxious to have Joseph work for him; consequently, he returned with the old gentleman; besides several others that who were picked up in the neighborhood, and commenced digging. After laboring about a month without success, Joseph prevailed on his employer to cease his operations. **It was from this circumstance, namely, working by the month at digging for a silver mine, that the very prevalent story arose, of his having been a money digger.**
>
> The full reference to Lucy Mack Smith is https://www.josephsmithpapers.org/paper-summary/lucy-mack-smith-history-1845/102

Contrary to the claims of the sentence in *Saints*, in this passage Lucy dismissively explains the origin of "the very prevalent story... of his having been a money digger." If there is something in Lucy's history that supports the *Saints* sentence, the editors should have cited it instead of this passage which expresses the opposite of what *Saints* claims.

Saints, volume 1, quotes Lucy Mack Smith's history 127 times. That's a legitimate and emphatic endorsement of her credibility and reliability, as well as her unique relationship with Joseph Smith and the insights that ensued. Why provide a reference that contradicts the editors' restatement of history?

Worse, *Saints* omitted every reference to Cumorah, including Lucy's account of what Moroni told Joseph that includes some important details available nowhere else.

A common theme among modern LDS scholars is that Joseph never identified the hill as Cumorah, or at least not until he wrote the letter that became D&C 128:20, by which time, according to these scholars, Joseph had adopted the false tradition that Cumorah was in New York. This false tradition, supposedly, was created by unknown persons at an unknown time in the early days of the Church.

Yet we have David Whitmer claiming repeatedly that he first heard about Cumorah directly from the divine messenger who had the abridged plates. This was in June 1829 before he had ever read a word in the Book of Mormon. We have Parley P. Pratt saying in 1831 that Moroni called the hill Cumorah anciently. We have Martin Harris referring to the hill as Cumorah in 1829.

What explains these accounts?

It's actually very simple and clear.

Lucy explained that Moroni identified the hill as Cumorah during his first visit to Joseph Smith!

> Now Joseph beware or when you go to get the plates your mind will be filled with darkness and all manner of evil will rush into your mind. To prevent you from keeping the commandments of God that you may not succeed in doing his work…
>
> **the record is on a side hill on the Hill of Cumorah** 3 miles from this place remove the Grass and moss and you will find a large flat stone pry that up and you will find the record under it laying on 4 pillars of cement— then the angel left him.[151]

Historians (and everyone else) are free to debate whether Lucy accurately remembered what Joseph told her, or whether her memory was "tainted" by a false tradition started later by Oliver Cowdery or someone else. But readers need to have the information to engage in that conversation. *Saints* undermines the "pillar of social trust" by erasing this account from Church history as part of an unacknowledged effort to erase and de-correlate the New York Cumorah for ideological reasons.

Censoring actual history is equivalent to inventing new history.

Apart from the Cumorah issue, Lucy's recollection is significant because of the details about the grass and moss. We don't get that detail

---

[151] https://www.josephsmithpapers.org/paper-summary/lucy-mack-smith-history-1844-1845/41

anywhere but in Lucy's account. Such a detail helps explain why the stone remained hidden for all these centuries—a detail that would help inform LDS artists. In one well-known painting, the artist depicted Joseph using a lever to raise a boulder with no moss on it. Rather than concealing the stone box, such a stone would have called attention to it.

Saints also omitted Cumorah from Lucy's account of the time when Moroni chastised Joseph Smith when he was coming home from Manchester. This event took place in January 1827, before Joseph obtained the plates. He referred to the hill as Cumorah on this occasion. Obviously, he could have learned the name Cumorah only from Moroni.

Below is a side-by-side comparison showing how this editing was done. Note how the section in the 1844-5 version was lined out on the original document, yet the *Saints* editors chose to use that version instead of the revised 1845 version—which was more detailed. In the 1845 version, Joseph referred to Cumorah to explain where he was when the angel chastised him, showing us that Lucy and her husband knew exactly where the hill was when Joseph referred to Cumorah.

Readers of *Saints* never learn this.

Nor do readers of the Joseph Smith Papers who search for "Cumorah." This reference to *Cumorah* does not show up in their search engine (possibly because it is hyphenated).

Saints, Vol. 1, p. 36	Lucy History 1844-5	Lucy History 1845
The Smiths liked having Joseph and Emma with them. But their son's divine call made them anxious. People in the area had heard about the gold plates and sometimes went looking for	Note 18 references this link: https://www.josephsmithpapers.org/paper-summary/lucy-mack-smith-history-1844-1845/59	But it does not reference this parallel link: https://www.josephsmithpapers.org/paper-summary/lucy-mack-smith-history-1845/111

them.18 One day, Joseph went to town on an errand. Expecting him back for dinner, his parents were alarmed when he did not return. They waited for hours, unable to sleep. At last Joseph opened the door and threw himself into a chair, exhausted. "Why are you so late?" his father asked.	<Soon after> this Mr. Smith had occasion to send Joseph to Manchester on buisness he set out in good season And we expected him <to be> at home as soon as 6 oclock but he did not arrive.... he did not return home till the night was considerably advanced his Father and myself were together I no one else was present when he entered the house he seemed threw himself into a chair seemingly much exhausted he was <as> pale as ashes his Father exclaimed Joseph why have <you> staid so late has anything happened you we have been in distress about you these 3 hours	Not long after this his father had occasion to send him to Manchester on business. <And,> as he started quite early in the morning, we expected him home, at the outside, by 6. o clock in the evening. But when 6. came he did not arrive.— we always had a peculiar anxiety about him whenever he was absent from us; for, it seemed as if something was always taking place to jeopardize his life. But to return, he did not get home till the night was far spent. On coming in, threw himself into a chair, apparently much exhausted. My husband did not observe his appearance, and immediately exclaimed, "Joseph, why have you staid so late? has anything happened you? we have been much distressed about you these three hours.

The Rational Restoration

"I have had the severest chastisement that I ever had in my life," Joseph said.	~~after Joseph recovered himself a little he said Father I have had the severest chastisement that I ever had in my life~~ - ~~Chastisement indeed! said Mr Smith Well upon my word I would like to [know?] who has been takeing you to task and what their pretext was its pretty well too if you are to be detained till this time of night to take lectures for your bad practises— Joseph smiled to see his Father so hasty and indignant. Father said he it was the angel of the Lord. he says I have been negligent~~	As Joseph made no reply, he continued his interrogations until I finally said: now, father, (as that was the manner in which I commonly addressed him) let him rest a moment— dont touble him now— you see he is home safe, and he is very tired; so pray wait a little....
"Who has been taking you to task?" demanded his father.		Presently he smiled, and said in a very calm tone, "I have taken the severest chastisement, that I have ever had in my life". My husband, supposing it was from some of the neighbors, was quite angry; and observed, "I would would like to know what business any body has to find fault with you."
"It was the angel of the Lord," Joseph replied. "He says I have been negligent."		"Stop, father, Stop." said Joseph, "it was the angel of the Lord— **as I passed by the hill of Cumorah,** where the plates are, the angel of the Lord met me and

239

		said, that I had not been engaged enough in the work of the Lord; that the time had come for the record to <be> brought forth; and, that I must be up and doing, and set myself about the things which God had commanded me to do: but, Father,' continued he, 'give yourself no uneasiness concerning the reprimand that I have received; for I now know the course that I am to pursue; so all will be well."
The day of his next meeting with Moroni was coming soon. "I must be up and doing," he said. "I must set myself about the things which God has commanded me to do."19	~~that the time has now come when the record should be brought forth and that I must be up and doing that I must set myself about the things which God has commanded me to do but Father give yourself no uneasiness as to this~~	

I've discussed these and similar problems with the *Saints* books at this blog: https://saintsreview.blogspot.com

Before concluding this chapter, though, we should consider one more problem in *Saints*: the Mary Whitmer story.

Long term, the biggest tragedy of *Saints* is the censorship of everything the early Church leaders said about the New York Cumorah and the translation with the Urim and Thummim.

But in the short term, the story of Mary Whitmer is causing confusion not only about history but about the doctrine of resurrection.

Chapter 7, titled "Fellow Saints," on pages 70-71 relates this account of David's mother seeing the plates. It's a fascinating account of a female witness of the plates. In the *Ensign* excerpt, the account is even accompanied by an illustration to draw attention to it.

The problem is, *Saints* relates a false version of the account.

The Rational Restoration

Now, thanks to *Saints*, future generations will believe it was Moroni who showed Mary the plates, solely because of (i) a mistake made by her descendants and (ii) the M2C agenda.

This has several repercussions.

- The "Moroni" version undermines the credibility of *Saints* because people who read *Saints* and believe this account will be confused when they read the actual history.
- The account in *Saints* will undermine belief in the reliability and credibility of David Whitmer, one of the Three Witnesses.
- Readers will wonder why Joseph and Oliver described Moroni so much differently than Mary Whitmer did. Does this mean resurrected beings can change their appearance, like shape-shifters, contrary to Alma's "perfect form" explanation?
- Readers will miss the far more fascinating aspect of the account that links the Book of Mormon to Church history.
- The Moroni narrative enables *Saints* to omit a key event in Church history that teaches us about the Hill Cumorah and the two sets of plates.

Here is the passage from *Saints*, starting on page 70, with my comments in brackets.

Once Joseph, Emma, and Oliver moved to Fayette, David's mother had her hands full. Mary Whitmer and her husband, Peter, already had eight children between the ages of 15 and 30, and the few who did not still live at home resided nearby. Tending to their needs filled Mary's days with work, and the three houseguests added more labor. Mary had faith in Joseph's calling and did not complain, but she was getting tired.17

Note 17 reads:
Orson Pratt and Joseph F. Smith, Interview with David Whitmer, Sept. 7-8, 1878, [10], in Joseph F. Smith to John Taylor and Council of the Twelve, Sept. 17, 1878, draft, Joseph F. Smith, Papers, Church History Library.

Jonathan Neville

https://catalog.churchofjesuschrist.org/assets/dca15baa-a0ac-4fc1-b2ec-7f3cd75e4906/0/43#churchofjesuschrist

[That link takes you to the hand-written version of the account. This is image 44 in the series. It's not easy to read, but it's a useful link because it relates David Whitmer's account of the messenger taking the plates to Cumorah—a portion of David's account that *Saints* omitted. I included transcripts of images 44-46 at the end of this chapter.]

Saints continued: The heat in Fayette that summer was sweltering. As Mary washed clothes and prepared meals, Joseph dictated the translation in an upstairs room. Oliver usually wrote for him, but occasionally Emma or one of the Whitmers took a turn with the pen.18 Sometimes, when Joseph and Oliver tired of the strain of translating, they would walk out to a nearby pond and skip stones across the surface of the water.
Mary had little time to relax herself, and the added work and the strain placed on her were hard to bear.

[So far, this is all reasonable conjecture and paraphrasing of the historical record.]

Saints continued: One day, while she was out by the barn where the cows were milked, she saw a gray-haired man with a knapsack slung across his shoulder. His sudden appearance frightened her, but as he approached, he spoke to her in a kind voice that set her at ease.
"My name is Moroni," he said. "You have become pretty tired with all the extra work you have to do." He swung the knapsack off his shoulder, and Mary watched as he started to untie it.19

Note 19 reads:
Skousen, "Another Account of Mary Whitmer's Viewing of the Golden Plates," 40; [Andrew Jenson], "Eight Witnesses," Historical Record, Oct. 1888, 621.

[The link given in the citation doesn't go to the correct page in the *Historical Record*, so if you want to see it, go here: https://catalog.churchofjesuschrist.org/assets/02b33f96-077a-47c7-b434-c45ee2f89897/0/638.

The Skousen article refers to the *Historical Record*. The relevant portion from page 621 is shown below:

Figure 9 - Historical Record on Mary Whitmer

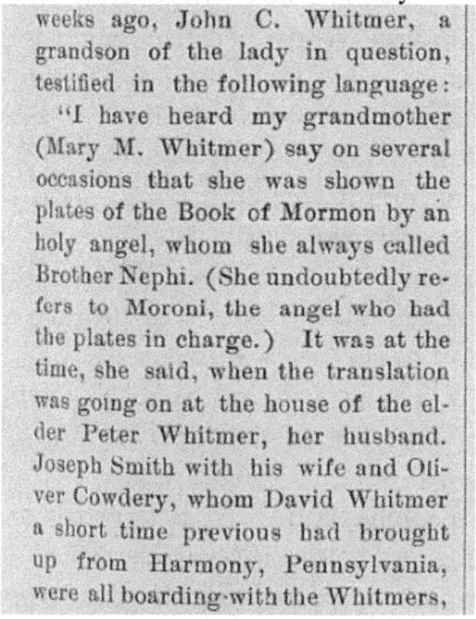

> weeks ago, John C. Whitmer, a grandson of the lady in question, testified in the following language:
> "I have heard my grandmother (Mary M. Whitmer) say on several occasions that she was shown the plates of the Book of Mormon by an holy angel, whom she always called Brother Nephi. (She undoubtedly refers to Moroni, the angel who had the plates in charge.) It was at the time, she said, when the translation was going on at the house of the elder Peter Whitmer, her husband. Joseph Smith with his wife and Oliver Cowdery, whom David Whitmer a short time previous had brought up from Harmony, Pennsylvania, were all boarding with the Whitmers,

The *Historical Record* purports to quote John C. Whitmer, Mary's grandson, as saying this in 1878:

"I have heard my grandmother (Mary M. Whitmer) say on several occasions that she was shown the plates of the Book of Mormon by an holy angel, whom she always called Brother Nephi. (She undoubtedly refers to Moroni, the angel who had the plates in charge.)"

Now you can see how the fake story of Moroni got started.

243

Mary Whitmer always referred to the messenger as "Brother Nephi."[152] This is consistent with what David Whitmer said about the messenger who took the Harmony plates to Cumorah; i.e., that, according to Joseph Smith, he was one of the Three Nephites. David's detailed description of a short, heavily bearded, portly old man also makes sense.

In this passage, Andrew Jensen, who compiled the 1889 *Historical Record*, used parenthesis to identify the grandmother (Mary M. Whitmer). But then he also used parenthesis to "correct" what Mary actually said!

Although Mary "always called [the angel] Brother Nephi," Andrew Jensen assumed she was wrong because (according to Jensen) it *had* to have been Moroni "who had the plates in his charge." Jensen changed/falsified the history by inserting the sentence that started the Moroni narrative.

Subsequent descendants apparently relied on this 1878 account and elaborated, inventing this quotation that was published by the family in 1958 and quoted, verbatim, in *Saints*: "My name is Moroni. You have become pretty tired with all the extra work you have to do. The Lord has given me permission to show you this record."

This account is related in Royal Skousen's article, which is available here: https://journal.interpreterfoundation.org/another-account-of-mary-whitmers-viewing-of-the-golden-plates/

If you read that article, you won't believe the attenuated hearsay links and assumptions that led to the 1958 article.

This leaves us with Andrew Jensen's speculation that Mary Whitmer was wrong (published in 1889 based on an interview in 1878), along with a family history account published in 1958 that, for the first time, directly quotes "Moroni" based on family lore.

The "Moroni" narrative directly contradicts the far more plausible direct testimony from David Whitmer. As a first-hand witness, David described the messenger who took the abridged plates to Cumorah. David said that, based on his mother's description, the messenger who

---

[152] While it is true that we don't know the names of the Three Nephites (3 Ne. 28:25-32), we do know that one of the disciples Christ called was named Nephi. (3 Ne. 19:4), so the chances are 3 in 12 that one of the Three Nephites was Nephi.

showed her the plates was the same individual he had seen. When David asked Joseph who it was, Joseph replied it was "one of the Nephites.

While on the return journey from Palmyra, David noticed a somewhat aged-looking man who approached them on the road. He had a very pleasant face, about which, however, there seemed something peculiar, and he carried a knapsack on his back fastened with straps which crossed his breast.

David asked him to take a ride, but he declined, saying: "I am going over to Cumorah," and then disappeared very suddenly, though there was no chance for him to secrete himself in the open country through which the party was then passing. All felt very strange concerning this personage and the Prophet was besought to inquire of the Lord concerning him.

Shortly afterwards, David relates, the Prophet looked very white but with a heavenly appearance and **said their visitor was one of the three Nephites to whom the Savior gave the promise of life on earth until He should come in power.**

After arriving home, David again saw this personage, and mother Whitmer, who was very kind to Joseph Smith, is said to have seen not only this Nephite, but to have also been shown by him the sealed and unsealed portions of the plates from which the Book of Mormon was translated.[153]

Edward Stevenson made a comment in his journal that corroborates the authenticity of David's statement. Zina Young and her family had been converted in 1832 by two missionaries: Hyrum Smith and David Whitmer. Edward reported that before he left Utah to visit David, Zina asked him to ask David about this incident.

---

[153] Edward Stevenson, "A Visit to David Whitmer," Juvenile Instructor, 22 (15 Feb 1887):55. See https://www.mobom.org/trip-to-fayette-references

"I wish to mention an Item of conversation with David Whitmer in regard to Seeing one of the Nephites, Zina Young, Desired me to ask about it. David Said, Oliver, & The Prophet, & I were riding in a wagon, & an aged man about 5 feet 10, heavey Set & on his back, an old fashioned Armey knapsack Straped over his Shoulders & Something Square in it, & he walked alongside of the Wagon & Wiped the Sweat off his face, Smileing very Pleasant David asked him to ride and he replied I am going across to the hill Cumorah.

Soon after they Passed they felt Strangeley and Stoped, but could see nothing of him all around was clean and they asked the Lord about it. He Said that the Prophet Looked as White as a Sheet & Said that it was one of the Nephites & that he had the plates."[154]

I find it astonishing that *Saints* omits the important and oft-repeated direct testimony of David Whitmer about the messenger taking the plates to Cumorah and then inserts this phony quotation from "Moroni" that contradicts not only David's direct testimony but what Mary Whitmer herself told her family.[155] It is both more interesting and historically accurate that she named one of the Three Nephites.

The Mary Whitmer account is awesome because we have a female witness of the plates, but replacing accurate history with a phony hearsay quotation composed over 100 years later leads us to wonder what the *Saints* editors were thinking and why they omitted the actual history for readers to at least evaluate.

When combined with the deliberate censorship of Cumorah throughout *Saints*, Volume 1, we can reasonably infer that the "Moroni"

---

[154] "Edward Stevenson Interview (1) 22-23 December 1877, Richmond, Missouri Diary of Edward Stevenson," LDS Church Archives, Lyndon W. Cook, ed., *David Whitmer Interviews*, 1993, p. 13; also Dan Vogel, ed., *Early Mormon Documents*, 2003, vol. v, p. 30.

[155] Those who defend the "Moroni" story also cite a typewritten manuscript from 1918 attributed to Joseph F. Smith, who had interviewed David in 1878. But as we see from the handwritten notes and his formal report to the Twelve, Smith and Pratt never said or implied that the messenger was Moroni. The 1918 manuscript (assuming it was created by Smith) apparently reflects the Jensen narrative.

The Rational Restoration

story was presented to deflect from David Whitmer's account of the messenger taking the abridged plates to Cumorah. Latter-day Saints and other readers deserve to learn accurate history, especially in the *Saints* books that the editors claimed would present a "historical present" that puts us in the times and places of the people we are reading about.

This is the transcript of the handwritten manuscript from Note 17 in *Saints*:

[Bottom of image #44]
When I was returning to Fayette with Joseph and Oliver, all of us riding in the wagon, Oliver and I on an old fashioned
[image #45]
wooden spring seat and Joseph behind us, we were suddenly approached by a very pleasant, nice looking old man in a clear open place, who saluted us with 'Good morning, it is very warm,' at the same instant wiping his face or forehead with his hand. We returned the salutation and by a sign from Joseph I invited him to ride if he was going our way, but he said very pleasantly, 'No, I am going to Cumorah.' This was something new to me, I did not know what Cumorah meant, and as I looked enquiringly at Joseph, the old man instantly disappeared so that I did not see him again."

Joseph F. Smith: "Did you notice his appearance?"

David Whitmer: "I should think I did. He was, I should think, about 5 feet 9 or 10 inches and heavy set, about such a man as James Vancleave, there, but heavier. His face was as large. He was dressed in a suit of brown, woolen clothes; his hair and beard were white, about like Brother Pratt's, but his beard was not so heavy. I also remember that he had a sort of knapsack on his back, and something was in it which was shaped like a book. It was the messenger who had the plates.

"Soon after our arrival home,
[image #46]
I saw something which led me to the belief that the plates were placed or concealed in my father's barn. I frankly asked Joseph if my supposition was right, and he told me it was.

247

"Sometime after this my mother was going to milk the cows when she was met out near the barn by this same old man, (as I suppose from her description of him) who said to her 'you have been very faithful and diligent in your labours but you are tried because of the increase of your toil, it is proper therefore that you should receive a witness, that your faith may be strengthened' and thereupon he showed her the plates. My Father and Mother had a large family of their own. The addition to it therefore of Joseph, Emma and Oliver very greatly increased the toil and anxiety of my mother and altho she had never complained she had sometimes felt that her labor was too much or at least she was beginning to feel so. This circumstance however completely removed all such feelings and nerved her up for her increased responsibilities."

Orson Pratt: "Have you any idea when the records will be brought forth?"

David Whitmer: "When we see things in the Spirit and by the power of God they seem to be right here present. The signs of the times indicate the near approach of the coming forth of the other plates, but when it will be, I cannot tell.

The Three Nephites are at work among the lost tribes and elsewhere. John the Revelator is at work, and I believe the time will come suddenly, before we are prepared for it."

15: Reframing *Rough Stone Rolling*

Richard Bushman's 2005 book *Rough Stone Rolling* has attracted praise and criticism from believers and non-believers alike. Some believers object to some aspects of the portrayal of Joseph Smith, such as him using a seer stone in a hat to produce the Book of Mormon.

In 2023, Richard Bushman published *Joseph Smith's Golden Plates: A Cultural History*. This book provides original sources and interpretations from many perspectives—multiple working hypotheses. I highly recommend it as an improvement over *Rough Stone Rolling* with respect to the origin (translation) of the Book of Mormon.

Every author writes from his/her personal bias and motivation, but few explain their own biases as well as Richard Bushman does in *Rough Stone Rolling*. His approach is exceptional and exemplary.

In the Preface, Brother Bushman wrote this:

> **it is unlikely there will ever be consensus on Joseph Smith's character or his achievements**... Everything about Smith matters to people who have built their lives on his teachings. To protect their own deepest commitments, **believers want to shield their prophet's reputation.**

> On the other hand, people who have broken away from Mormonism-and they produce a large amount of the scholarship-**have to justify their decision to leave.** They cannot countenance evidence of divine inspiration in his teachings without catching themselves in a disastrous error. Added to these combatants are **those suspicious of all religious authority who find in Joseph Smith a perfect target for their fears.** Given the emotional crosscurrents, agreement will never be reached about his character, his inspiration, or his accomplishments.

> **A believing historian like myself** cannot hope to rise above these battles or pretend nothing personal is at stake. For a character as controversial as Smith, **pure objectivity is impossible.**

> **What I can do is to look frankly at all sides of Joseph Smith**, facing up to his mistakes and flaws. Covering up errors makes no sense in any case. Most readers do not believe in, nor are they interested in, perfection.

Flawless characters are neither attractive nor useful. We want to meet a real person....

Joseph Smith did not offer himself as an exemplar of virtue. **He told his followers not to expect perfection.** Smith called himself a rough stone, thinking of his own impetuosity and lack of polish. He was sensitive to insults and could not stand to be crossed. Twice he was brought to trial before one of his own church councils for scolding offenders too severely. He so dominated the rooms he entered that some thought him arrogant. But it was his iron will that brought the church, the cities, and the temples into existence.

If people read and consider this preface, the rest of the book makes sense. Bushman does not set out to write an encyclopedia. Nor does he intend the book to be either apologetic or critical. "Frankly" means "open, honest, direct." That's not technically the same as "objective," but objectivity is an elusive goal. Probably an impossible one.

As any author must, Professor Bushman decided to include some facts and omit others. For example, he omitted some of the most direct historical statements about the Urim and Thummim. In some cases, he described a version of history in narrative form. This style of writing—framing theories as facts—can be misleading to readers who don't understand that this is *interpretation* of the facts, not purely *reporting* of the facts.

Critics naturally take unfair advantage of this, telling their audiences that the *Rough Stone Rolling* narrative is the "true" history. Some believers also fall into this trap, not being able or willing to do their own research on the complete historical record.

To help people separate facts from assumptions, inferences, and theories, I wrote a detailed, line-by-line analysis of the section of *Rough Stone Rolling* that deals with the translation of the Book of Mormon. This covers pages 71-76. The analysis is too long to include in this book, but here are the first two entries.

1. *Rough Stone Rolling*, p. 71. "Day after day," Cowdery reported in 1834, "I continued, uninterrupted, to write from his mouth, as he translated with the Urim and Thummim."

My comment. This truncated quotation from Oliver Cowdery's Letter I omits an important part of Oliver's statement, bolded here: "as he translated with the Urim and Thummim, **or, as the Nephites would have said, 'Interpreters,' the history or record called 'The Book of Mormon.'**"

Oliver described the translation instrument as the Nephite interpreters. He did not write "*a* Urim and Thummim" and he did not write "a seer stone." Oliver's statement, first published in October 1834, was a direct response to the claim in *Mormonism Unvailed* that there were two alternative explanations for the translation, one being a "peep stone" and the other the Urim and Thummim.

Oliver also specified that Joseph translated the "history or record," invoking Moroni's description of the plates. In Letter IV, Oliver reported that during his first visit to Joseph in 1823, Moroni "gave a history of the aborigenes [sic] of this country... He said this history was written and deposited not far from that place."

Proposed emendation: complete the full sentence in the quotation to clarify that Oliver referred to the specific instrument that came with the plates.

2. *Rough Stone Rolling*, p. 71. When Martin Harris had taken dictation from Joseph, they at first hung a blanket between them to prevent Harris from inadvertently catching a glimpse of the plates, which were open on a table in the room. By the time Cowdery arrived, translator and scribe were no longer separated.

My comment. This is a reasonable inference, given that Cowdery, too, attempted to translate, which would require him to use the Urim and Thummim and the plates. But the evidence does not preclude a divider that would prevent Emma (and others) from seeing Joseph and Oliver working with the plates and Urim and Thummim.

Proposed emendation: Replace the second sentence so the passage reads like this:

"When Martin Harris had taken dictation from Joseph, they at first hung a blanket between them to prevent Harris from inadvertently catching a glimpse of the plates, which were open on a table in the room. When Cowdery arrived, he sought and obtained permission from the Lord to translate the same as Joseph did, which eliminated the need for a blanket separating them."

You can read the entire analysis here:
https://www.mobom.org/rsr-review

16: All/Some/None—Book of Mormon geography

Book of Mormon geography is a disfavored topic among many Latter-day Saints, but it is a natural question that every reader of the book poses. "Where did all this take place?"

Those who disfavor the topic explain that the setting of the Book of Mormon is inconsequential compared with the primary purpose, which is to convince the world that Jesus is the Christ. While that seems axiomatic, many readers point out that to be convincing, the book must be authentic, and to be authentic, it must be a real history of real people.

For this reason, many believers find the setting to be an important issue, albeit less important than the primary purpose. Critics likewise point to the setting as a test of authenticity. "If there's no evidence of the events, then how can anyone say they occurred?"

The easy (and obvious) way to have no more contention about Book of Mormon geography is through clarity, charity, and understanding. For a thorough discussion, we could apply the FAITH model, but that is a book in itself. in this section, we can summarize the issues using the all/some/none filter.

We seek to understand and respect one another by recognizing there are multiple working hypotheses, all subject to revision and improvement.

We seek charity by recognizing that well-intentioned people have different perspectives, such that we're fine with people believing whatever they want.

We seek clarity through explicit explanations of assumptions, inferences, etc., by using the all/some/none filter.

It is often difficult to obtain clarity. Sometimes people aren't clear themselves about what they believe, about the foundation of their beliefs, or the implications of their beliefs. Bias confirmation (accepting only what confirms one's beliefs) is a common way to avoid thinking about these things, but it doesn't help others understand with clarity. Vague thinking can help assuage cognitive dissonance but it produces confusion, not clarity.

I compiled the table below to promote clarity, charity and understanding.

All of the positions in this table reflect published material. For references, see https://www.mobom.org/church-history-issues

If you have suggestions for more clarity, email me at lostzarahemla@gmail.com and I'll incorporate them.

Setting of the Book of Mormon		
Relative belief in what Joseph Smith and Oliver Cowdery taught		
All	Some	None
Cumorah of Mormon 6:6 is an actual place in the real world and is the same location as the Jaredite Ramah (Ether 15:8)	Cumorah of Mormon 6:6 is an actual place in the real world and is the same location as the Jaredite Ramah (Ether 15:8)	Cumorah and Ramah are both fictional locations.
Cumorah/Ramah is in New York.	Cumorah/Ramah is anywhere but New York (such as southern Mexico, known as M2C for the Mesoamerican/two-Cumorahs theory), or Panama, Baja, Peru, Malaysia, Eritrea, etc.	Cumorah/Ramah is fictional
The identification of the New York hill as Cumorah originated during Moroni's first visit to Joseph Smith, as reported by Lucy Mack Smith.	We don't know when the false New York Cumorah theory originated, but Lucy Mack Smith's history is unreliable because she didn't dictate it until after Joseph died in 1844.	Cumorah is fictional so this doesn't matter anyway, but the "some" group rejects Lucy Mack Smith's history only when it contradicts their own theories.

The Rational Restoration

The identification of the New York hill as Cumorah originated during Moroni's first visit to Joseph Smith, as explained in D&C 128:20 (Glad tidings from Cumorah! The book **to be** revealed)	We don't know exactly what Joseph Smith meant when he wrote D&C 128:20.	Cumorah is fictional so this doesn't matter anyway, but D&C 128:20 does imply that Joseph invented Cumorah before he got the plates, which corroborates his mother's account.
In early 1829 Joseph Smith referred to the hill as Cumorah even before he got the plates because Moroni had taught him the name of the hill, as related by Lucy Mack Smith.	Joseph Smith did not refer to the hill as Cumorah because he didn't know the name until he dictated the text in 1829. Lucy Mack Smith's history is unreliable because she didn't dictate it until after Joseph died in 1844.	Cumorah is fictional so this doesn't matter anyway, but the "some" group rejects Lucy Mack Smith's history only when it contradicts their own theories.
David Whitmer told Joseph F. Smith and Orson Pratt that he first heard the name "Cumorah" during a conversation with the divine messenger to whom Joseph had given the abridged plates before leaving Harmony, PA, in late May or early June 1829. Remembering this was the first time he heard the name "Cumorah" is an indicia of reliability	David Whitmer told Joseph F. Smith and Orson Pratt that he first heard the name "Cumorah" during a conversation with the divine messenger to whom Joseph had given the abridged plates before leaving Harmony, PA, in late May or early June 1829. However, David must have conflated his experience with the messenger with later beliefs about	Cumorah is fictional so this doesn't matter anyway. David probably saw a random guy on the road and Joseph invented the story of the messenger.

and credibility.	Cumorah.	
The messenger had the abridged plates in his knapsack and said he was going to Cumorah.	The messenger had the plates in his knapsack and said he was going to Cumorah. But even if David recalled the conversation correctly, the messenger could not have been referring to the hill in New York as Cumorah/Ramah. He must have been speaking metaphorically or referring to a hill somewhere else, such as in Mexico.	The messenger didn't have any plates. Notice how the "some" group rejects the Cumorah aspect of David Whitmer's account only because it contradicts their own theories about geography.
David Whitmer separately told Edward Stevenson that the messenger declined a ride and said "I am going over to Cumorah."	David Whitmer separately told Edward Stevenson that the messenger declined a ride and said "I am going over to Cumorah." Again, David must have conflated his experience with the messenger with later beliefs about Cumorah.	Another account by David of the story Joseph made up.
David Whitmer told Edward Stevenson that "the Prophet looked very white but	David was wrong about this because, according to historian Andrew Jensen, it was	The confusion between Nephi and Moroni shows that it was all made up.

with a heavenly appearance and said their visitor was one of the three Nephites."	Moroni who had charge of the plates.	
David Whitmer likely told his experience with the messenger to Zina Young in 1832 because he was one of the missionaries who baptized her family and she asked Edward Stevenson to ask David about the account before he left Utah to visit David.	It is merely speculation that David related the account to Zina Young in 1832 because she could have had another reason to ask Edward Stevenson to ask David about the account when he left Utah to visit David.	Whether Zina heard David's story in 1832 doesn't make it any more credible because Joseph invented the story about the messenger, who was really just a guy on the road.
During their mission to the Lamanites (DC 28, 30, 32) in 1830, Parley P. Pratt reported that Oliver Cowdery explained to the Indians that Moroni had anciently called the hill in New York "Cumorah."	During their mission to the Lamanites (DC 28, 30, 32) in 1830, Parley P. Pratt reported that Oliver Cowdery explained to the Indians that Moroni had anciently called the hill in New York "Cumorah." However, Oliver was merely relating the false tradition that he or someone else had invented or assumed.	During their mission to the Lamanites (DC 28, 30, 32) in 1830, Parley P. Pratt reported that Oliver Cowdery explained to the Indians that Moroni had anciently called the hill in New York "Cumorah." However, Oliver was merely relating the false tradition that he or someone else had invented or assumed.
As Assistant President of the Church, Oliver Cowdery wrote an essay about Cumorah	As Assistant President of the Church, Oliver Cowdery wrote an essay about Cumorah	As Assistant President of the Church, Oliver Cowdery wrote an essay about Cumorah

to refute charges that the Book of Mormon was fiction (published as Letter VII).	to refute charges that the Book of Mormon was fiction (published as Letter VII.	to refute charges that the Book of Mormon was fiction (published as Letter VII).
He declared it is a fact that the Cumorah of Mormon 6:6 is the hill in New York where Joseph found the plates.	He declared it is a fact that the Cumorah of Mormon 6:6 is the hill in New York where Joseph found the plates.	He declared it is a fact that the Cumorah of Mormon 6:6 is the hill in New York where Joseph found the plates.
Oliver had good reason to know it was a fact because he and Joseph had visited the repository of Nephite records in the hill on multiple occasions, as reported by Brigham Young, Heber C. Kimball, Wilford Woodruff and others.	Oliver was merely relating his own opinion that Cumorah is in New York and he was wrong. The accounts of Oliver and Joseph visiting the repository of Nephite related multiple visions of another location, probably the mountain in southern Mexico.	The "some" group is correct to the extent that there never was any such repository of Nephite records.
Oliver never claimed revelation about Cumorah because he relied on his own experience at the hill, as well as what Joseph told him. He also never claimed revelation about the restoration of the Priesthood because he related his actual experience.	Oliver never claimed revelation about Cumorah, except that whatever experience he related to Brigham Young must have been a vision of a hill somewhere other than in New York.	Despite what they claimed, neither Oliver nor Joseph had any experience with an angel who restored the Priesthood, nor any experience with actual ancient records.

Prophets, including members of the First Presidency speaking in General Conference, have reiterated what Joseph and Oliver taught about Cumorah and were correct.	Prophets may have reiterated what Joseph and Oliver taught about Cumorah but they were merely expressing their own opinions and they were wrong because Cumorah/Ramah cannot be in New York.	Prophets have reiterated what Joseph and Oliver taught about Cumorah but were wrong because they were merely expressing their own opinions about a fictional location.
Extrinsic evidence corroborates the New York Cumorah because the text and Oliver explained only thousands of Jaredites and tens of thousands of Nephites/Lamanites died there.	Extrinsic evidence does not corroborate the New York Cumorah because Oliver was wrong and the text says millions of Jaredites and hundreds of thousands of Nephites/Lamanites died there.	Extrinsic evidence does not corroborate the New York Cumorah because scholars say millions of Jaredites and hundreds of thousands of Nephites/Lamanites died there.

17: All/Some/None—Book of Mormon translation

A similar chart can explain the alternative approaches to the origin (translation) of the Book of Mormon. The chart below is merely an example. There are dozens of statements by Joseph, Oliver, and their contemporaries that can be assessed through this model.

A good starting place is the "Question and Answer" Joseph Smith published in the Elders' Journal in July 1838.

How, and where did you obtain the book of Mormon?

Moroni, the person who deposited the plates, from whence the book of Mormon was translated, in a hill in Manchester, Ontario County, New York, being dead; and raised again therefrom, appeared unto me, and told me where they were, and gave me directions how to obtain them. **I obtained them, and the Urim and Thummim with them, by the means of which, I translated the plates**; and thus came the Book of Mormon. (*Elders' Journal,* July 1838)[156]

Origin of the Book of Mormon		
Relative belief in what Joseph Smith and Oliver Cowdery taught		
Facts		
All	Some	None
Joseph Smith wrote that he "obtained [the plates] and the Urim and Thummim with them, by the means of which I translated the plates."	Joseph Smith wrote that he "obtained [the plates] and the Urim and Thummim with them, by the means of which I translated the plates."	Joseph Smith wrote that he "obtained [the plates] and the Urim and Thummim with them, by the means of which I translated the plates."

---

[156] https://www.josephsmithpapers.org/paper-summary/elders-journal-july-1838/10

The Rational Restoration

Assumptions		
All	Some	None
When he wrote "by the means of which," we assume Joseph explicitly referred to the Urim and Thummim that came with the plates. This excluded alternative explanations for the translation, such as using a seer stone or having a vision.	Other evidence shows that Joseph produced the Book of Mormon by reading words off the stone in the hat (SITH), which we assume is accurate.	Other evidence shows that Joseph produced the Book of Mormon by reading words off the stone in the hat (SITH), which we assume is accurate.
Inferences		
All	Some	None
Joseph's explanation is so clear no inferences are required.	We infer that Joseph referred to the Urim and Thummim generically. By 1838, Joseph used the term Urim and Thummim to refer to any translation instrument, including the "seer stone" he had found in a well.	We infer Joseph wrote this to mislead people into thinking he didn't use the stone to distract them from Joseph's magical world view.
Theories		
All	Some	None
Joseph translated the plates by means of the Urim and Thummim that came with the plates.	Joseph produced the Book of Mormon by reading words off a seer stone he placed in a hat and did not use either the plates or the Urim and Thummim that came with the plates.	Because there were no plates or Urim and Thummim, Joseph fooled his followers by putting a stone in a hat and dictating a story he composed.

Hypotheses		
All	Some	None
Because Joseph translated by means of the Urim and Thummim, contrary accounts will have evidentiary problems or relate Joseph's use of a stone for other reasons, such as a demonstration.	Because Joseph produced the Book of Mormon with SITH, he did not use the term "translate" in the normal sense and the accounts by the SITH witnesses are accurate.	Because Joseph misled everyone about the translation, it's easy to see how he misled everyone about his other truth claims as well.

Appendix 1: Recommended Reading

We've been reminded that, "as all have not faith, seek ye diligently and teach one another words of wisdom; yea, seek ye out of the best books words of wisdom; seek learning, even by study and also by faith." (Doctrine and Covenants 88:118)

I've cited and quoted from a variety of sources in this book. Actually, I wrote this book drawing from years of experience with a wide variety of people and innumerable secular and religious sources. I've compiled many times more information than I could put in this book, but because people ask me what I read, I'm providing this representative list of resources that can help us understand the Restoration in its many facets.

"One of the grand fundamental principles of Mormonism is to receive truth let it come from where it may." Joseph Smith, Jr.

Holy Bible, Book of Mormon, Doctrine and Covenants, Pearl of Great Price, Conference Reports, Journal of Discourses, Joseph Smith Papers, WordCruncher databases, Church Gospel Library
Adams, Scott. *Reframe Your Brain: The User Interface for Happiness and Success*
Bushman, Richard. *Joseph Smith's Gold Plates: A Cultural History*
Cialdini, Robert B. *Presuasion: A Revolutionary Way to Influence and Persuade*
Edwards, Jonathan. *The Works of President Edwards* (8 vol. 1808) (kindle)
Harris, Matthew L. *The LDS Gospel Topics Series: A Scholarly Engagement*
Heinrichs, Jay. *Thank you for Arguing*
Kahneman, Daniel. *Thinking: Fast and Slow*
Lucas, James W. and Woodworth, Warner P. *Working Toward Zion: Principles of the United Order for the Modern World*
Maxwell, Neal A. *Of One Heart*
Meyer, Stephen C. *Darwin's Doubt*
Nibley, Hugh, *Approaching Zion*
Pinker, Steven. *Enlightenment Now* and *Rationality: What it Is, Why it Seems Scarce, Why it Matters*
Reiss, Jana. *The Next Mormons*
Seel, David John. *The New Copernicans: Millennials and the Survival of the Church*
Taylor, Jill Bolte. *Whole Brain Living*
Tolle, Eckhart. *A New Earth: Awakening to Your Life's Purpose* and *The Power of Now*
Welch, John W. *Opening the Heavens*

Short references on rational thinking:
Packer, Boyd K. "I Say unto You, Be One," https://speeches.byu.edu/talks/boyd-k-packer/say-unto-one/
Welch, John W. "The Role of Evidence in Religious Discussion," https://rsc.byu.edu/no-weapon-shall-prosper/role-evidence-religious-discussion

The Joseph Smith Papers

Today, the best source of historical information relating to Joseph Smith is the Joseph Smith Papers. I encourage everyone interested in Church history to buy the books or access the web page (or both). You'll find a wealth of original documents, as well as extensive and useful commentary.

(I like to tell people to throw away the old *History of the Church*, but you need those to follow footnotes in Church-related publications. A few authors still cite *History of the Church*, but hopefully that won't continue because of all the problems with the way that series was compiled.)

The web address is easy to remember and find: http://www.josephsmithpapers.org/.

Footnotes in this book include links to the Joseph Smith Papers.

By way of caution, the editorial content in the Joseph Smith Papers sometimes promotes the M2C and SITH agendas at the expense of accuracy and completeness. For examples, see my paper here: https://www.academia.edu/67756647/Agenda_driven_editorial_content_in_the_Joseph_Smith_Papers

Useful blogs.
My blog on historical narratives:
http://www.ldshistoricalnarratives.com/
My blog on avoiding contention:
www.nomorecontention.com
General Book of Mormon blog:
www.mobom.org

Appendix 2: The Restoration according to Joseph Smith and Oliver Cowdery

Excerpts from the writings of Joseph Smith and Oliver Cowdery.

That our narrative may be correct, and particularly the introduction, it is proper to inform our patrons, that our brother J. Smith Jr. has offered to assist us. Indeed, there are many items connected with the fore part of this subject that render his labor indispensible. With his labor and with authentic documents now in our possession, we hope to render this a pleasing and agreeable narrative, well worth the examination and perusal of the Saints. To do Justice to> this subject will require time and space: we therefore ask the forbearance of our readers, assuring them that it shall be founded upon facts.
https://www.josephsmithpapers.org/paper-summary/history-1834-1836/48

Near the time of the setting of the sun, sabbath evening, April 5th. 1829, my natural eyes for the first time beheld this brother. He then resided in Harmony, Susquehanna county Penn. On Monday the 6th. I assisted him in arranging some business of a temporal nature, and on Tuesday the 7th. commenced to write the book of Mormon.

These were days never to be forgotten—to <sit> under the voice sound of a voice dictated by the inspiration of heaven, awakened the utmost gratitude of this bosom! Day after day I continued, uninterrupted, to write from his mouth, as he translated with the Urim and Thummim, or, as the Nephites should have said, "Interpreters," the history, or record, called "the book of Mormon."

On a sudden, as from the midst of eternity, the voice of the redeemer spake peace to us, while the vail was parted and the angel of God came down clothed with glory, and delivered the anxiously looked for message, and the keys of the gospel of repentance!...

we received under his hand the holy priesthood, as he said, "upon you> my fellow servants, in the name of Messiah I confer this priesthood, and this authority, which shall remain upon earth, that the sons of Levi may yet offer an offering into the Lord in righteousness!

On the evening of the 21st of September, 1823, previous to retiring to rest, our brother's mind was unusually wrought up on the subject which had so long agitated his mind... While continuing in prayer for a manifestation in some way that his sins were forgiven; endeavoring to exercise faith in the scriptures, on a sudden a light like that of day, only of a purer and far more glorious appearance and brightness, burst into the room... and in a moment a personage stood before him...

Though fear was banished from his heart, yet his surprise was no less when he heard him declare himself to be a messenger sent by commandment of the Lord, to deliver a special message...

"Therefore, says the Lord, I will proceed to do a marvelous work among this people, even a marvelous work and a wonder...

"This cannot be brought about untill first certain preparatory things are accomplished, for so has the Lord purposed in his own mind. He has therefore chosen you as an instrument in his hand to bring to light that which shall perform his act, his strange act, and bring to pass a marvelous work and a wonder. ... Therefore, marvel not if your name is made a derission, and had as a by-word among such, if you are the instrument in bringing it, by the gift of God, to the knowledge of the people."

He then proceeded and gave a general account of the promises made to the fathers, and also gave a history of the aborigines of this country... He said this history was written and deposited not far from that place, and that it was our brother's privilege, if obedient to the commandments of the Lord, to obtain and translate the same by the means of the Urim and Thummim, which were deposited for that purpose with the record.

https://www.josephsmithpapers.org/paper-summary/history-1834-1836/68

I must now give you some description of the place where, and the manner in which these records were deposited You are acquainted with the mail road from Palmyra, Wayne Co. to Canandaigua, Ontario Co. N.Y. ... about four miles from Palmyra, you pass a large hill on the east side of the road. Why I say large, is because it is as large perhaps, as any in that country. ... At about one mile west rises another ridge of less height, running parallel with the former, leaving a beautiful vale between. The soil is of the first quality for the country, and under a state of cultivation, which gives a prospect at once imposing, when one reflects on the fact, that here, between these hills, the entire power and national strength of both the Jaredites and Nephites were destroyed.

By turning to the 529th and 530th pages of the book of Mormon120 you will read Mormon's account of the last great struggle of his people, as they were encamped round this hill Cumorah....

This hill, by the Jaredites, was called Ramah: by it, or around it pitched the famous army of Coriantumr their tents.

https://www.josephsmithpapers.org/paper-summary/history-1834-1836/90

Appendix 3: Restoration Timeline Summary

1805: Joseph Smith, Jr. (JS) born 23 December in Sharon, Vermont.

1812: JS has serious leg surgery, accompanies Uncle Jesse to Massachusetts to recuperate near the sea, requires crutches until family moves to Palmyra.

1816: Smith family moves to Palmyra, New York.

Circa 1816-1825: JS visits the Palmyra print shop/book store weekly to get the newspaper for his father; a store employee, Orsamus Turner, remembers Joseph as a "meddling inquisitive lounger;" JS participates in juvenile debating society and as an exhorter.

1820: Traditional year of First Vision.

1823: On 21-22 September, JS visited by angel Moroni, who tells him about a record of the aboriginal inhabitants of this country that was "written and deposited not far" from Joseph's home; Moroni tells Joseph to go to the Hill Cumorah, where Joseph views the abridged plates, the Urim and Thummim (U&T) and the breastplate.

1824-6: JS visited by angel Moroni at the hill Cumorah each September.

1827: JS marries Emma Hale in Jan., meet Moroni at Cumorah and receives chastisement and encouragement, on Sept. 22 obtains abridged plates with U&T and breastplate; they move to Harmony, Penn., in Dec.

1828: Using the U&T, JS begins copying and translating the characters from the engravings on the abridged plates; in Feb. Martin Harris (MH) takes transcript of characters to NYC; from Apr. 12-Jun. 14 JS translates plates with MH as scribe; in June MH loses the manuscript (the 116 pages); JS forfeits U&T; in July JS travels to Palmyra; on Sept. 22, JS receives back the U&T and the plates. He resumes translating with Emma and Samuel Smith as scribes.

1829: Joseph and Emma translate until March, when Martin Harris visits (D&C 5);

April-May 1829. At Harmony, PA, Oliver writes as Joseph continues the translation of the original plates he obtained from Moroni, as described on the Title Page: Mormon's abridgment of the record of the Nephites, Moroni's abridgment of the record of Ether, and Moroni's concluding comments. This is Mosiah through Moroni in the current Book of Mormon. In April, the Lord promises Oliver that when he and Joseph finish the record they have in Harmony, there are other records that Oliver will have power to assist to translate (D&C 9:1-2)

May 1829. When Joseph and Oliver near the completion of the Harmony translation, they consider starting over at the beginning. The Lord tells them not to retranslate the Book of Lehi (the 116 pages lost by Martin Harris). Instead, they must translate the unabridged plates of Nephi directly (D&C 10:38-51). But they don't yet have the small plates.

May 1829. Through the Urim and Thummim, Joseph receives a revelation to ask David Whitmer to come to Harmony immediately to transport Joseph and Oliver to the home of Peter Whitmer (David's father) near Fayette. Oliver writes the letter.

May 1829. Before leaving Harmony, Joseph and Oliver translate the Title Page from the last leaf of the original plates. They have this page printed to submit as part of a copyright application, which is filed on June 11 at Utica, NY.

May 1829. Before leaving Harmony, Joseph gives the plates to a divine messenger with a promise that when he gets to Fayette, he will receive the plates he needs to translate there.

May 1829. David Whitmer receives Oliver's letter but can't leave because of farm work. Miraculously, three unknown persons plow his fields and spread plaster (fertilizer) so he can go.

May-June 1829. Joseph monitors David's progress using a seer stone and relates the details to Oliver Cowdery, who writes them down. David verifies every detail on the return trip.

June 1829. On their way from Harmony to Fayette, New York, Joseph, Oliver, and David meet a divine messenger who is carrying the plates and says he is going to Cumorah, a place David never heard of before.

June 1829. In Fayette, Joseph receives the plates of Nephi from a divine messenger (who presumably brought them from the Cumorah repository). He translates the small plates of Nephi (1 Nephi - Words of Mormon 1-11).

June 1829. Joseph, Oliver, David and Martin Harris see the plates as shown to them by an angel.

June or July 1829. The Eight Witnesses see and handle the plates as shown to them by Joseph Smith.

1829-1830. On multiple occasions, Joseph, Oliver and others visit the room in Cumorah that contains Mormon's repository of Nephite records and artifacts (Mormon 6:6). They apparently move the records from Cumorah to a nearby location.

1830: Book of Mormon published; Church organized; first missionaries sent to Lamanites (American Indians) in New York and Ohio.

1831: LDS gather to Kirtland; New Jerusalem in Missouri revealed.

1832: Grammar in the early revelations is changed (which to who, etc.).

1834: In response to *Mormonism Unvailed*, JS and OC publish the first formal history of the Church, affirming U&T; OC ordained Assistant President of the Church.

1837: JS edits the Book of Mormon to correct grammar.

1840: JS edits the Book of Mormon again.

1844: Joseph and Hyrum Smith are martyred in Carthage, IL.

A complete chronology is available online here: http://www.josephsmithpapers.org/reference/events

Jonathan Neville

Appendix 4: The *New* New Mormon History

The *New* New Mormon History builds on the contributions of the "New Mormon" historians to take a fresh look at the original truth claims made by Joseph Smith and Oliver Cowdery. This updated interpretation corroborates what Joseph and Oliver said all along, helping to clarify lingering issues in Church history.

Background: The following overview describes the term and the leading participants.

> The phrase "New Mormon history" refers to a 20th century style of reporting the history of Mormonism by both Mormon and non-Mormon scholars which departs from earlier more polemical or faith-based styles of history. ... Because it is a break from past historical narratives, new Mormon history tends to be revisionist. ...
>
> LDS historian Richard Bushman described the "New Mormon History" as "a quest for identity rather than a quest for authority." New Mormon historians include a wide range of both Mormon and non-Mormon scholars, the most prominent of which include Bushman, Jan Shipps, D. Michael Quinn, Terryl Givens, Leonard J. Arrington, Richard P. Howard, Fawn Brodie, and Juanita Brooks.[157]

The New Mormon History has done many useful things, particularly gathering scattered source material (e.g., the Joseph Smith Papers project). However, some of the New Mormon Historians have drifted into revisionism seemingly for its own sake, possibly in the pursuit of something "new" to publish about. They have developed a new consensus to replace the earlier, faith-based consensus. For example, the new consensus reframes Joseph as dictating a *revealed* text instead of a *translated* text. Instead of translating the plates by means of the Urim and Thummim, Joseph read words that appeared on a seer stone (or in his mind), while not even using the plates. Some even claim that Joseph and

---

[157] https://en.wikipedia.org/wiki/New_Mormon_history

Oliver misled people about the translation as well as the historicity of the Book of Mormon, with the Hill Cumorah being located in New York.

This revised New Mormon History narrative has faced resistance from traditional and conservative historians (and members generally). In my view, if the evidence requires a revised narrative, then by all means let's revise. But there are important areas where revisionism under the rubric of New Mormon History appears to have distorted or ignored the actual historical record.

Ideally, we should consider multiple working hypotheses based on accepted facts.

Proposed *New* New Mormon History

This *New* New Mormon History transcends prior consensus to offer an alternative evidence-based narrative; i.e., that Joseph did translate the engravings on the plates, that there were two sets of plates, and that the Hill Cumorah in New York is both the site of the repository of Nephite records and the setting for the final battles of the Jaredites and Nephites.

1. Joseph as a young religious seeker.

Traditional view: Joseph was an uneducated, barely literate prophet uniquely capable of receiving revelation from God, including the text of the Book of Mormon. Alternative view: Joseph was a gifted religious genius whose "inspired eclecticism" who drew on contemporary sources to channel inspiration. Alternative view: Joseph was a charismatic conman whether pious or not.

New view: Joseph became a religious seeker when he survived life-threatening leg surgery. During his years of convalescence and after his family moved to Palmyra, he acquired "an intimate acquaintance with those of different denominations" by reading Christian literature, including the works of Jonathan Edwards. Most of the non-biblical language in the Book of Mormon and early revelations draws from Jonathan Edwards. He translated the text using his own lexicon as any translator would do, albeit inspired in his choice of words and phrasing. See *Infinite Goodness: Joseph Smith, Jonathan Edwards, and the Book of Mormon*.

2. Two sets of plates.

Traditional view: Joseph obtained the plates from the hill in New York and returned them to the messenger when he was finished with the translation.

New view: Moroni deposited only the abridged record in the stone box in the hill. Joseph took these plates to Harmony and translated them there. He and Oliver planned to re-translate the Book of Lehi (the lost 116 pages), but the Lord told him to translate the plates of Nephi instead (D&C 10). Except Joseph didn't have the plates of Nephi. Those plates were still in the depository of Nephite records. Before he left Harmony, Joseph gave the abridged plates to a messenger (one of the three Nephites). The messenger returned the abridged plates to the repository, picked up the plates of Nephi, and took those plates to Fayette, which is why Joseph translated those plates there. See *Whatever Happened to the Golden Plates?*

3. Joseph as an actual translator.

Traditional view: Joseph translated the engravings by the gift and power of God and by means of the Urim and Thummim. Alternative view: Joseph read words that appeared on a stone in the hat (SITH), and the words were provided by a supernatural translator because Joseph didn't even use the plates. Alternative view: Joseph was a conman who composed or copied the texts he produced.

New view: Joseph's claim that he translated the characters (engravings) on the plates is consistent with the language he dictated and the evidence from witnesses and the Original Manuscript. Whatever the witnesses who described the stone-in-the-hat (SITH) were witnessing, it could not have been the translation because Joseph explained that he could not display the plates or Urim and Thummim that he used to translate. Evidence indicates Joseph conducted one or more demonstrations with SITH, just as he later did when people asked for revelations through the stone. Later, witnesses related SITH to refute the Spalding theory. See *A Man that Can Translate* and *By Means of the Urim and Thummim: Restoring Translation to the Restoration.*

4. The New York Cumorah.

Traditional view: Moroni identified the hill as Cumorah the first night he met Joseph, and Joseph and Oliver reaffirmed that setting. Alternative view: Joseph and Oliver merely speculated about Cumorah, and/or early Church members created a false tradition about Cumorah that Joseph and Oliver adopted. Alternative view: Because the text is fiction, no Cumorah exists in the real world.

New view: *Mormonism Unvailed* claimed the Book of Mormon was fiction, taken from a novel by Solomon Spalding. In response, Joseph and Oliver affirmed it was a fact that the hill in New York was the same hill Mormon described in Mormon 6:6 (Letter VII). This reality has important implications for interpreting the text. See *Between these Hills: A Case for the Hill Cumorah, Moroni's America,* and *Letter VII: Oliver and Joseph explain the Hill Cumorah*.

5. Mesoamerican/two-Cumorahs theory (M2C).

Traditional view: Early Latter-day Saints speculated about a hemispheric setting for the Book of Mormon. Some, such as Orson Pratt and Benjamin Winchester, cited ruins in Mesoamerica as evidence. Anonymous articles in the 1842 *Times and Seasons* promoted the Mesoamerican setting. Because they were signed "Ed." and Joseph was listed as the editor of the paper, he must have written or approved of these articles. Because Mesoamerica is so distant from New York, the real Cumorah must be in southern Mexico.

New View. In the Wentworth letter, Joseph sought to correct Orson Pratt's Mesoamerican theory. The 1842 articles in the *Times and Seasons* were erroneously attributed to Joseph Smith, who was listed as the nominal editor but had little input other than for material he personally signed, such as the Wentworth letter. Joseph approved the republication of Letter VII in Mormon newspapers, and his brothers published Letter VII in the *Times and Seasons* (1841) and in *The Prophet* (1844). In D&C 128:20, Joseph referred to Moroni explaining the New York Cumorah when the book was yet to come forth. See *The Lost City of Zarahemla, Brought to Light, The Editors: Joseph, Don Carlos, and William Smith* and *Mesomania*.

NOTES:

Made in the USA
Las Vegas, NV
20 March 2024